Proust
in Love

Proust
in Love

WILLIAM C. CARTER

Yale University Press ✻ *New Haven & London*

Published with assistance from the foundation established in memory of Philip Hamilton McMillan of the Class of 1894, Yale College.

Designed by Mary Valencia

Set in Fournier type by Keystone Typesetting, Inc.

Printed in the United States of America by Vail-Ballou Press.

Library of Congress Cataloging-in-Publication Data

Carter, William C., 1941–

Proust in love / William C. Carter.

   p.   cm.

Includes bibliographical references and index.

ISBN–13: 978-0-300-10812-5 (cloth : alk. paper)

ISBN–10: 0-300-10812-5 (cloth : alk. paper)

1. Proust, Marcel, 1871–1922—Sexual behavior. 2. Novelists, French—20th century—Sexual behavior. 3. Homosexuality and literature—France. I. Title.

PQ2631.R63Z545486 2006

843′.912—dc22

2005025261

A catalogue record for this book is available from the British Library.

The paper in this book meets the guidelines for permanence and durability of the Committee on Production Guidelines for Book Longevity of the Council on Library Resources.

10 9 8 7 6 5 4 3 2 1

For Josephine and Terence Monmaney,
who, through Proust, found love

Love alone is divine.
—Marcel Proust

Contents

Illustrations follow page 96

Acknowledgments

I wish to express my sincere thanks to those who encouraged me in the research, writing, and production of this book. The list of those to whom I am deeply and happily indebted includes Robert Bowden; Elyane Dezon-Jones; Anne-Marie Bernard; Marie-Colette Lefort; Robert Blumenfeld; Bob Borson; the late Dr. L. M. Bargeron Jr.; J. P. Smith; Claudia Moscovici; Caroline Szylowicz, Kolb-Proust Librarian at the Kolb-Proust Archive for Research, University of Illinois Library; my friends and colleagues at the University of Alabama at Birmingham's Mervyn H. Sterne Library; my editors at Yale University Press, John Kulka and Dan Heaton; and, as always, and especially, my wife, Lynn.

Introduction

Proust in Love portrays the novelist Marcel Proust's amorous adventures—and misadventures—from his adolescence through his adult years, applying, where appropriate, his own sensitive, intelligent observations about love and sexuality, which are often disillusioned and at times highly amusing. These observations are drawn from his correspondence, his novel *In Search of Lost Time,* and his other writings.

Proust's achievement is unique in a number of ways. Widely recognized as one of the world's great novelists, he wrote only one novel, but one of vast proportions, consisting of seven principal parts whose English titles are *Swann's Way, Within a Budding Grove, The Guermantes Way, Sodom and Gomorrah, The Captive, The Fugitive,* and *Time Regained.* The central figure, who tells us his life's story in the first person and whose enchanting voice we come to know intimately, never identifies himself with a name. We refer to him simply as the Narrator.

Proust in Love inevitably contains some overlap of material covered in my recent biography *Marcel Proust: A Life,* but I focus here on the links between Proust's amorous relationships and his transposition of these into the Narrator's erotic experiences and his depictions of a variety of sexual types, particularly homosexuals and bisexuals. I have tried to avoid weighing down the book with too many academic analyses, but in the notes I do refer the curious reader to those works that I consider most useful in probing the various critical and psychological interpretations of Proust's ideas about love and sexuality.

The new Forssgren documents—*The Memoirs of Ernest Forssgren, Proust's Swedish Valet* (Yale University Press, 2006) and Paul Morand's recently and posthumously published private diary, *Le*

Journal inutile (The useless diary), available only in the original French edition—add interesting details to the portrait of Proust in love and provide new glimpses of his modus operandi when attempting to seduce young men from the servant class. Morand was a young writer and diplomat who met Proust in 1916. He and his future wife, Princess Hélène Soutzo, quickly became part of Proust's intimate circle of friends and remained closely associated with him until his death.

It is clear from the memoirs of those who knew Proust, his letters, testimony by witnesses, and scenes from the novel that the vicious, sadistic side of sexuality intrigued him. Whether he participated in such acts or merely observed them, it is certain that the dark side of passion both attracted and repulsed him. Indeed, jealous, obsessive, and sometimes sadistic love is a profane theme that runs throughout Proust's novel in direct counterpoint to the transcendent, sacred theme of art, which ultimately triumphs as the Narrator concludes his quest. Along the way, Proust brilliantly portrays and analyzes the manifestations of such love in the heterosexual couples Swann and Odette, the young Narrator and Gilberte, the mature Narrator and Albertine, and Robert de Saint-Loup and the actress Rachel, and in homosexuals such as Mlle Vinteuil and her friend (a key figure, but one with no name), Charlus and Charlie Morel, and the bisexual lovers Saint-Loup and Morel. In spite of the dark, anxious overtones issuing from the bitter experiences of jealous, disappointed lovers, Proust often brings to bear his trenchant wit or mischievous sense of humor as he delights in showing how frequently and how thoroughly love makes fools of us all.

Abbreviations of Titles of Proust's Works

All quotations from *In Search of Lost Time* are from the Modern Library Edition in 6 volumes, translated by C. K. Scott Moncrieff and Terence Kilmartin, revised by D. J. Enright, New York, 1992. Each section of the novel is cited by its title, volume number, and page number:

1. *Swann's Way*
2. *Within a Budding Grove*
3. *The Guermantes Way*
4. *Sodom and Gomorrah*
5. *The Captive* and *The Fugitive*
6. *Time Regained*

The following abbreviations are used for the correspondence and miscellaneous writings of Marcel Proust:

Corr.	*Correspondance de Marcel Proust*, edited by Philip Kolb. Paris: Plon, 21 vols., 1970–93.
SL 1	*Selected Letters in English, 1880–1903*, edited by Philip Kolb, translated by Ralph Manheim, introduction by J. M. Cocking. New York: Doubleday, 1983.
SL 2	*Selected Letters, 1904–1909*, vol. 2, edited by Philip Kolb, translated with an introduction by Terence Kilmartin. London: Collins, 1989.
SL 3	*Selected Letters, 1910–1917*, vol. 3, edited by Philip Kolb, translated with an introduction by Terence Kilmartin. New York: HarperCollins, 1992.
SL 4	*Selected Letters, 1918–1922*, edited by Philip Kolb, translated with an introduction by Joanna Kilmartin. London: HarperCollins, 2000.

Carnet 1908 *Le Carnet de 1908*, edited by Philip Kolb. Paris: Gallimard, 1976.

CSB *Contre Sainte-Beuve*, edited by Pierre Clarac with the collaboration of Yves Sandre. Paris: Gallimard (Pléiade), 1971.

For those works and documents that exist only in French, all translations are my own, unless otherwise indicated.

Proust
in Love

CHAPTER ONE

Promiscuous Proust

The principal trait of my character: *The need to be loved and, to be more precise, the need to be caressed and spoiled even more than the need to be admired.*

Marcel Proust attended high school at the lycée Condorcet from 1882 to 1889. Among his "intimate circle" of classmates were an astonishing number of future writers. Daniel Halévy wrote biographies of Friedrich Nietzsche, Jules Michelet, and Sébastien Vauban; Louis de La Salle, who died young, published a volume of poetry and a novel; Robert Dreyfus became an important historian of the Third Republic. Two other high school friends, the poet Fernand Gregh and the playwright Robert de Flers, were elected to the Académie Française, an honor not bestowed upon Proust, whose belated achievement as a novelist was to eclipse those of his brilliant schoolmates.

Proust's classmates did not always enjoy his company. His obvious literary gifts awed them, but his personality, especially his jealous need for their exclusive attention, often repulsed them. Jacques-Émile Blanche, who painted a famous oil portrait of Proust, recalls in his memoirs a mutual childhood friend who confided that whenever he played with the future writer, he was always "gripped with fear when I felt Marcel seize my hand and declare to me his need for total and tyrannical possession."[1] With the callousness common to adolescent boys, Proust's classmates teased and snubbed their sensitive and clinging companion, curtly rejecting his offers of greater intimacy, thus wounding him deeply.

Daniel Halévy was a handsome, towheaded, freckle-faced boy with hazel eyes who, like Proust, came from a liberal, bourgeois Parisian family with a distinguished literary and musical pedigree. The two boys had a solid but difficult friendship. Halévy, who liked to be seen as domineering and tough, tormented the pining Marcel with his angry gestures and the ability to keep silent for days on end. In an interview many years later, Halévy recalled the "beastly" manner in which he and his friends treated Marcel: "He figured among us as a sort of archangel, disturbed and disturbing . . . with his great oriental eyes, his big white collar, his flying cravat. There was something about him we found unpleasant. . . . His kindnesses, his tender attentions, his caresses . . . we often labeled as mannerisms, poses, and we took occasion to tell him so to his face. . . . We were rough with him. The poor wretch!"[2]

In 1888, at age seventeen, brimming with literary ambition and adolescent lust, the poor wretch, impervious to earlier rebuffs, upped the ante and sent his classmates poems and letters celebrating love between boys and offering himself as an eager partner for sexual initiations. Marcel focused his attention on Halévy's slightly younger cousin Jacques Bizet, son of the distinguished composer Georges Bizet. The elder Bizet had died in 1875, a few months after the première of *Carmen,* when Jacques was only three years old. Bizet's widow, Geneviève, daughter of the renowned composer Fromenthal Halévy, later married the lawyer Émile Straus. Geneviève was to become Proust's beloved Mme Straus, confidante and model for the wit of the duchesse de Guermantes in the novel. Although Bizet had inherited the Halévy family curse of mental illness, which led ultimately to drug addiction and suicide, none of this was yet apparent in the bright, handsome, popular boy who loved the outdoors and hiking.

In a letter to Jacques, Marcel said that he needed reassurance of his friendship because of so many problems at home. Hoping to win sympathy and—above all—affection, Proust confided that his parents had threatened to send him far away to a boarding school in the provinces. He pleaded with Bizet to be his "reservoir," the recipient of his overflowing sorrows and love: "My only consolation when I am really sad is to love and be loved." He ended his short, desperate appeal by declaring: "I embrace you and love you with all my heart."[3]

Not long afterward, between classes at school, Proust thrust a letter into Bizet's hand, inviting him to have sex. At the next change of classes, Bizet passed his answer back to Proust, who was headed to history class. Once at his desk, Proust skimmed the letter and then, disappointed but persistent, took a sheet of paper and wrote his reply. Feigning acceptance of Bizet's refusal, Proust praised his friend's intellectual gifts while gently pressing his case to have sex by arguing that such behavior would prove harmless now, because they were young, innocent, and inexperienced:

My dear Jacques,

Under the stern eye of M. Choublier, I have just raced through your letter, propelled by my fear. I admire your wisdom, while at the same time deploring it. Your reasons are excellent, and I am glad to see how strong and alert, how keen and penetrating your thinking has become. Still, the heart—or the body—has its reasons that are unknown to reason, and so it is with admiration for you (that is, for your thinking, not for your refusal, for I am not fatuous enough to believe that my body is so precious a treasure that to renounce it required great strength of character) but with sadness that I accept the disdainful and cruel yoke you impose on me. Maybe you are right. Still, I always find it sad not to pluck the delicious flower that we shall soon be unable to pluck. For then it would be fruit . . . and forbidden.[4]

Bizet again shrugged off the invitation. From the secure vantage of his own exclusively heterosexual yearnings, he apparently found Proust's seductive overtures harmless fun. Fellow classmate Robert Dreyfus recorded that Bizet "liked only women who also found him very attractive and so did not see himself at all compromised by Marcel's bizarre behavior; on the contrary, it flattered him."[5]

That spring Proust informed Bizet in a letter that his parents, having discovered the nature of his sexual desires and his obsessive need to masturbate, had prohibited him from seeing Bizet.[6] Bizet, who was perplexed, wrote back that he did not understand why they could not continue to play together. Proust replied that perhaps his mother feared that his "somewhat excessive affection" for Bizet might "degenerate" into "*sensual* love" because she feared that the two boys shared "the same faults . . . independent spirit, nervousness, a disordered mind, and perhaps even masturbation."[7]

Bizet gave the letter to Halévy, already the historian, who recorded it in his diary, noting as he did so, "Poor Proust is absolutely crazy."[8] Halévy, as he continued to read the letter, saw that Mme Proust had reason to be concerned. Dr. Proust had caught Marcel masturbating: "This morning, dearest, when my father saw me . . . he begged me to stop masturbating for at least four days." Proust swore to Bizet that, if necessary, he would defy his parents by fleeing the family prison to find his friend and love him "outside the walls" in a nearby café.

Like all adolescents, Proust felt isolated and misunderstood. In his early writings and later in the novel, he described the feeling of being alone, plotted against, made a prisoner by his family, all of which provoked "that old desire to rebel against an imaginary plot woven against me by my parents, who imagined that I would be forced to obey them, that defiant spirit which drove me in the past to impose my will brutally upon the people I loved best in the world, though finally conforming to theirs after I had succeeded in making them yield."[9] In *Jean Santeuil,* his first attempt at novel writing, Proust, whom his classmates considered spoiled, wrote, in words that closely echo the letter to Bizet, that Jean's childhood resembled a prison, that his "parental home had seemed to him a place of slavery."[10]

In *Swann's Way*, Proust's young Narrator, while engaging in onanistic practices, dreams of finding someone to love, a heterosexual someone. When he first sees Gilberte, the daughter of Swann and Odette, she makes a gesture that he interprets as obscene and insulting, but whose true meaning is the opposite. Transfixed by what he assumes to be her unattainable beauty, he continues to stare at her. Gilberte's gesture is so ambiguous and he so innocent that it leaves him bewildered and humiliated. His only recourse is to continue his solitary, sensual practices, which he does by secluding himself in "the only room whose door I was allowed to lock, whenever my occupation was such as required an inviolable solitude: reading or day-dreaming, tears or sensual pleasure." As he explores and seeks to relieve his sexual urges, he gazes at the distant tower of Roussainville:

> Alas, it was in vain that I implored the castle-keep of Roussainville, that I begged it to send out to meet me some daughter of its village, appealing to it as to the sole confidant of my earliest desires when, at the top of our house in Combray, in the little room that smelt of orris-root, I could see nothing but its tower framed in the half-opened window as, with the heroic misgivings of a traveller setting out on a voyage of exploration or of a desperate wretch hesitating on the verge of self-destruction, faint with emotion, I explored, across the bounds of my own experience, an untrodden path which for all I knew was deadly—until the moment when a natural trail like that left by a snail smeared the leaves of the flowering currant that drooped around me.[11]

The tower of Roussainville is indeed phallic, not only because the protagonist gazes at it from the window while masturbating and yearning for a girl but also because years later he learns that the tower had been the scene of sexual experimentations by the young people of the village and that what he had mistaken for Gilberte's obscene gesture of repulsion on first seeing him had in fact been intended as an invitation to join her in the games at the tower.[12] Many years later, when Gilberte is married to Robert de Saint-Loup, the Narrator visits her at Combray. One evening when they are out for a walk, she reminisces about her sexual awakenings: "I was in the habit . . . of going to play with little boys I knew in the ruins of the keep of Roussainville. And you will tell me that I was a very naughty girl, for there were girls and boys there of all sorts who took advantage of the darkness."[13]

As an adolescent, Proust enjoyed flirting and playing innocent games of tag with the two Benardaky sisters, Marie and Nelly, the primary models for Gilberte Swann. He wrote about their games, using the sisters' real names, in *Jean Santeuil*. Proust later claimed that Marie was "the intoxication and despair" of his youth.[14] The Narrator's late adolescence corresponds to that period in Proust's own life when he, with his ideals and illusions firmly intact, believed, like his young hero "in love with Gilberte . . . that Love did really exist outside ourselves."[15] At play with Gilberte in the gardens of the Champs-Élysées, the Narrator unexpectedly experiences the fulfillment of those "baser" needs, much more easily satisfied than the desire for reciprocated passionate devotion.[16] As he wrestles with her in a lighthearted tussle over a letter, the struggle quickly becomes a simulation of coitus, leading to an unanticipated ejaculation that the circumstances leave him no time to appreciate. Equally aroused, Gilberte is reluctant to stop the contest:

> [Gilberte] thrust [the letter] behind her back; I put my arms round her neck, raising the plaits of hair which she wore over her shoulders . . . and we wrestled, locked together. I tried to pull her towards me, and she resisted; her cheeks, inflamed by the effort, were as red and round as two cherries; she laughed as though I were tickling her; I held her gripped between my legs like a young tree which I was trying to climb; and, in the middle of my gymnastics, when I was already out of breath with the muscular exercise and the heat of the game, I felt, like a few drops of sweat wrung from me by the effort, my pleasure

express itself in a form which I could not even pause for a moment to analyze; immediately I snatched the letter from her. Whereupon Gilberte said good-naturedly: "You know, if you like, we might go on wrestling a bit longer."[17]

This premature and unanticipated ejaculation during a puerile game is charming in its innocence and bears no guilt or shame, unlike many of the adult characters' sexual games, some of which involve sadism and masochism and are homosexual in nature.

The letter to Jacques Bizet about running away together astounded Halévy not only because of its revelations about Proust's private life at home but also as a piece of writing that made him envious. Halévy knew something about literary production. His father, Ludovic, was a dramatist who also wrote, with Henri Meilhac, the libretto for Bizet's *Carmen*, as well as libretti for many of Jacques Offenbach's wildly popular operettas. As Halévy reread Proust's letter, his awe increased; his schoolmate had dashed off this remarkable letter without crossing out a single word, an amazing feat, which led Halévy to conclude: "This deranged creature is extremely talented, and I know NOTHING that is sadder and more marvelously written than these two pages." Halévy expressed his belief that the excesses of genius should be tolerated, but worried that his friend's sensual obsessions might destroy his gifts. "More talented than anyone else. He overexerts himself. Weak, young, he fornicates, he masturbates, he engages, perhaps, in pederasty! He will perhaps show in his life flashes of genius that will be wasted."[18]

Amazingly enough, Halévy thus anticipated the major plotline of Proust's future novel: Will the Narrator discover his vocation and learn his craft as a writer in time to transform the experiences of his wasted years into the material of a novel? Decades later, when asked whether any of Proust's schoolmates had a premonition of his genius, Halévy replied that while they all recognized Marcel's talent, no one believed that he had "the willpower to achieve a masterpiece."[19]

Proust's parents agonized over the threat to his future success, a threat linked in their minds and in Dr. Proust's scientific writings to neurasthenia and a lack of willpower: masturbation. This practice, widely viewed in Proust's day as one of the gravest dangers to a young man's health and morality, became, for that reason, a "prime obsession" of parents and teachers. Masturbation was also suspected of being a significant contributing factor in causing homosexuality. Given the inevitably high rate of masturbation among adolescents, it is not surprising that family-sanctioned visits to prostitutes began in high school. Business in the brothels boomed during "holidays and the Thursday half-days" when the houses "swarmed with school boys" seeking cures for the bane of self-abuse.[20] "Some doctors . . . prescribed frequent visits to the brothel, preceded by large doses of alcohol. The idea was that an experienced prostitute would know how to generate the correct response, even in a nervous, drunken invert."[21]

Edmond de Goncourt's famous diary relates the description of one such "successful" treatment conducted by Dr. Jean-Martin Charcot, perhaps the most distinguished French physician of the era. Charcot had taught Sigmund Freud and steered him in "a direction in which he had already shown some telling signs of going: psychology."[22] Charcot had prescribed a visit to a prostitute for a patient of his, a thirty-two-year-old Belgian law professor. At age seven, the Belgian had seen a statue of Hercules, which "had given him a preference for men and a kind of horror of women. As a young man, he never made love, all the while struggling to resist his unnatural penchants. After undergoing Charcot's prescribed treatment in a Parisian house of prostitution, the man exited the brothel and shouted to the world: 'I can do it! Yes, I can!' " When last heard from, he was preparing "to marry one of his cousins."[23] Such testimony from an authority like Charcot provided additional incentive for desperate parents to try the brothel cure. It was the best remedy that science and lore had to offer.

Proust's sexual proclivities truly alarmed his parents, who felt that something must be done. Dr. Proust, who, like Charcot, believed that excessive masturbation and homosexuality were linked, gave his son ten francs and sent him to a brothel. Proust obeyed, but at the brothel he became so nervous that he broke a chamber pot, thereby losing both his erection and his money. Distraught but determined to successfully conclude the experiment, Proust sent his grandfather Nathé Weil an urgent plea for thirteen francs: "Here's why. I so desperately needed to see a woman in order to put an end to my bad habit of masturbating that papa gave me ten francs to go to a brothel. But first, in my agitation, I broke a chamber pot 3 francs and, second, in this same agitated state I was unable to screw. So here I am still awaiting each hour ten francs to satisfy myself and in addition three francs for the chamber pot." His request ended on a humorous note: "But I dare not ask papa for money again so soon and I hope you will be able to come to my aid in this instance, which, as you know, is not only exceptional but unique: it can't happen twice in one lifetime that a person's too upset to screw."[24] We do not know if his plea was granted, enabling him to return to the brothel. Whatever the outcome, Proust was not cured of his longings to have sex with boys.

That spring Proust wrote Halévy a long note from M. Choublier's "boring" geography class. After some literary chitchat about his favorite authors, Proust expressed his desire to meet him after school one day. In the postscript, he offered to share information that he had obtained about homosexuality among adolescents. Halévy had apparently raised the issue by hinting that he had an acquaintance whom he suspected of being a homosexual, or at least a latent one. Proust warned Halévy that he might very well be mistaken about the youth's inclinations as he himself had been:

(and if this interests you and you promise me *absolute secrecy,* not to tell even Bizet, I will give you documents of very great interest, belonging to me, addressed to me) from young men and especially ones in age from eight to seventeen who love other guys, eager always to see them (as I do Bizet) who cry and suffer far from them, and who desire only one thing to embrace them and sit in their lap, who love them for their *flesh*, who devour them with their eyes, who call them darling, my angel, very seriously, who write them passionate letters, and who would not for anything in the world practice pederasty.

After admitting that some of the boys could not resist touching each other, Proust expressed his opinion about homosexual love: "However, generally love wins out and [the boys] masturbate together. But don't mock them and the friend of whom you speak, if he is like this. They are simply in love. And I do not understand why their love is any more unclean than normal love."[25] Proust remained steadfast in this tolerant attitude throughout his life. In his early twenties, he elaborated this viewpoint in a short story "Avant la nuit" (Before the night), using an aesthetic argument to justify lesbian love.[26] "If fruitful love, meant to perpetuate the race, noble as a familiar, social, human duty, is superior to purely sensual love, then there is no hierarchy of sterile loves, and such a love is no less moral—or, rather, it is no more immoral for a woman to find pleasure with another woman than with a person of the opposite sex."[27]

In the autumn of 1888 Proust sent Halévy a sonnet depicting his dreams of romance; its title was all in capital letters: PEDERASTY. If he had a large sack of gold, he would run away to an ideal country "forever to sleep, love or live with a warm boy, Jacques, Pierre or Firmin," whose delicious "scent" he would "breathe . . . until he dies . . . far from the mournful knell of importunate Virtue."[28]

Around the same time, Proust submitted a prose poem about homosexuality to *La Revue lilas*, one of several little literary reviews he and his friends created while at the lycée Condorcet.[29] The editors of the review were shocked by the poem and rejected it. The poem, obviously the result of adolescent wishful desire, paints an idealized, albeit somewhat decadent, ancient Greece, where love between boys is not merely tolerated but openly celebrated. A beautiful lad named Glaukos, who shares Proust's love of philosophy, poetry, and young men, surrounds himself with stacks of letters from boys who cherish his "little, soft body" and reciprocate his affection by loving him "madly," "infinitely." Glaukos delights in basking half-naked under the sun in the company of these handsome, devoted youths. Proust clearly yearned to inhabit such a world in which he could perch on the lap of a lovely boy while blissfully satisfying his sensual and intellectual longings: "Often seated on the sturdy knees of one of them, cheek to cheek, bodies entwined, [Glaukos] discusses with him Aristotles' philosophy and Euripides' poems, while they embrace and caress each other, making elegant, clever remarks in the sumptuous room, near magnificent flowers."[30]

Proust's friends, unlike those of the fortunate Glaukos, rejected his sexual overtures and tormented him because he dared to make such advances and because his clinging possessiveness annoyed and exasperated them. The crisis of sexual identity is one of the most traumatic and dangerous that an adolescent can face. An important element of Proust's literary genius lies in his ability to see and depict the humorous as well as the serious side of such human predicaments.

Young Proust, seen by others and often depicted by himself in early letters as the incarnation of the wretched, insecure mama's boy, proved to be a precocious psychologist and a gifted comic, who loved to mimic his friends and professors. Knowing how ridiculous he often appeared to his friends, he frequently amused them with outrageous parodies of himself. One September day, elated by the beautiful fall weather as he headed off to a riding lesson in the Bois de Boulogne, Proust sent Robert Dreyfus this self-caricature in which he imagined himself to be a great lord, who could "order up a play" and do anything he liked. First, he would declare his love to Jacques Bizet. Then, to compensate for his unrequited love, he'd go for a carriage ride in the Acacia Gardens, where elegant, wealthy Parisians went to see and be seen. "That, to my taste, is the height of Parisian beauty in 1888." He next imagined two courtesans gossiping while riding through the park. One asks the other if she knows "M.P." and then tattles about Proust's crushes on his schoolmates, revealing that he is nothing but a little hypocrite, because, although he had proclaimed "quite a feeling" for her and merely paternal love for a schoolmate, she has learned the truth that he "loves" the youth as he "would a woman." According to the courtesan, Proust can't help being fickle, even among the boys: "The nasty part of it, *ma chère*, is that after making a fuss over B he drops him and cajoles D, whom he soon leaves to fling himself at the feet of E and a moment later into the lap of F. Is he a whore, is he mad, is he a charlatan, is he an imbecile?" Although Proust wrote the parody in the third person, the answer he gives to the courtesan's question is clearly personal: Proust is "all of these at once."[31] The ambiguous, protean nature of Proust's sexuality depicted in these self-portraits from his schooldays was later to be transposed for his fictional characters.

By the end of September, perhaps under parental pressure or because he himself saw the need to reform, Proust wrote Dreyfus again about his "new" love interests, this time heterosexual ones, claiming to have a platonic "passion" for a "famous" but unnamed "courtesan." He also mentioned, again without naming her, a pretty Viennese girl he had met in dance class, giving Dreyfus to understand that he was involved in an "absorbing liaison" with the girl and that his attachment "threatens to go on at least a year for the greater good of the *café-concerts* and other places of the same kind, where one takes this sort of person."[32] Nothing more is known about the Austrian beauty met in dance class, except that—if she really did exist—he quickly forgot her. This letter, unlike those written to and about boys, has a hollow ring.

Proust did make one audacious attempt at heterosexual seduction whose authenticity cannot be contested because the scene was witnessed and recorded by Halévy, his coconspirator. Halévy had told Proust about a beautiful woman he had noticed behind the counter in a dairy shop on the slopes of Montmartre.[33] One day after school, Halévy led the intrigued Proust to the shop, where the two randy boys stopped on the sidewalk and simply stared, transfixed by the sight of Mme Chirade busily serving her customers delicious cheeses and creams. Struck by the splendor of her black hair, fair skin, and fine features, Proust whispered in Halévy's ear: "How beautiful she is!" A short silence ensued during which Proust, absorbed in admiration, tried to imagine what it might be like to possess such a gorgeous creature. Then, he startled Halévy by asking, "Do you think we can sleep with her?" Halévy, who had never considered such bold action, felt a sudden respect for the friend he had considered a sissy. Inflamed by desire and eager for action, Proust quickly proposed: "Let's bring her some flowers."

A few days later, the boys returned to Montmartre, Proust bearing an armload of roses. Arriving in front of the shop, they looked in and saw Mme Chirade at her usual place, tending to customers. Unaccountably shy, Halévy remained glued to the sidewalk, his eyes wide and darting as he wondered whether Proust would actually dare to approach the woman. Holding the roses before him, Proust advanced into the shop and went straight to Mme Chirade. Halévy watched Proust's back as he spoke to the captivating creature. Halévy saw her smile gently but firmly, her lips forming the word *non* as she shook her head. Proust apparently insisted, at which point, the beautiful lady, still smiling and determined, advanced in slow, invincible steps, forcing him to retreat until, before he knew it, he found himself back out on the sidewalk standing next to his amazed and flustered friend.

We might speculate that Halévy was the pawn in an elaborate ruse by Proust, who had marched into the shop certain of two things: that the lady would certainly refuse and that Halévy would testify to all their friends that Proust was not only sexually attracted to women but also audacious beyond belief in his attempts to seduce them. His homosexual overtures, the boys were bound to conclude, were simply the result of that common schoolboy phenomenon of raging sexual urges seeking a handy outlet. Had not Proust, who knew that homosexuals were despised and considered effeminate, said as much himself in the letter to Bizet, when he observed that once the "flower" of youth had ripened into "fruit" it would be "forbidden"? Proust may have decided, no doubt with strong parental approval, that the best public stance was to appear heterosexual.

In his private life, however, Proust remained true to his love for those of his own sex, even though he was not immune to the temptations offered by girls who—like Marie Benardaky and Jeanne Pouquet—when still in the tomboyish stage had masculine qualities that complemented his own feminine attributes. In his novel such girls are represented by Gilberte and especially by the athletic Albertine.

The somewhat burlesque attempt to seduce Mme Chirade and Proust's disastrous visit to the brothel were initiatives within the range of normal sexual behavior that one expected from lusty young men. Such initiatives obviously pleased Dr. Proust, who had, as we have seen, ordered his son to demonstrate his manhood by having sex with a prostitute, in keeping with the practice of generation upon generation of young men coming of age.

Paul Morand recounted the standard sexual initiation that he and his adolescent companions underwent. The eager boys went to read dirty novels in the bookstores or lingered on the street to watch whores solicit men arriving at the Gare Saint-Lazare. Once aroused, they ran round to public toilets where they formed a circle and masturbated, but solo—Morand insists—with no contact between them. When they turned sixteen, the age of majority, they pocketed five francs and headed for the nearest whorehouse in the rue de Hanovre or the rue des Moulins. Once the boys had completed this rite of passage and become young men, they "ceased their solitary games" of masturbation.[34]

In his senior year at the lycée Condorcet, Proust studied philosophy under the man who became his most respected teacher, Alphonse Darlu. From Darlu he learned, as an antidote to Hippolyte Taine's positivism, the lessons of Platonic and Kantian idealism and rationalism. These philosophies, with the later addition of Ruskin's aesthetics, served Proust well until he advanced beyond these systems to formulate his own aesthetics and ethics.[35] Proust admired in Darlu's discourses the strength of his convictions, his enthusiastic and contagious love of philosophy, and his firm belief in the progress of civilization, made possible by the succession of great minds in all domains of creativity. Darlu believed as strongly in science as in philosophy and in the role of religion in its proper domain; his idea of God was as a spirit embodying truth.[36]

Sometime in the autumn of his senior year, Proust wrote Daniel Halévy a letter showing that his thoughts in Darlu's class were fixed, at times, on subjects less idealistic and transcendental than Plato and Kant. Having apparently received a verbal lashing from Halévy, who had also called him a pederast, Proust replied that his "ethical beliefs" allowed him "to regard the pleasures of the senses as a splendid thing." He then attempted to explain why affectionate caresses between boys need not be corrupt:

> You think me jaded and effete. You are mistaken. If you are delicious, if you have lovely eyes which reflect the grace and refinement of your mind with such purity that I feel I cannot fully love your mind without kissing your eyes, if your body and mind, like your thoughts, are so lithe and slender that I feel I could mingle more intimately with your thoughts by sitting on your lap, if, finally, I feel that the charm of your person, in which I cannot separate your keen mind from your agile body, would refine and enhance "the sweet joy of love" for me, there is nothing in all that to deserve your contemptuous words, which would have been more fittingly addressed to someone surfeited with women and seeking new pleasures in pederasty. I am glad to say that I have some highly intelligent friends, distinguished by great moral delicacy, who have amused themselves at one time with a boy. . . . That was the beginning of their youth. Later on they went back to women.[37]

This argument, justifying homosexual love between innocent youths as a rite of passage, reads like a more mature and sophisticated version of Proust's plea to Jacques Bizet about savoring the delicious flower of the fruit not yet forbidden. It also anticipates the explanation later given in the novel regarding the disappearance of "conventional homosexuality" in the modern, decadent era, as is seen in his examples of the "old masters" Socrates and Montaigne, who "permit men in their earliest youth to 'amuse themselves' so as to know something of all pleasures, and so as to release their excess tenderness."[38] (Proust realized later that he was mistaken about Montaigne's attitude regarding homosexuality.) Although he claimed to believe that the "old masters" were wrong, he did accept the "general tenor of their advice." Then he urged Daniel to relent: "Don't call me a pederast, it hurts my feelings."[39]

When Proust realized that Darlu was going to question him, he had to stop his letter writing and concentrate on philosophy. First, though, he found the time to pose a quick question to Daniel: "But tell me what you mean by saying that your hands are not pure...."[40] The indirect question, placed as though it were a casual afterthought, shows Proust typically eager to learn all he could about his friends' secrets. Daniel's earlier reference to "impure hands" was, Proust surmised, a confession that he engaged in masturbation.

We see that young Proust remained trapped in the struggle between a boy's desires to remain pure on the one hand and on the other to taste the forbidden fruit. Ever overflowing with tenderness, he sought an ethics that sanctioned the physical possession of his masculine ideal: intelligent beauty. *My ethical beliefs allow me to regard the pleasures of the senses as a splendid thing.*

Darlu may not have known that his admiring pupil spent part of his class time writing letters justifying homosexual love between youths, but he certainly knew about Proust's frequent infatuations with classmates. One day when Darlu saw him at Condorcet with yet another new friend, he made a point of inquiring afterward: "What number did you give him when he passed through the door of your heart?"[41] Clearly young Proust wore his heart on his sleeve.

In 1892, when Proust was twenty-one, he and his former Condorcet classmate Fernand Gregh wrote portraits of each other. Gregh took his name for Proust from the character "Fabrice" that Proust had created in his sketches of Italian comedy, later published as part of *Pleasures and Days*. In the first line Gregh stated his friend's defining characteristic: "Fabrice needs to be loved," demonstrating that even after having completed his military service and begun university studies, Proust still had not outgrown his excessive thirst for affection.[42]

CHAPTER TWO

Mighty Hermaphrodite

My favorite qualities in a man: *Feminine charm.*

My favorite qualities in a woman: *Manly virtue and openness in friendship.*

Proust's youthful role-playing of a boy-girl or whore sitting seductively in the laps of his male friends gave him an early understanding of what it is to be an androgynous being. He routinely looked for feminine traits among his male friends and their male relatives, and for masculine traits among his female friends and their relatives, in search of the types that were to become the men-women or women-men of his novel. When Proust wrote to the actress Louisa de Mornand to express his condolences for the death of her eighteen-year-old brother, Ernest, killed during the war, he recalled having seen a photograph of the young man, known for his good looks, that had made the writer eager to meet him, "for I have always been curious about the effects of the transposition of a friend's or loved one's face from the masculine sex into the feminine and vice versa."[1]

Proust used such transpositions for some of his principal characters. The youthful Saint-Loup's masculine beauty and his striking resemblance to his aunt Oriane de Guermantes are the first clues of his latent homosexuality. The tomboyish Mlle Vinteuil resembles her father; Charlus resembles his female relatives. These androgynous likenesses were intended in part to prepare for the profanation scenes, although the scene in which Mlle Vinteuil defiles her father's photograph is the only one that Proust fully developed and integrated into the story as a key plot element.

Proust's interest in all aspects of sexuality is demonstrated in the many pages he devoted to the topic in his writings. He was not, however, the only member of the family to produce documents regarding sexual behavior. His father, Dr. Adrien Proust, and his younger brother, Dr. Robert Proust, studied human sexuality in a clinical sense in their treatment of patients who suffered from sexual disorders that were physiological or psychological in nature. Marcel's friend Robert de Billy saw the elder Dr. Proust's influence in his son's attempts to diagnose the various manifestations of sexuality, in his refusal to establish a "hierarchy" of such passions, in striving to remain objective, in the belief that no "disorder should be glorious or shameful," and in understanding the relative nature of sexual mores. Billy, a well-read and widely traveled diplomat, recognized such relativity himself: "Some sentiments are accepted as natural on certain continents and punished on others." In any case, "such feelings" obviously "influence the societies wherein they exist" and therefore more than justified the studious attention to which Proust subjected them.[2]

Adrien Proust dealt with sexual anomalies as would a psychiatrist, treating both mind and body, in his firm conviction that "the patient's mental state . . . determines in large measure the dysfunctions of the genital organs."[3] This same belief in the importance of mind over matter led him to diagnose his son's relentless asthma attacks as psychosomatic in origin, a conclusion that infuriated Proust and further alienated the two men.[4] Proust adopted the same point of view in his novel, however, to explain Charlus's evolution from a virile homosexual to a more flamboyant, effeminate type. The baron's "ladylike" behavior stems directly from his mental state. His desire for men is so powerful that it alters his body chemistry, causing him to become a woman:

> Although other reasons may have dictated this transformation of M. de Charlus, and purely physical ferments may have set his chemistry "working" and made his body gradually change into the category of women's bodies, nevertheless the change that we record here was of spiritual origin. By dint of thinking tenderly of men one becomes a woman, and an imaginary skirt hampers one's movements. The obsession, as in the other instance it can affect one's health, may in this instance alter one's sex.[5]

Proust considered this portrait of Charlus innovative and explained why in a letter to André Gide: "I tried to portray a homosexual infatuated with virility, because, without knowing it, he is a Woman. I don't in the least claim that he is the only type of homosexual. But he's an interesting type which, I believe, hasn't ever been described."[6]

Other passages support the view that Proust accepted his father's notion that nervous conditions cause behavior seen as aberrant. In his writings intended for publication, Proust concedes that given the persecutions and social intolerance of homosexuals, the only ones who existed in his time were those who could not help themselves. Intolerance and intense social pressures had long since stifled those youths who might have been tempted to indulge their desires for members of their own sex. Faced with opprobrium or worse, the only homosexuals who dared express such inclinations were those whose "nervous" condition made it impossible for them to conform to society's norm. In *Sodom and Gomorrah,* the Narrator promises to explain more fully "what we mean by nervous weakness, and why it is that a Greek of the time of Socrates, a Roman of the time of Augustus, might be what we know them to have been [homosexual or bisexual] and yet remain absolutely normal, not men-women such as we see around us today."[7]

Proust had first tested this argument in "Before the Night," where Leslie uses it to justify Dorothy's love affair with a soprano: "The cause of such love is a nervous impairment which is too exclusively nervous to have any moral content. . . . Furthermore . . . if we refine sensuality to the point of making it aesthetic, then, just as male and female bodies can be equally beautiful, there is no reason why a truly artistic woman might not fall in love with another woman. In a truly artistic nature, physical attraction and repulsion are modified by the contemplation of beauty."[8]

As promised, the Narrator returns to the subject in *The Captive*, offering a fuller explanation of why "conventional homosexuality" no longer exists and arguing that neuroses often prove beneficial not only to those who suffer from them but also to society. Charlus's sensitivity and artistic nature, which he neglects to cultivate, are said to result from his homosexual nature: "[Charlus] refused to see that for nineteen hundred years . . . all conventional homosexuality—that of Plato's young friends as well as that of Virgil's shepherds—has disappeared, that what survives and increases is only the involuntary, the neurotic kind, which one conceals from other people and misrepresents to oneself."[9]

The Narrator paints an idyllic picture of homosexual love among the ancients that recalls the argument for yielding to his advances that Proust himself had made, many years earlier, to Jacques Bizet in the note written at the lycée Condorcet: the "delicious flower" of adolescence, Proust had written in the note, was not yet "forbidden fruit." Among the ancients, such liaisons were deemed appropriate or, in any case, were tolerated between youths who were expected later to engage in normal sexual relations: "The shepherd in Theocritus who sighs for love of a boy will have no reason later on to be less hard of heart, less dull of wit than the other shepherd whose flute sounds for Amaryllis. For the former is not suffering from a disease; he is conforming to the customs of his time." In Proust's day, at least according to the Narrator, homosexuality determined by a nervous condition had its compensations in the enhancement of one's overall awareness of the inner and exterior worlds, creating a sensitivity that is extremely useful to the artist: "It is the homosexuality that survives in spite of obstacles, shameful, execrated, that is the only true form, the only form that corresponds in one and the same person to an intensification of the intellectual qualities."[10]

It seems evident that by "conventional homosexuality" Proust means socially acceptable behavior and that he yearned for a return to the attitude of those ancient days when tolerance prevailed and love in all its forms was accepted and even celebrated. It may also be reasonable to conclude that if sexual tolerance were universal, homosexuals would lose the advantage that Proust claims they have over heterosexuals. For example, Charlus might become more like his brother, the duc de Guermantes, who, although married to one of the most beautiful women in Paris, has a string of mistresses. The duke lacks any artistic sensitivity because he fits the norm so well: "One is dismayed at the relationship that can exist between these [intellectual qualities] and a person's bodily attributes when one thinks of the tiny dislocation of a purely physical taste, the slight blemish in one of the senses, that explains why the world of poets and musicians, so firmly barred against the Duc de Guermantes, opens its portals to M. de Charlus." Here Proust is endorsing the view—widely held then and now—that homosexuals are more artistic than heterosexuals.[11]

In his letters and in conversations with other homosexuals such as André Gide, Proust removed the stigma of same-sex love. He did so not to placate Gide, who abhorred Proust's depiction of homosexuals, but because he never wavered in his belief, expressed publicly in "Before the Night," and earlier as a schoolboy to Daniel Halévy, that he finds no moral or hygienic distinctions between heterosexual and homosexual love. Likewise, the Narrator refuses to pass judgment on the liaison between Charlus and the violinist Charlie Morel: "I had no opinion as to the proportion in which good and evil might be blended in the relations between Morel and M. de Charlus."[12] At times, he engages the reader in the debate about homosexuality by asking a rhetorical question: "Why, when we admire in the face of this man a delicacy that touches our hearts, a grace, a natural gentleness such as men do not possess, should we be dismayed to learn that this young man runs after boxers?"[13]

Apparently, Proust's only rule of conduct regarding sexual ethics is that one must be true to one's fundamental sexual nature, simple or complex as it may be, and not betray that nature out of mere curiosity by engaging in sexual experimentation. The Narrator condemns Charlus when he commits this transgression on reaching "the stage when the monotony of the pleasures that his vice has to offer had become wearying." Unable to resist the urge for "novelty," he sometimes spends "the night with a woman, just as a normal man may once in his life have wished to go to bed with a boy, from a similar though inverse curiosity, equally unhealthy."[14]

Dr. Robert Proust had specialized in gynecology and titled his dissertation "Female Genital Surgery." From 1904 to 1914 he worked as Dr. Samuel Pozzi's assistant at the Hôpital Broca, during which time he studied "andrologie" (the physiology and pathology of male genitalia) and gynecology. The two men collaborated closely on a number of articles on hermaphrodites, a specialty of Pozzi's. In particular, Robert examined Adèle H., a famous hermaphrodite, and contributed to Pozzi's studies of the patient, the results of which were published in *Le Journal de chirurgie*. Robert served as the journal's codirector, and the copies for some of these articles are in his handwriting.[15] Their work was interrupted by the war; then only a few months before the armistice, a deranged patient murdered Pozzi.

Because Dr. Pozzi was also one of the models for Proust's fictional Dr. Cottard, it may be well to say a word about this accomplished, colorful figure whose unusually handsome looks were captured in one of John Singer Sargent's most remarkable full-length portraits. The doctor's skills matched his appearance, and he operated on many of the era's celebrities, including Sarah Bernhardt, on whom he performed a hysterectomy. So successful were the results in rejuvenating the actress that Bernhardt began to call Pozzi Dr. God, which is the glorifying attribute that Mme Verdurin uses in Proust's novel to de-scribe Dr. Cottard.[16] Pozzi was a notorious womanizer, and his ex-ploits earned him yet another nickname: *l'Amour médecin*, Dr. Love. Geneviève Straus was rumored to have succumbed to his charms. Mme d'Aubernon, a leading salon hostess, dubbed Pozzi's long-suffering wife "Pozzi's mute" because she never said anything about his repeated infidelities. Far from denying his liaisons, Pozzi tried to reassure his spouse by joking, "I didn't betray you, I complimented you!"[17] The surgeon was so vain that Léon Daudet, a former medical student himself, liked to joke that although Pozzi had the reputation of being a good surgeon, Daudet would not even let him cut his hair for fear that if there were a mirror anywhere nearby Pozzi would become so lost in admiring himself that he might slice Daudet's face.[18]

There is no evidence that the research conducted by Pozzi and Ro-bert Proust directly influenced Marcel's ideas about human sexuality. Indeed, Proust came to resent the vulgarization resulting from inten-sive scientific studies in the new field of sexology. Apparently, he feared the demystification of "vice" or attempts to make an arid scientific study of physical love. At least that is how Paul Morand interpreted his reaction when the diplomat returned from Berlin in 1922 and placed on the writer's bed "the enormous volume" compiled by the pioneer Magnus Hirschfeld at his Institute for Sexual Science, the world's first sexological institute. Far from finding the gift appeal-ing or amusing, Proust shrugged his shoulders "in despair."[19] Even though there are no references in Proust's known letters to his broth-er's research on hermaphrodites, these beings became important fig-ures in Proust's depiction and explanation of human sexuality. Such creatures clearly preoccupied him; he occasionally sketched portraits of hermaphrodites in the margins of his notebooks.[20]

When Charlus, normally "so obsessed with virility," lets down his guard and unwittingly imitates the gestures and attitudes of a female relative, he is said to do so under "the influence of the transit of Venus Androgyne."[21] There are ancient statues representing this type of Venus, often bald and bearded and endowed with male and female genitalia, who served as the protector of all births.[22] Such figures were fairly common among the ancients, whose creation myths often credited androgynous births with engendering the divine and human races and associated hermaphroditic Venus with creation and fertility rites. This interpretation differs little from Proust's idealized notion of the androgyne or hermaphrodite as the perfect, united (or reunited) creature. According to the Narrator, when we sleep and dream, we revert to our primitive, androgynous origins: "The race that inhabits [the realm of sleep], like that of our first human ancestors, is androgynous."[23]

Charlus's great infatuation, Morel, is not—as one might expect, given the baron's obsession with masculinity—a virile heterosexual, but a bisexual: "Anyone looking at Morel at that moment, with his girlish air enshrined in his masculine beauty, would have understood the obscure divination which marked him out to certain women no less than them to him." A true androgyne, Morel "was sufficiently fond of both women and men to satisfy either sex with the fruits of his experience with the other."[24]

Proust's answers to a questionnaire in a friend's keepsake book regarding his preferred qualities in men (feminine charm) and women (manly virtue and openness in friendship) underscore his belief, determined in his youth, that neither sex is complete in itself and that humanity consists of a variety of sexual types, each in search of the ideal partner whose sexual makeup best complements his or her own.[25] The encounter and union of two people whose sexual needs are a perfect match can be seen only as a positive event. When such unions take place between men, they do not represent same-sex couplings— which is why Proust preferred the term *invert* to *homosexual*—but a true union of opposite or complementary needs.[26] Thus Proust's treatment of lesbianism has recently been viewed as the only "homosexual" part of the novel.[27] This notion of seeking what is missing in one's own sexual makeup leads him to elaborate a variety of sexual types, including spouses who adjust, as needed, either by the altered sexual identity of one (the Vaugoubert couple) or by the husband's satisfying his desire for "inverted" sex with another man by seeking partners outside the marriage, while remaining happily and heterosexually bound to his wife (the Courvoisiers).

> The young Vicomte de Courvoisier thought he was the only man alive, perhaps the only man since the beginning of the world, to be tempted by someone of his own sex. Supposing this inclination to come to him from the devil, he struggled against it, married an extremely pretty wife and had children by her. Then one of his cousins taught him that the tendency is fairly wide-spread and was even so kind as to take him to places where he could indulge it. M. de Courvoisier became fonder than ever of his wife and redoubled his philoprogenitive zeal, and he and she were quoted as the happiest couple in Paris.[28]

The Narrator, who clearly approves of this arrangement, regrets that Robert de Saint-Loup—also madly in love with Morel—has failed to adopt it, a failure that has ruined his marriage to Gilberte: "Robert, instead of being content with inversion, made his wife ill with jealousy by keeping mistresses without pleasure to himself."[29] (Charlus also endorses the idea that homosexuals can make their wives happy, as he apparently had his late spouse: "I've always said that they [homosexuals] made the best husbands.")[30] And the Narrator continues his ruminations on sexual attraction and the importance of complementary traits in a clear endorsement of the idea that opposites attract and a repetition of the notion that sexual tastes are biologically inherited: "It is possible that Morel, being excessively dark, was necessary to Saint-Loup in the way that shadow is necessary to the sunbeam. Can one not imagine some golden-haired aristocrat sprung from an ancient family such as his, intelligent and endowed with every kind of prestige, concealing within him, unbeknown to his friends, a secret taste for negroes?"[31]

In the case of M. and Mme de Vaugoubert, Proust allows for the influence of both nature and nurture on her altered sexuality. I will quote here only the nature part, which, like the comparison of the union of Charlus and Jupien to the encounter of the bumblebee and the rare flower which only it can fertilize, shows Proust seeking to endow all sexual varieties with a natural sanction:

> Mme de Vaugoubert was really a man. Whether she had always been one, or had grown to be as I now saw her, matters little, for in either case we are faced with one of the most touching miracles of nature which . . . makes the human kingdom resemble the kingdom of flowers. . . . If the woman has not at first these masculine characteristics, she adopts them by degrees, to please her husband, and even unconsciously, by that sort of mimicry which makes certain flowers assume the appearance of the insects which they seek to attract.[32]

In the "dumb show" of the mating ritual performed by Jupien and Charlus, Proust insists on its "beauty," a word that occurs throughout the relatively brief chapter on homosexuality that opens the volume *Sodom and Gomorrah*.[33] The "scene was not, however, positively comic; it was stamped with a strangeness, or if you like a naturalness, the beauty of which steadily increased." The strange beauty that the Narrator sees in the Charlus-Jupien encounter comes from the chance meeting of two different but complementary homosexual types: "[Jupien is] the man predestined to exist in order that they [men like Charlus] may have their share of sensual pleasure on this earth: the man who cares only for elderly gentlemen." Some pages later, Proust returns to this idea: "It is no small matter for a person to be able to encounter the sole pleasure which he is capable of enjoying, and that 'every soul here below' can impart to some other 'its music or its fragrance or its flame.' "[34] He pursues this theme, comparing Charlus and Jupien to Romeo and Juliet, and expands it to include biological and cosmic destiny:

> [They] may believe with good reason that their love is not a momentary whim but a true predestination, determined by the harmonies of their temperaments, and not only by their own personal temperaments but by those of their ancestors, by their most distant strains of

heredity, so much so that the fellow-creature who is conjoined with them has belonged to them from before their birth, has attracted them by a force comparable to that which governs the worlds on which we spent our former lives.[35]

In the light of contemporary society's sensitivity, or lack thereof, to the plight of gays, such passages may be read as an impassioned plea for tolerance and a justification for same-sex unions.

Can a case be made for a bisexual Proust? Those who knew him well and those who have written about his sexuality are divided into two camps: those, like Jean Cocteau and Paul Morand, who believe he was telling the truth when he told André Gide that he had known love only with men and those, like Robert Dreyfus, Lucien Daudet, and Robert Soupault, who believe he did have brief affairs with such women as the courtesan Laure Hayman and the actress Louisa de Mornand.

Dreyfus, who knew Proust well from the time of their schooldays, when he observed the adolescent Proust playing with the Benardaky sisters, later wrote that he believed his friend's attraction to women was genuine. Dreyfus goes so far as to say, in making a strong case for Proust's bisexuality, that he frequented "whores in houses of prostitution" and "engaged in flirtations with actresses and courtesans." Dreyfus is categorical in his conclusion about Proust's sexuality, at least in his youth: "But what is certain, is that he loved . . . both sexes, which horrified us [his schoolmates] because we only liked women." Regretting the intolerant attitude of Marcel's classmates, the older and wiser Dreyfus noted that "life has taught me to be indulgent" toward homosexuals because he had concluded that sexual orientation is genetic and that "one cannot choose" one's sexuality, an attitude that matches Proust's in the novel.[36]

We can use the case of Louisa de Mornand to represent the mature women with whom Proust carried on intense flirtations. He became well acquainted with Mornand during and after the period when she was the mistress of his friend the Marquis Louis d'Albufera. Albufera and Mornand inspired to a large degree the Marquis Robert de Saint-Loup's liaison with the actress Rachel in the novel.

In the copy of *La Bible d'Amiens* that Proust inscribed for Louisa de Mornand, he used biblical language and a play on her name to suggest the carnal attraction that he felt for her. The first sentence warned that what followed was risqué: "*Dedication not to be left lying around*. To Louisa Mornand, ringed by the blaze of her adorer's eyes. For men who have seen Louisa, but have had no success with her—that is to say everyone—other women cease to be attractive. Whence this couplet: 'He who Louisa cannot win / Must be content with Onan's sin.' I love and admire you with all my heart. Marcel." Proust used the archaic French verb *morner*, which meant to blunt a lance or to render it harmless by fitting a ring to its tip, a clear allusion to copulation. Since Mornand refuses to "blunt the lances" of the men who desire her, they must resort to Onan's sin of masturbation.[37]

On another occasion, Mornand invited Proust to her apartment, where he watched her read in bed before falling asleep. Afterward, she sent him an autographed photograph from "The Original who is so fond of little Marcel. Louisa. April 1904." In thanking her for the photograph, which he was "mad about," he opined that what she had written to him would "become a reality for me and will have the power to bind my fickle heart."[38] He enclosed a mildly titillating poem of thirty-three lines, evoking the rosy vision of her in bed. This bedside visit inspired, at least in part, the episode in which the Narrator rapturously describes his ritual of watching Albertine in slumber before he lies beside her and caresses her.

Mornand, who never achieved celebrity as an actress, later capitalized on her relationship with Proust by selling his letters and giving interviews in which she hinted that they may have been lovers: "We had a loving relationship which was neither an ideal flirtation nor an exclusive liaison, but, on Proust's side, a keen passion balanced between affection and desire, and on mine a deeply felt attachment which was more than friendship."[39]

The only person to whom Proust avowed his homosexuality and

who left a record of it is André Gide. Gide had called on Proust and brought a copy of *Corydon*—Gide's book about sexuality—for him to read, asking that he not reveal to anyone the book's contents. During the visit Gide discussed some of the more intimate episodes from his projected memoirs, whereupon Proust suggested, "You can tell everything provided you don't say 'I.'" Gide did not find this a useful hint for someone intent on writing his memoirs. As Proust began to talk about his own sexuality, Gide was somewhat astonished to hear that "far from hiding his homosexuality, he exposes it and I could almost say prides himself on it." Proust admitted that he had "never liked women except platonically and had only known love with men." This revelation surprised Gide, who had never thought that Proust was "exclusively homosexual." Unfortunately, Gide does not tell us why he had assumed that Proust was bisexual.[40]

Is it possible that Proust was telling Gide what he wanted to hear? A notorious flatterer, Proust often tailored his remarks to suit his listener. Henri Bonnet maintained that Proust would never have made such a confession "had he known Gide was keeping a diary in which he would tell all."[41] This seems a particularly weak case to make, given that Gide had just told Proust about his plans to write his memoirs.

We cannot identify with certainty any of Proust's sexual partners based on the evidence we now have. It does seem reasonable to conclude from Proust's letters, testimony left by his friends, and the vivid and psychologically complex female characters that he created in his novel, that women clearly fascinated him and that he observed and studied them closely.

Was Proust's often-proclaimed physical attraction to girls genuine? If Mme Chirade had said "Oui!" would he indeed have slept with her? Was he truly attracted to Jacques Bizet's maid or only seeking information for a story when he asked his driver Jossien whether the maid was someone one could sleep with?[42] Letters dating from his adolescent years prove that he enjoyed flirting with girls, a practice he continued with attractive women, especially those who were the wives and mistresses of his friends. As a result he could observe them very closely, but safely, from behind the barrier of fidelity imposed by jealous possession on the part of the men and respect for the duties of friendship on Proust's part. Proust's rather frequent remarks about being attracted to beautiful girls and women have been taken as smokescreens to hide his homosexuality; still, one could cite many letters in which he flirts with the female recipient, or letters to male friends in which he comments on the beauty of women seen in cafés and in society, or in which he declares his love for a particular girl or woman, or in which he refers, always obliquely and mysteriously, to mistresses or to a girl or woman he might be on the verge of marrying.

Proust's basic idea about the human personality, demonstrated in his novel, was that most people are androgynous, containing both male and female elements. This is particularly true, he believed, of artists. What Proust consistently denied were homosexual acts, not homoerotic attraction, which he obviously felt and frankly expressed, both in his letters to male friends and in his writings. He may have been lying, of course, about being attracted to women and about not engaging in homosexual acts, but there is some evidence that he was telling the truth. He also maintained that people are not necessarily fixed in their sexual preferences, but may vary over time, a premise confirmed by scientific research at least as early as Alfred C. Kinsey's 1948 *Sexual Behavior in the Human Male*. Kinsey's research also revealed that, as Proust had proposed, people do not fall into neatly defined sexual categories: "Males do not represent two discrete populations, heterosexual and homosexual. The living world is a continuum in each and every one of its aspects. The sooner we learn this concerning human sexual behavior the sooner we will reach a sound understanding of the realities of sex."[43]

The specific nature of Proust's own sexuality does not really matter, of course, if we accept his demonstrations about the highly subjective nature of love and his conclusion that, no matter the object, the experience and the emotions are the same whether heterosexual or homosexual.

CHAPTER THREE

My Heart Beats Only for You

My favorite occupation: *Loving.*

On October 29, 1895, Proust's short story "The Death of Baldassare Silvande, Viscount of Sylvania" appeared in the *Revue hebdomadaire.* Proust received 150 francs for the piece, apparently the first money he had earned as a writer. He had dedicated the story "To Reynaldo Hahn, poet, singer, and musician."[1] Hahn thanked Proust for the honor and received this reply: "I would like to be the master of all that you desire on earth in order to bring it to you—the author of all you admire in art in order to dedicate it to you. I'm beginning in a very small way! But, who knows, if you encourage me . . ."[2]

The two men had met a year earlier at a large party given by the society hostess and artist Madeleine Lemaire. That evening, Mme Lemaire's guests were entertained by a tenor from the Opéra-Comique who sang Count Robert de Montesquiou's poems from *Les Chauves-souris* (The bats) set to music by Léon Delafosse, a young pianist, making his debut on the social scene. Proust, who prided himself on being a matchmaker, had introduced Delafosse, a blond with pretty features, to the volatile count, who quickly made the musician his protégé and began to manage his career.[3]

While Delafosse played his accompaniments to the songs about bats, Proust's eyes were drawn to another young man in the crowd, the handsome, dark-complexioned Reynaldo Hahn, whose musical talent far exceeded Delafosse's. At nineteen, three years younger than Proust, Hahn was already a successful composer and accomplished performer in Paris's most exclusive drawing rooms. He had recently completed his first opera, *L'Ile du rêve,* based on Pierre Loti's novel *Le Mariage de Loti.* The "little Venezuelan," as his professors and classmates called him, had made his debut at the age of six in the salon of Princesse Mathilde, where he had sung in a thin but strong voice arias from opéras bouffes by Jacques Offenbach.

A star of the Conservatoire de Musique de Paris, where he had begun his studies at age ten, Hahn had been trained by three of the era's most distinguished composers: Jules Massenet, Charles Gounod, and Camille Saint-Saëns. When Hahn was only fourteen, he set to music Paul Verlaine's poems *Chansons grises,* a collection of songs that made the young composer famous overnight. Two years later, *Le Figaro* published Hahn's musical setting of Victor Hugo's poem "Si mes vers avaient des ailes" (If only my poems had wings).[4] This piece quickly became popular in Paris salons, where Hahn often performed it.

Hahn's professors ranked him among the best students in composition and piano performance. When the noted author Alphonse Daudet sought a composer for an important commission, Massenet recommended Hahn. Daudet was delighted with Hahn, who quickly became a regular guest at the Daudet home and a friend of Daudet's sons, Léon and Lucien. Through Hahn, Proust was to become a close friend of the Daudets' as well.

During his adolescent years, Hahn had carried on an intense flirtation with Cléo de Mérode, a beautiful young dancer in the corps de ballet at the Opéra. By age thirteen, the precociously seductive Cléo had already posed for the painters Jean-Louis Forain and Edgar

Degas. Had Hahn felt a genuine attraction to her, or was he merely engaging in the sort of flirtation that Proust had enjoyed with courtesans like Laure Hayman? Did Hahn himself even know the true nature of his feelings?

Although Hahn brimmed with talent and energy and had a generally optimistic air, his friends at times detected a melancholy streak and a tendency to be sarcastic. Perhaps he agonized over his sexual identity. This brings to mind the Narrator's observation regarding youth and self-knowledge: "No one can tell at first that he is an invert, or a poet, or a snob, or a scoundrel."[5] A rumor circulated that Hahn had been the lover of his teacher and mentor, Saint-Saëns, a closeted homosexual, who routinely vacationed in North Africa or the Canary Islands where he could indulge, without fear of discovery, the "vice" to which he never made reference at home.[6]

At the time he met Proust, Hahn still viewed homosexuals with scorn, as seen in a letter to his fellow student and accomplished pianist Édouard Risler. Writing about the musical offerings in Paris, Hahn said that he enjoyed the outdoor concerts in the Tuileries Gardens, except for one "drawback: there are always a lot of *homosexuals*." In another letter to Risler, Hahn condemned Verlaine's homosexuality: "I've heard that the great Verlaine's disciples attribute his talent to his horrible vice. [Alphonse] Daudet told me, so it must be true. Soon people will believe that to be a genius you have to shit on your music paper."[7] Hahn may have concluded that those aspects of homosexuality that he found so objectionable in others did not apply to him—an attitude that Proust describes in the novel: "But when they [homosexuals] see another man display a particular predilection towards them . . . this predilection, exalted by them as long as it is they themselves who feel it, is regarded as a vice."[8] In any case, Hahn's disapproval of Verlaine's behavior did not diminish his profound appreciation of the beauty and musicality of his poems. Proust must have had the occasion to hear Hahn sing in one of the salons that he regularly attended, because he soon began asking friends whether they knew Hahn, "the most enchanting voice I have ever heard."[9]

It was apparently Proust who pursued Hahn, although we have almost no details about the beginnings of their relationship. A few months after the party at Madeleine Lemaire's, he expressed his eagerness to meet Hahn, using his curiosity about Léon Delafosse's recent trip to England as "the only pretext I have for asking you to see me." Proust made himself available "any afternoon any time soon at my place or yours or on the terrace by the pond in the Tuileries gardens or anywhere you like, I would be charmed to hear you relate to me Delafosse's success in London."[10] Soon the two were inseparable; in their more leisurely hours, they delighted in the glitter and gossip of high society and all the riches that the City of Light offered in exhibitions, concerts, salons, and brilliant conversation.

Proust believed that he had at last found the ideal companion who both merited and reciprocated his love. He and Hahn had much in common: each had one Catholic and one Jewish parent, and they shared a passion for art, literature, and especially music, although they disagreed about their favorite composers. More modern in his tastes, Proust fervently admired the operas of Richard Wagner and later Claude Debussy's innovative *Pelléas et Mélisande,* choices derided by Hahn. Not long after becoming intimate friends, they decided to collaborate on a biography of Frédéric Chopin, a composer each esteemed, especially the more musically conservative Hahn. The Chopin project never got off the ground, having been nothing more than a dream born of their affection. Each had ambitions and pursued objectives that were important to his career. Hahn sought a producer for his first opera, *L'Ile du rêve,* while Proust assembled stories, poems, and sketches for a book entitled *Les Plaisirs et les Jours* (Pleasures and days), a deluxe volume prefaced by Anatole France and illustrated by Madeleine Lemaire. Hahn contributed to that project by setting to music Proust's poems in praise of painters and composers, "Portraits de peintres" and "Portraits de musiciens."[11] Proust never missed an opportunity to express his love; on receiving praise from a friend for poems occasioned by his affection for Hahn, he forwarded the compliment to the composer, observing that "one is always inspired when speaking of what one loves. The truth is that one should never speak of anything else."[12]

Proust and Hahn invented, as lovers always do, their own terms of endearment. At times, considering how accomplished Hahn was for someone so young, Proust addressed him as "my master." Or thinking only of Hahn's youthful charms and engaging mischievousness, he called him "my child." Hahn's pet name for Proust was "pony." On hearing himself compared to an equine animal, Proust at first reacted with dismay, finding the name too derisive: "Why 'Marcel the pony'? I don't care for this novelty. It makes me think of Jack the Ripper or Louis the Headstrong." But then he changed his mind: "Don't forget that it's not a nickname and that I am really and truly, Reynaldo, Your pony Marcel." In this same letter, written at Trouville in mid-September 1894, only a few months after they had apparently become lovers, Proust addressed Hahn in English as "My little master" and invited him to come and "comfort me" after the departure of his mother, who had been staying with him at the Hôtel des Roches Noires.[13] That Hahn's presence could provide the antidote for the absence of Proust's mother indicates how deeply the author loved him. This claim is reinforced by a 1912 letter in which Proust told Hahn that he "wouldn't have been able to go to sleep without having embraced you, without having given you the Combray kiss, I kiss your little hand my Gunibuls."[14] In the novel, the mother's consoling, reassuring kiss bestowed on the child Narrator in their nightly ritual is assumed by Albertine for the adult Narrator. Thus we see again that all Proust's major characters are composites of those he knew, including himself, as well as products of his own creation.

In the letters to Hahn, one finds an astonishing number of variations of Proust's pet name for him, "Buncht," the origin of which is unknown. Alphabetically, these range from "Bersnilch" to the next-most-frequent "Bunibuls" and "Buninuls" to "Burnuls." One can count forty-eight variations under "B" alone. For the rest of the alphabet, there are forty-four versions, including "Mintchniduls" and "Ounl rch ni buls." And, of course, Proust often used Hahn's real name as well. They also invented code words for fun and mystification, or perhaps to mislead any nosy person who might chance to read one of their letters. For example, "moschant," an obvious corruption of "méchant" (bad or mean) often indicated homosexual behavior or an individual known or thought to be gay. One should mention that there is a large gap for the years 1897–1903 in the correspondence between Proust and Hahn.

Doting lovers always appear silly to their friends, but the affectionate nonsense found in the exchanges between Proust and Hahn exceeds even the tolerated bounds. Proust feared most the accusation of being ridiculous, which to any Frenchman is worse than death. Nor did he want to be seen as a homosexual. Since his high school outpourings, Proust had learned to be discreet, and he now implored the impetuous Hahn to keep their letters secret: "Don't show anyone our *bininulseries,* which I assure you would only serve to make us appear ridiculous, even to the most kindly disposed."[15]

Proust often adorned the margins of his letters with whimsical drawings. A favorite motif was stained-glass windows. In one sketch, "The Master and the Pony," Proust drew himself lying in bed while Hahn sits next to him. The caption reads "Pony smokes. The master raises his arm in a gesture of discouragement and says 'Poor Pony!'" Proust often sent Hahn caricatures of friends, architectural drawings of sites that he visited or imagined, and pastiches of contemporary artworks.[16] In later years, he frequently signed his letters to Hahn with the drawing of a woman with an elongated nose that resembles a penis. In a variation on this motif, Proust also drew hermaphrodites in the margins of his manuscript.[17] In one of these the trunk of the "woman's" clothed body and her head clearly suggest an erect penis.

Hahn gave Proust a photograph of himself seated at the piano; on the back of the picture he scribbled a musical dedication from that "detestable queer" Verlaine, whose poem "Green" Hahn had set to music and which opens with the line: "Voici des fruits, des fleurs, des feuilles et des branches." The lines are spoken by a young and eager lover who runs through green fields gathering offerings to bring to the beloved: "Here are fruits, flowers, leaves and branches." Proust knew, of course, that the next line reads: "Et puis voici mon cœur qui ne bat que pour vous." "And here is my heart which beats only for you."[18]

In late April 1895 Proust had made plans to meet Hahn after first escorting, at her insistence, Madeleine Lemaire to a silly social affair called the "pink cotillion." After the ball, Proust, confused about the time, arrived too late to meet Hahn, who had grown tired of waiting and left. Distraught, Proust raced around Paris to all their late-evening haunts, but Hahn was nowhere to be found. The suffocating anxiety Proust felt on not being able to find him was nearly as wrenching as the misery experienced as a child on those occasions when he feared that his mother might leave him.

The following morning, Proust wrote to apologize for the missed rendezvous. What he had felt on not finding Hahn there had been so intense and painful that he might transpose the experience for a story: "Wait for my boy, lose him, find him, love him twice as much on hearing that he had come back . . . to get me, wait two minutes for him or make him wait for five, that for me is the true, throbbing, profound tragedy, which I shall perhaps write some day and which in the meantime I am living."[19]

A short time later, Proust wondered whether it might be wise to wean himself from depending too much on Hahn's presence. Perhaps they should practice going for a week or two without seeing each other so as to harden themselves against future "tempests" on his part. But Proust lacked the strength to endure more deprivation after his panic over the missed rendezvous: "Let's not begin yet, please." The recent experience had made him realize, as never before, the depth of his affection for Hahn and how painful it was to be separated from him.[20]

Years later Proust described an identical moment when Swann fails to find Odette where he expected her to be waiting for him. The resulting trauma crystallizes his love for her:

He arrived at the house so late that Odette, supposing that he did not intend to come, had already left. Seeing the room bare of her, Swann felt a sudden stab at the heart; he trembled at the thought of being deprived of a pleasure whose intensity he was able for the first time to gauge, having always, hitherto, had that certainty of finding it whenever he wished which (as in the case of all our pleasures) reduced if it did not altogether blind him to its dimensions.[21]

While analyzing the case of Swann, made desperate by his inability to find Odette that evening, Proust switches to the inclusive pronoun *we,* thus inviting the reader to reflect on "all the modes by which love is brought into being." Few of these are "so efficacious as this gust of feverish agitation that sweeps over us from time to time. For then the die is cast, the person whose company we enjoy at that moment is the person we shall henceforward love." We may not even have found that person, "up till then," particularly attractive. "All that was needed was that our predilection should become exclusive. And that condition was fulfilled when—in this moment of deprivation—the quest for the pleasures we enjoyed in his or her company is suddenly replaced by an anxious, torturing need, whose object is the person alone, an absurd, irrational need which the laws of this world made it impossible to satisfy and difficult to assuage—the insensate, agonising need to possess exclusively."[22]

This "irrational need" for exclusive possession inevitably results in jealous suspicions that can be allayed only, if at all, by the willingness of the object of such an obsession to accept nearly impossible demands. Proust himself, like his characters Swann and the Narrator, was to prove helpless, in spite of his remarkable intelligence and lucidity, in the face of such overwhelming jealous emotion.

At twenty-four, handsome, wealthy, and single, Proust watched his friends begin to marry and settle into their careers. Proust's parents apparently made no serious attempts to encourage him to take a wife. Dr. Robert Soupault, who became acquainted with the family as a medical student under Robert Proust, believed that although Proust was homosexual, he was not exclusively so. Yet Soupault could not imagine Proust's getting married and setting up a household, not because the young man found intimacy with women repugnant, but simply because marriage "requires a modicum of practicality and self-denial of which he was quite incapable."[23]

In the summer of 1895, Proust and Hahn spent two exceptionally happy weeks at Saint-Germain-en-Laye with Hahn's sisters, Maria and Clarita. From there the two men journeyed to Dieppe, where Madeleine Lemaire had invited them to stay in her seaside villa, before their departure for Belle-Île-en-Mer, off the coast of Brittany, where they were to be the guests of Hahn's friend the actress Sarah Bernhardt at her new summer home. Hahn, who worshiped Bernhardt and often accompanied her on tour, later wrote a biography of *La Grande Sarah* (The great Sarah). In Dieppe, Proust recalled his childhood visits to the town with his mother and grandmother, when he had first seen the old ramparts that encircled the medieval village. From Lemaire's villa, he and Hahn enjoyed the vistas of sea and watched the strollers on the fashionable boardwalk that embraced the shore.

Two days after their arrival, Proust became slightly ill, which made Hahn fear that the trip to Brittany might be canceled. Very early that morning, Hahn wrote Maria that he felt "great" and was enjoying himself in Dieppe, where he and Proust had been taking long walks. Then he described for his sister the deep nocturnal setting and the slumbering household: "It is four in the morning and I am writing while facing the sea, blue as a flower, or gray as the wing of a migratory bird. Everyone is sound asleep: the ladies downstairs, Proust next door, but with one eye open, so that even the sound of my pen gives me terrible anxieties." Noise was one of the many stimuli to which Proust was known to be hypersensitive. Hahn had quickly learned how uncertain any activities involving Proust must be and expressed his concerns for their plans to Maria: Proust had "had a mild asthma attack. May his parents allow him this trip to Brittany that I so much desire!"[24]

Proust, who seemed to improve, listened to the sounds of the sea with Hahn and explored the surrounding dunes and glens. Growing more relaxed, he enjoyed lying in the dunes and losing himself in nature. On one excursion to nearby Petit-Abbéville, his admiration of the beech woods inspired a prose poem, "Forest Scene," for his forthcoming book *Pleasures and Days*. Toward the end of their stay, Lemaire introduced him to another vacationer in Dieppe, Camille Saint-Saëns, whose *Sonata for Violin and Piano No. 1 in D Minor* Proust later used as an inspiration for Vinteuil's sonata in the novel.

Although Lemaire, playing surrogate mother to both young men, remained concerned about their well-being and health, especially Proust's, she had absolute faith in the salubrious atmosphere of Dieppe and the curative powers of her own regimen and program of activities. She wrote Maria Hahn to express her apprehensions about her guests' imprudent plans to leave the haven of her villa for what she regarded as the wilds of Brittany: "Ah! if only they would give up their Brittany trip. I dare not mention it to them for fear of making them think about leaving—it seems to me that they will get more rest here than in bad hotels. I make them eat at regular hours. But once they are on their own who knows when they will take their meals?"[25]

Lemaire felt genuinely hurt when she saw her entreaties go unheeded. Not only did she dread losing such delightful company, but her maternal instincts, which often bordered on the tyrannical, told her that the pair might be in danger if allowed to roam. Lemaire's determination to keep these two of her "faithful" close at hand, while managing their lives, was a trait Proust later gave to Mme Verdurin, the bourgeois society hostess in his novel who makes virtual prisoners of her group.[26] One can hear comic echoes of Lemaire's possessiveness in this passage in which Mme Verdurin, who always predicts disaster when any member of her "little clan" ventures abroad without her, expresses her horror on learning that Dr. and Mme Cottard have planned an Easter trip: "In Auvergne? To be eaten alive by fleas and all sorts of creatures! A fine lot of good that will do you!"[27] Although slightly unwell, Proust did not want to disappoint Hahn.

Besides, in spite of the asthma, to which he had long been accustomed, and a mild stomach disorder, he was enjoying immensely the extended vacation with the man he loved.

On September 5, 1895, Proust and Hahn sailed across the Bay of Biscay to Belle-Île-en-Mer, the largest of the islands in the Atlantic Ocean off the Brittany Coast. Arriving in the port known as Le Palais, they observed the high walls of the seventeenth-century citadel, built by famed military engineer Sébastien Le Prestre de Vauban. Belle-Isle, as treacherous as it is beautiful, offers spectacular panoramas of sheer seaside cliffs rising two hundred feet above the water. Even today, signs posted near the edge of the cliffs warn visitors: "Danger of Sudden Death." After centuries of battering the cliffs, the sea has, in many spots, carved out fantastic grottoes and rock formations, and when waves pound these jagged rocks, their force hurls thick spouts of spray high into the air. Claude Monet, among other artists, had earlier taken up residence on the island in order to paint Belle-Isle's dramatic and unparalleled natural beauty.

Two years before Proust's visit, Sarah Bernhardt had scored a triumph by reprising one of her most famous roles as Jean Racine's Phèdre. That same year she purchased an old Napoleonic fort built on a high promontory with grand, sweeping vistas of the sea. With her usual zeal and flair for the grandiose, Bernhardt converted the ancient fort into her summer home, complete with gardens, tennis courts, menagerie, and other amenities that she, her entourage, and a large retinue of adoring servants began to enjoy in the summer of 1895.

Proust and Hahn had barely arrived at Fort Sarah Bernhardt, where the flagpole flew a blue and white banner with the initials SB, when Mme Lemaire's predictions began to come true: Proust fell ill with a stomachache and fever. Soon he had but one thought: to return to the mainland as quickly as possible. Hahn concurred, and they left Belle-Isle; their premature departure deprived Proust of the opportunity to observe "the Divine Sarah" in her island retreat.

A few days after returning to the mainland, Proust and Hahn arrived in the seaside village of Beg-Meil, where, on a gentle hill overlooking the sea, stood a small hotel, the Fermont. Run by an enterprising couple who had converted their farmhouse into a hotel, the Fermont had become popular with painters, who stayed as late as possible in the season and often left their pictures behind as payment for the modest bills. Since the main building's four or five rooms were all taken, Hahn and Proust had to lodge in the annex, located some hundred yards away, with rooms renting for a mere two francs a night. Guests who stayed in the annex joined the others for their meals in the hotel's dining room.

Hahn signed the hotel register first, giving his profession as musician, followed by Proust, who gave his as "a man of letters." With at least three other guests listed as painters, the addition of a composer and a writer made the obscure Beg-Meil suddenly resemble a budding artists' colony. After a pleasant dinner, Hahn wrote Maria to inform her of their whereabouts. There were apple trees everywhere, he told her, and "real Breton flowers, genista, heather, golden furze." All around were seascapes bounded by hills where "apple trees slope down to the rocky beach."[28] Hahn realized that this peaceful, secluded spot might be the perfect place to finish the opening section and the andante of his trio.[29] As it turned out, Beg-Meil instead inspired Hahn to begin composing a "Breton choral" work, which he eventually called *Là-bas* (Over there).[30]

Proust explored the surrounding area, finding the air intoxicating—he could breathe once more with refreshing ease—and the views superb: "On one side there is the sea, very Breton and sad. On the other the Bay of Concarneau, which is blue with, in the background, a vista exactly like Lake Geneva."[31] He began to feel much better; his recent stomach troubles disappeared, and he began to eat heartily, which pleased Hahn, who had feared many times during the trip that Proust's illnesses would shorten their itinerary.

Proust had brought along books to read—Balzac's *Splendeurs et misères des courtisanes* and Thomas Carlyle's *Heroes and Hero-Worship* in a French translation—but had not anticipated that he would find himself in such a primitive place in need of other supplies. Robert de

Billy received a letter scribbled on the backs of two calling cards: "My dear Robert, . . . I am in a village where there is no paper. It's called Beg-Meil, the apple trees come down to the sea, and the smell of cider mingles with that of seaweed. The mixture of poetry and sensuality is just about right for me." He asked Billy to watch for his story about Baldassare Silvande, due to appear soon in *La Revue hebdomadaire*.[32] Proust managed to secure one sheet of decent writing paper and used it to inform another friend that they had landed in

> a primitive and delightful spot . . . where, however, there are not even any water closets. And indeed, this would be just the place to air Vigny's line:
>
> *Never leave me alone with nature.*
>
> For it is to nature that we consign everything, and I assure you that nothing is so *irritating* as the excessive zeal of the nettles, which try to make themselves *indispensable*, if you will forgive the pun, and their way of doing it is piquant but harsh.[33]

Proust had made a pun on the latest French euphemism for toilet paper, *indispensables*. Accustomed to only the finest hotels, Proust adapted well to his two-franc room and to all the other hardships, even to squatting in the bushes to answer nature's call.

Beg-Meil proved vital to his development as a novelist. One of the painters with whom Proust and Hahn immediately formed a close bond was the American expatriate Thomas Alexander Harrison, a longtime visitor to Beg-Meil.[34] A gifted though now nearly forgotten artist, Harrison spent every summer in the coastal town, where he painted sunrises and sunsets. Hahn recalled having seen one of his works, *Blue Lake*, in Paris's Luxembourg Palace, which then served as an important art museum. Harrison rented a ramshackle studio constructed of unpainted planks on a nearby farm. Fanatical about the beauty of the sunsets at Beg-Meil, every evening he ran down to the dunes to watch the sun sink into the sea. Soon Proust and Hahn were joining him for the late afternoon race to catch the sunsets, whose brilliant, shifting colors Hahn described to Maria: "We have seen the sea successively turn blood red, purple, nacreous with silver, gold, white, emerald green, and yesterday we were dazzled by an entirely pink sea specked with blue sails."[35]

Proust began to draft the episodes for a story that he began sometime during the summer, most likely at Beg-Meil. These fragments formed the basis of *Jean Santeuil,* the sprawling novel on which he was to labor intermittently for the next five years until the manuscript grew to nearly a thousand pages. Proust named his hero Jean (John), probably as a tribute to his mother, whose name was the feminine form of the same name: Jeanne. While in Beg-Meil he wrote descriptions based on his explorations of the seacoast, but he also found himself re-creating scenes from the past, especially memories of his childhood in Paris, Auteuil, and Illiers, which he often transposed to suit his fancy or the lives of the characters he struggled to infuse with life. Proust's encounter with Harrison inspired the key character known simply as the writer C. C is the original of *In Search of Lost Time*'s Elstir, who is, like Harrison, a painter.[36] Elstir's name bears the sound of the way the French pronounce the name of another and much greater American expatriate painter, whom Proust was later to meet: James McNeill Whistler.[37]

Proust and Hahn enjoyed Beg-Meil so much that they decided to extend their special thirty-three-day "Seaside Resorts" train passes, purchased for this trip, for another ten days into October.[38] Harrison, with his painter's eye and native's knowledge of the area, advised them on using their passes to see the most beautiful views and sunsets. Of all the places they visited along the coast, Proust "infinitely" preferred "Penmarch . . . a sort of mixture of Holland and the Indies and Florida (according to Harrison). Nothing could be more sublime than a tempest seen from there."[39] He liked Penmarch best, no doubt, because he saw it as metaphorical in nature, embodying not a single place but many. Proust always chose the complex over the simple, seeing many things in one, which led him to seek the harmony that unites them. The views of land and sea elements in such beautiful sites as Penmarch deepened his impressions and later inspired seascapes found in his novel and in Elstir's painting *The Port of Carquethuit*.

The trip to Brittany might be viewed as a kind of honeymoon for Proust and Hahn. In any case, that period was apparently the happiest they spent together. One can detect in Proust's brief descriptions of lovers lying in the dunes wisps of the sea and the apple-scented air of Beg-Meil.

Although Proust expressed admiration for Camille Saint-Saëns's work, he thought less highly of the composer's accomplishments than did his former pupil Hahn.[40] But one section of the first movement of Saint-Saëns's *Sonata I for piano and violin, opus 75,* had a haunting melody that completely captivated the author. Proust never tired of hearing it, and he must have asked Hahn to play it for him on more than one occasion. Saint-Saëns's melody inspired the "little phrase" that Swann asks Odette to play for him again and again.[41]

Saint-Saëns receives no credit in the novel, where the "little phrase" is the creation of Proust's fictional composer Vinteuil, but Proust did later acknowledge in a letter to Antoine Bibesco that the model was indeed Saint-Saëns's sonata.[42] Proust had also used this music earlier in the drafts of *Jean Santeuil,* where Saint-Saëns does receive credit when the "little phrase" makes its literary debut as the love song of Jean and Françoise. But there the music is described nostalgically, recalling the days when the two lovers were blissfully content:

> He had recognized that phrase from the Saint-Saëns Sonata which almost every evening in the heyday of their happiness he had asked for, and she had played endlessly to him, ten times, twenty times, over, making him sit quite close to her so that she could embrace him while she played. . . . Far from her now and all alone, having had this evening not so much as a single kiss, and not daring to ask for one, he listened to the phrase which when they were happy, had seemed to greet them with a smile from heaven, but now had lost its power to enchant.[43]

Proust and Hahn may well have considered that musical passage from Saint-Saëns to be "the national anthem of their love," as do Swann and Odette. Swann can't hear it often enough, even though "Odette played [it] vilely, but often the most memorable impression of a piece of music is one that has arisen out of a jumble of wrong notes struck by unskilful fingers upon a tuneless piano. The little phrase continued to be associated in Swann's mind with his love for Odette."[44]

Proust continued to show the drafts of *Jean Santeuil* to Hahn, who seemed to be the story's primary, if secret, inspiration, at least in its nascent state. He wanted Hahn to tell him whether the pages contained anything that recalled too obviously their being together, anything "too pony." If so, Hahn must help him correct those parts, not that Proust wanted to remove the traces of his friend from the book— on the contrary, he wanted Hahn to be present in everything he wrote, "but like a god in disguise, invisible to mortals. Otherwise you'd have to write 'tear up' on every page."[45]

One does find traces of Hahn in the book that Proust was later to abandon after writing drafts of nearly one thousand pages. Beyond the use of the Saint-Saëns sonata, Jean's closest friend is Henri de Réveillon, whose initials are those of Hahn reversed. Réveillon is the name of Madeleine Lemaire's château; not only had she provided the occasion for Proust to meet Hahn, but she had also encouraged the relationship, inviting them both for holidays at Réveillon and at her villa in Dieppe. In the novel, Proust observes that "the good offices of the procuress are part of the duties of the perfect hostess."[46] But in his novel as in his life, the "evil deity" of jealousy that ruins the happiness of such lovers was soon to rear its ugly head and drive Proust and Hahn apart.[47]

CHAPTER FOUR

Jalousie

It was through Hahn that Proust met Lucien Daudet, who soon became the object of his attention. Only sixteen, Daudet had delicate features, a fine olive complexion, and soft dreamy eyes. He was a pretty boy whose sexual nature was apparent, but his family, conservative and devoutly Catholic, chose to ignore the implications of his androgynous beauty and effeminate manners. Like Proust, Daudet had certain neurotic tendencies and was often moody and temperamental. Theirs was not a match one could expect to last.

Daudet had ambitions to be a painter and was enrolled at the prestigious Académie Julian on the Left Bank, not far from Saint-Germain-des-Prés. Proust began to meet him after class, occasionally dashing off notes to be delivered to Daudet in class. In one such note, Proust apologized for disturbing him during his art class again—he swore this would be the last time—and asked Daudet to meet him outside the Académie.

Proust's public behavior with Daudet often appeared childish and outlandish. The two were frequently afflicted with what the French call *le fou rire,* mad laughter. Just before one dinner party, Count Robert de Montesquiou received a strange letter from Proust and Daudet, who claimed that for the past week whenever they were together it was impossible for them to avoid "being seized and held by the most irrational, painful and irresistible laughter." Having accepted Montesquiou's invitation to the party that evening, they were writing to beg his indulgence and ask that he warn the others: "Since [Léon] Delafosse or [Fernand] Gregh might take offense, would you be so kind as to tell them not to be offended and that M. and Mme Daudet have been patiently tolerating this for a week while trying to calm this hideous disorder with their sympathetic understanding." They closed the letter by assuring Montesquiou of their affection and respect.[1]

The letter infuriated Montesquiou, who saw the whole affair as a conspiracy to ruin his dinner party, an event that he always planned with the care one would expect from the esthete considered by others —and certainly by himself—as the arbiter of taste in Parisian high society. That evening, as soon as Proust and Daudet entered the room, Montesquiou's severe, suspicious demeanor bent them over into peals of laughter, and they had to rush out of the room, gasping for air. Daudet said that Montesquiou *"never* forgave" them for this impropriety.[2]

Proust and Daudet also enjoyed a game that inevitably provoked bouts of mad laughter. It consisted of compiling lists of what they called *louchonneries*—trite or pretentious expressions—such as "the Big Blue" for the Mediterranean Sea or "our little soldiers" for the French army. Daudet later recalled that whenever someone at a social event uttered a word or phrase from their list, he and Proust exchanged a knowing look, then Proust lowered his eyes. In those eyes Daudet saw "gleaming the diabolical light of uncontrollable laughter," which he found contagious.[3] Proust seemed to take pleasure in the juvenile game; before arriving at the Daudets', he would alert

Lucien with telegrams asking him to warn his parents and appeal to their indulgence.

By Christmas 1895, only a few months after Proust and Hahn had returned from Beg-Meil, their relationship was becoming strained. Their affection for each other apparently remained strong, but Proust had become infatuated with Daudet. Hahn's emotions fluctuated between jealousy and exasperation over Proust's apparent devotion to the boy. For Daudet's New Year's present, Proust purchased a rare, expensive eighteenth-century carved ivory box. At the same time, Proust showed no signs of wanting to relinquish his hold on Hahn. Clearly, trouble lay ahead.

Hahn wrote a letter reproaching Proust for his excessive attention to Daudet. Hahn would be free to see Proust later that day, but urged him not to pass up an evening with Daudet solely for his sake. Then he apologized for the scolding tone of his letter: "Life is so short and so boring" that Proust was right not to forsake "those things (even the most trivial) that amuse or give pleasure, when they are blameless or harmless—thus, forgive me, dear little Marcel. I am sometimes quite unbearable; I'm aware of it. But we're all so imperfect. Affectionately, Reynaldo."[4]

Flattered by Hahn's apparent jealousy, Proust did nothing to discourage the idea that he preferred to spend his time with Daudet. Proust later wrote of betrayals that prove too costly: "A woman whom we love seldom satisfies all our needs and we deceive her with a woman whom we do not love."[5] In late spring, Proust and Daudet spent a day together reading Robert de Montesquiou's *Les Hortensias bleus* (Blue hydrangeas), the count's latest volume of poetry, prefaced by José-Maria de Heredia, a distinguished poet and member of the Académie Française.[6] That evening Proust went to Mme Lemaire's soirée for the première of Hahn's Breton choral work *Là-bas,* begun when the two had been so happy during their holiday in Brittany. Among the distinguished guests at the première were Anatole France, Montesquiou, and Minister of Finance Raymond Poincaré. According to the journal *Le Gaulois,* Hahn's composition was performed with great success.

A short time later Hahn accompanied Sarah Bernhardt and her troupe to London for a brief stay. Soon after he returned to Paris, his relationship with Proust reached a crisis point.[7] Fearing that Hahn was slipping away from him, Proust proposed a pact according to which each promised to tell the other everything about himself, especially any love relationships or sexual encounters, past, present, and future. Out of weariness or in a desperate attempt to placate Proust, Hahn agreed to the absurd proposal and swore to uphold it. The agreement was so preposterous, so unrealistic that in no time at all Hahn found himself in violation of it. Each man was to learn the accuracy of a statement that Proust later placed in the novel: "There can be no peace of mind in love, since what one has obtained is never anything but a new starting-point for further desires."[8] The pact and Proust's increasingly fragile physical and emotional condition only exacerbated the misunderstandings between them. A short time later Proust sent Hahn a letter full of recriminations.

In May and June 1896 Proust was saddened by the deaths first of his great uncle Louis Weil and then his grandfather Nathé Weil. Hahn sent his condolences from Hamburg, where he was visiting one of his sisters, and offered to return and comfort his bereaved friend. Although deeply touched by Hahn's kindness, Proust told him not to come; the sacrifice would be too great and was not really necessary. "Stay as long as you enjoy it," he insisted. Proust's main concern was not the death of close relatives but Hahn's fidelity. Using *mosch,* their code word for homosexual, Proust implored him:

> Just tell me from time to time in your letters no mosch, have seen no mosch, because, even though you imply as much, I'd be happier if you'd say it now and then. And I am happy—without self-abnegation—that you're staying on. But I shall also be very happy, ah, my dear little Reynaldo, very very happy when I'm able to embrace you, you whom along with Mama I love best in all the world.

Proust quickly changed the subject: "I am determined not to write you anything that will irritate or annoy you, since at this distance I can't soothe you with the thousand little pony endearments that I reserve for your return."[9] The reminders to behave himself and uphold the pact only served to irritate Hahn.

Soon after Hahn's return from Hamburg, he and Proust quarreled bitterly and Hahn threatened to renounce their pact of fidelity and confession. The rift apparently started when Proust tried to guess the name of someone Hahn found attractive, someone who may have been "mosch" and whose name the composer adamantly refused to divulge. In a letter filled with resentment, Proust vehemently protested Hahn's violation of the agreement. He began with a half-hearted apology for his anger, then quickly resumed his accusations of betrayal:

> Reynaldo, I had a spell of bad humour this evening, you mustn't be surprised or take it amiss. You said, I'll never tell you anything again. If that were true, it would be a breach of your oath; even untrue, it's still the cruelest of blows. That you should tell me everything has been my hope, my consolation, my mainstay, my life since the 20th of June. For fear of making you unhappy, I hardly ever speak of it, yet I think of it almost all the time.

During the confrontation, Hahn had made a "cutting" remark when the implacable Proust had persisted in interrogating him in order "to fill in the gaps in a life which is dearer to me than anything else, but which will be a source of sorrow and torment to me as long as it remains unknown to me even in its most innocent aspects." Conceding that his demands were excessive and irrational, Proust nonetheless insisted that Hahn fulfill his promise. And, as he had done so often with his parents, Proust pleaded his ill health as a cause for special consideration:

> Alas, it's an impossible task, and when in your kindness you try to satisfy my curiosity with a little of your past, you are undertaking a

labor of the Danaïds. But if my fantasies are absurd, they are the fantasies of a sick man, and for that reason should not be crossed. Threatening to finish off a sick man because his mania is exasperating is the height of cruelty. You will forgive these reproaches because I don't often make any and always deserve some myself, which will appease your pride. Be indulgent to a pony.[10]

Not long afterward, Proust fired off another angry letter to Hahn, acknowledging that their affection for each other had considerably diminished. Among his grievances, he cited Hahn's refusal to accompany him home after a soirée at Mme Lemaire's, preferring instead to remain for supper. He repeated Hahn's warning, made earlier in the evening, that one day Proust would regret having made him promise to tell all. Proust declared that he had attempted to remain faithful to Hahn in order to avoid painful confessions: "Wretch, you don't understand, then, my daily and nightly struggles where the only thing that holds me back is the thought of hurting you." Then he observed, "Just as I love you much less now, you no longer love me at all, and that my dear little Reynaldo I cannot hold against you." He signed the letter, "Your little pony, who after all this bucking, returns alone to the stable where you once liked to say you were the master."[11]

Proust and his mother left soon afterward for a spa at Mont-Dore in the Puy-de-Dôme, where he sought treatment for his persistent bouts of asthma. From here he sent Hahn a letter of apology, urging him to forget the pact and claiming that he was no longer jealous:

Forgive me if you're angry with me, but I'm not angry with you. Forgive me if I've hurt you, and in future don't tell me anything since it upsets you. You will never find a more affectionate, more understanding (alas!) and less humiliating confessor, since, if you had asked silence of him as he has asked a confession of you, your heart would have been the confessional and he the sinner, for that is how weak he is, weaker than you. Never mind, and forgive me for having added, out of egoism as you say, to the sorrows of your life. I have no sorrows, only an enormous tenderness for my boy, whom I think of, as I said of my nurse when I was little, not only with all my heart, but with all of me.

Claiming that he was over his unreasonable jealousy, he ended his plea for a resumption of their relationship on a lighter note: "I embrace you tenderly, your sisters too, except the one with the jealous husband. I, who am no longer jealous but have been, respect jealous people and have no wish to cause them the slightest unhappiness or to lead them to suspect any secret."[12]

If Proust had hoped Hahn would come running to protest the assertion "you no longer love me at all," he was to be disappointed. Hahn did love him deeply, but no longer with passion. Proust had no choice but to recognize that the love affair was over. In a short while, the bitterness disappeared, leaving nothing but the true affection of his deep friendship. No matter how great his attraction to Daudet, Proust knew that no one could ever take Hahn's place. And he knew, lucid reader of the human heart that he was, that he had no one to blame but himself. In *The Captive*, the Narrator finally has to admit to himself that his jealous grillings of Albertine are pointless: "For there is no one who will willingly deliver up his soul."[13]

Proust had become, in many ways, the obsessed lover he had depicted in a short story "The End of Jealousy." There jealousy ends with the hero becoming a wise man just before dying from injuries sustained in an accident. Another (posthumously published) text from this period reveals his anguish and his utter helplessness to summon the will to act otherwise, in spite of his keen recognition of the inappropriateness of his behavior. One is, he observed, jealous not of the happiness of the person one loves but of the pleasure she gives or the pleasure she takes. There are no remedies: "Intelligence is disarmed when faced with jealousy as with sickness and with death."[14] Proust most often describes the "love" that Swann feels for Odette as pathological. For example, Swann's jealous obsession is likened to a cancer that slowly gnaws away at his insides until it kills him:

And this malady which Swann's love had become had so proliferated, was so closely interwoven with all his habits, with all his actions, his thoughts, his health, his sleep, his life, even with what he hoped for after his death, was so utterly inseparable from him, that it would have been impossible to eradicate it without almost entirely destroying him; as surgeons say, his love was no longer operable.[15]

Louis de Robert, who read *Swann's Way* in manuscript, told Proust that the section called "Swann in Love" presented his readers with "a study of jealousy like none other in our literature."[16] Among these passages we find echoes of Proust's implementation of the pact with Hahn in the many scenes where the suspicious, desperate lover demonstrates his tenacity in pursuit of his beloved by spying on her, bribing prostitutes for information about her past behavior, and subjecting her to intensive interrogations. This psychological torture only serves to make him and the object of his obsession more miserable. For example, Swann, who pretends to know more about Odette's presumed infidelities than he does, including her occasional lesbian affairs, grills her relentlessly, seeking to catch her in a lie or fool her into telling the truth. He even makes her swear on the religious medallion that she holds sacred that her denials are true. And when he finally does wring from Odette the admission that she may have had sex with women, he keeps pressing her for more details, more confessions: "For his jealousy, which had taken more pains than any enemy would have done to strike him this savage blow, to make him forcibly acquainted with the most cruel suffering he had ever known, his jealousy was not satisfied that he had yet suffered enough, and sought to expose him to an even deeper wound. Thus, like an evil deity, his jealousy inspired Swann, driving him on towards his ruin."[17]

The imagery used for sexual jealousy throughout *In Search of Lost Time* is Dantesque, with its many references to evil demons, hell, and the fire and brimstone that fell on Sodom and Gomorrah: "By what trap-door suddenly lowered had [Swann] . . . been precipitated into this new circle of hell from which he could not see how he was ever to escape."[18]

Proust pointed out to Lionel Hauser what should be obvious to any reader of *In Search of Lost Time:* the love depicted therein is not true love, or love in its purest, noblest form. Indeed, it is that opposite of such love:

> Nothing is further from the "heart" than this egotistical sentiment called love, and which even in Racine's tragedies leads to murder or suicide whenever its object fails to share the same sentiment. This does not at all mean that I find this kind of love uninteresting. Such love is important for the philosopher, full of lessons for whoever analyzes, atrocious, as I know only too well, for him who falls under its spell. But I have never pretended to identify it with a true heart.[19]

Harold Bloom sees Proust as Shakespeare's rival "at portraying sexual jealousy, one of the most canonical of human affects for literary purposes, handled by Shakespeare as catastrophic tragedy in *Othello* and near-catastrophic romance in *The Winter's Tale.* Proust gives us three magnificent sagas of jealousy: the ordeals, in sequence, of Swann, Saint-Loup, and Marcel [the Narrator]." Bloom finds that Proust is unmatched in his analysis of "the passion that jealousy initially augments and then replaces. Here the genius of Proust goes beyond Shakespeare, beyond Freud, as an insight into erotic obsession."[20]

One of Proust's most successful tactics to engage the reader is the way in which, after providing a detailed and brilliant analysis of the situation and emotions of his highly individualized and vivid characters, he states his observations or conclusions in gemlike maxims in the tradition of French moralistes, maxims that are deftly woven into the fabric of the narrative. The shift from "I" to "we" immediately engages the reader by inviting comparisons between the Narrator's experience and our own. Here are some samples of such maxims or laws that Proust formulated from the Narrator's experiences. As we read them, we can see that while they may be taken as universal truths, they can also be specifically applied to Proust's jealous love for Hahn and his insistence on obeying the pact by which neither man would keep an erotic secret from the other.

> More often than not, a body becomes the object of love only when an emotion, fear of losing it, uncertainty of getting it back, is merged into it. Now jealous anxiety has a great affinity for bodies. It adds to them a quality that surpasses beauty itself, which is one of the reasons why we see men who are indifferent to the most beautiful women fall passionately in love with others who appear to us ugly. To such beings, such creatures of flight, their own nature and our anxiety fasten wings.

> Jealousy . . . is a demon that cannot be exorcised, but constantly reappears in new incarnations.

> It is because human bodies contain within themselves the hours of the past that they have the power to hurt so terribly those who love them, because they contain the memories of so many joys and desires already effaced for them, but still cruel for the lover who contemplates and prolongs in the dimension of Time the beloved body of which he is jealous, so jealous that he may even wish for its destruction.[21]

That August 1896 at Mont-Dore, Proust stayed in a repentant mood and wrote an apologetic letter to Daudet for having failed to see him before leaving Paris. He had been worried that his own exemption from this year's military reserve training would be denied, obliging him to report for duty at Versailles on August 31. Trying to resolve this problem before leaving for the spa had prevented him from saying good-bye to his "dear little one. I think of you so often that it's unbelievable." He told Daudet that he was unhappy with the lack of progress on *Jean Santeuil* and that, if his condition did not improve soon, he would take the train home. Did Lucien, he wondered, still harbor some feelings of friendship for him? Or had he completely forgotten him? He invited Daudet to visit him after his return to Paris in order to select one of the photographs Proust had had made at Otto's studio, where fashionable Parisians had themselves photographed. Lucien would see that there were many "ridiculous poses from which to choose." Although he signed the letter "Your little Marcel," he knew that his romantic friendship with the young art student was rapidly cooling.[22]

There had been signs of this distancing earlier in the year. In February, Proust had become confused about Daudet's schooling and thought he had just passed his baccalaureate exams. He sent the supposed graduate a congratulatory telegram, saying he had heard the news by chance, and gently reproached Daudet for having failed to inform him. This oversight, Proust bitterly observed, fit the pattern of Daudet's apparent determination to avoid him. Somehow Proust and Hahn had managed to fall out of love while keeping intact their profound respect and admiration for each other in spite of outbursts of anger and recriminations, a happy resolution that enabled them to continue to delight in their many affinities and in each other's extraordinary company. Lucien was simply too young and too unstable, compared with the remarkably solid Hahn, to be any match in the realm of true friendship. Proust acknowledged as much in a letter to Daudet's mother, perhaps because he felt the need to explain why he and Daudet were seeing less of each other. He tactfully blamed himself for not being a better companion for her son: "Unfortunately, I am not the right kind of friend for him, I too am too nervous. He needs someone who, along with similar intellectual and moral aspirations, has the opposite sort of temperament, calm rather than agitated, resolute and happy. I should like to find him a friend of that sort, or become so myself."[23]

In an ironic and disturbing twist, just when Proust and Daudet were drifting apart, the nature of their relationship became a subject of gossip as a result of the long-awaited publication of *Pleasures and Days*. Although the expensive volume received a few encouraging reviews, sales were practically nonexistent, given the relative obscurity of the author and the exorbitant price tag. The book did, however, provoke a highly public insinuation of a homosexual relationship between Proust and Daudet.

Such scandals involving men of letters were in the public mind because little more than a year had passed since the trial in England of Oscar Wilde, who, convicted of "gross indecency," had received the harsh sentence of two years at hard labor. Proust ran no comparable risks in France, where the revolutionary Code Pénal of 1791 had "decriminalized sexual relations between men by deliberately omitting any reference to them," but homosexuals were often arrested on other charges, such as public indecency and corruption of the young.[24] Still, social prejudices remained so strong against homosexuality that men feared being branded as such, and hence were subject to blackmail or opprobrium. One historian of the era has written that by mid-nineteenth century in France "male prostitution and blackmail was said to have become 'an industry of almost unbelievable dimensions.' "[25] Another commentator maintains that in spite of "the legal tolerance of homosexuality, France was more dangerous for homosexuals than England. For most of the nineteenth century, raids on homosexual clubs and cruising-grounds were even more common in Paris than they were in London."[26] There were many legal and social incentives for homosexuals to stay in the closet or at least to be exceptionally discreet.

On Wednesday, February 3, 1897, the journalist Jean Lorrain wrote a virulent article in his "Pall Mall" column for *Le Journal*, mocking Proust and his friends by attacking *Pleasures and Days*. After deriding Anatole France for having contributed a preface and ridiculing Madeleine Lemaire's drawings, Lorrain fired his most poisonous dart: "Rest assured," he alerted his readers, "that for his next book, M. Marcel Proust will obtain a preface from M. Alphonse Daudet . . . who will not be able to refuse this preface either to Madame Lemaire or to his son Lucien."

The scurrilous columnist was himself a homosexual, but one who despised effeminate men; he preferred rougher trade. Those who knew Lorrain and found his excesses amusing savored the ironies and contradictions that constituted his character. Although Lorrain liked to seduce manly men, in order to do so he wore makeup, a practice that made even those who were kindly disposed toward him regard him with derision.

Cornelia Otis Skinner provides a colorful portrait of this "screaming homosexual," whose "torso, big as that of a porter from the Halles, was held in by a corset so tight it gave him a bosom. His hair, which he wore in bangs and a pompadour, was dyed a peroxide blond. With his cheeks garishly rouged, his eyes heavily made up, he looked like a Place Pigalle streetwalker."[27] (Although Proust never wore makeup or anything else suggesting drag, it is ironic that both Maurice Duplay and André Gide thought that, in his later years, Proust's features and physique resembled Lorrain's.)[28]

Lorrain lived in Auteuil, not far from the writer and diarist Edmond de Goncourt, who tolerated the journalist's company because once the summer crowd returned to Paris, Auteuil became a lonely place. Goncourt found in "this hysterical gossiper," who worked hard to support his elderly mother, a strange combination of "filthy passions and family virtues." Lorrain's scandalous gossip amused Goncourt, as did the reaction of the less sophisticated citizens who saw him out strolling with Goncourt and who recoiled in disbelief on seeing the journalist's rouged lips and mascaraed eyelashes. Goncourt would hear passersby muttering, behind Lorrain's back, the insulting remark used for men who wore makeup, "Oh, le *platré!*"[29]

Always on the prowl for fresh blood for his vituperative column, Lorrain had noticed with contempt Daudet's pretty face and androgynous nature. The acid-penned chronicler frequently attacked men on the social scene who shared his sexual proclivities but whose effeminate appearance aroused his scorn. Even though he wore jewelry, doused himself with perfume, and dyed his mustache red with henna, he apparently regarded himself as more manly because he fancied tough homosexuals or male prostitutes, sailors or butcher boys, from the lower classes. His taste in sexual partners, in short, mirrored those of Proust's future homosexual character the baron de

Charlus. Lorrain's letters and memoirs recount narrow escapes from severe beatings. Once sailors, outraged by his blatant sexual overtures, tried to drown him. Goncourt's diary contains descriptions of Lorrain's routinely turning up with various mysterious wounds. "The other day he had his hand in a sling and said that he had slashed it while cutting bread in an awkward way. Today, I find him at home with a black eye and a hole in his head that required the application of six leeches."[30]

On reading Lorrain's attack in *Le Journal*, Proust knew at once that he must defend his honor against the insinuation that he was homosexual, not only for his own sake but also to protect his parents from public humiliation. A few years later, when rumors once again circulated about his possible homosexuality, Proust denied such behavior and pleaded with Prince Antoine Bibesco, who loved to gossip and tease him about these apparent tendencies, not to drop such "innuendoes" in the presence of others, "not only on my account, I also owe it to my family not to let myself be taken for a Salaïst, gratuitously, since I'm not one."[31] *Salaïst* is a word invented by Proust as a code for homosexual; he took it from the name of Count Antoine Sala, an overt homosexual, whom the novelist observed on the social scene.

It seems likely that Proust's parents knew about his homosexuality and may have hoped he would be "cured" of it or would, like many other men, take a wife and begin a family. The most convincing testimony that his parents did know came from Maurice Duplay, who knew Proust well and whose parents, Dr. and Mme Simon Duplay, had been for many years friends of Adrien and Jeanne's. When Mme Duplay died in 1911, Maurice received what he called a "desperate" letter of condolence from Proust, who expressed his envy of Maurice for not having caused his mother so many "worries" and "sorrows" as Proust had his mother. In his memoir, Maurice comments that the worries Proust had in mind were "his deplorable health and its demands, the whims of an eternal invalid," and his sexual "mores."[32]

Faced with Lorrain's scandalous implications, Proust knew that he had no choice; he must protect the family honor by challenging the columnist to a duel. In spite of being nervous and sickly, he did not shrink from exposing himself to danger or even death. When provoked, Proust could be hot-tempered. Léon Daudet wrote that although Proust was normally the most amiable of men, he responded, when offended, like dynamite or a lion who had been given a flick of the finger.[33] A year earlier, during the summer vacation with his mother at Mont-Dore, Proust had exchanged heated words with another guest and nearly fought a duel. When creating his fictional counterparts, Jean Santeuil and, later, the Narrator, Proust endowed both with his own touchy temperament.[34]

One often finds in Proust's letters nostalgic remarks about his duel. For example, nearly two decades later, on learning that Bernard Grasset, the publisher of *Swann's Way*, had recently fought a duel in which he received a sword cut in the arm, Proust congratulated him, saying that he did not pity him because he knew from experience "how agreeable such occasions are; a duel is one of my best memories."[35] Proust's letters contain frequent "macho" remarks regarding duels, a trait he gave to the Narrator.

To make arrangements for the agreeable occasion with Lorrain, Proust secured as his seconds Jean Béraud, a distinguished painter, and Gustave de Borda, a delightfully witty socialite with impeccable credentials for the business at hand. Borda had fought so many duels with such dexterity and finesse that he was known as "Sword-Thrust Borda." As his seconds, Lorrain also chose members of the bohemian set, the painter Octave Uzanne and the novelist Paul Adam. The four seconds met at Béraud's residence but failed to resolve their differences, and a duel was judged necessary. It was agreed that the duel would be fought with pistols on Saturday, February 6, in the forest of Meudon, just outside Paris. Proust's primary worry, he later told Robert de Montesquiou, was not the bullets but having to rise, dress, and go out in the morning. He was greatly relieved on learning that Borda and Béraud had managed to negotiate an afternoon confrontation.

The day of the duel dawned cold and rainy. Before leaving for his encounter with Lorrain, Proust calmly wrote a note to congratulate the poet Henri de Régnier on his recent election to the Légion d'honneur.[36] Hahn accompanied Proust on the carriage to the dueling place outside Paris at the Tour de Villebon. Once both parties had arrived, the men went quickly about their business. Proust was later to recall, with some derision, that Adam became "hysterical" over the dangerous situation.[37] After stepping off twenty-five paces, Proust and Lorrain each fired one shot at the other, neither scoring a hit. Proust had apparently taken aim at Lorrain, because his bullet hit the ground very near the journalist's right foot.[38] After the exchange of fire, the seconds for both parties declared the matter resolved.

Later that day Hahn recorded in his diary: "Today Marcel fought with Jean Lorrain, who had written an odious article about him in *Le Journal*. For the last three days he has shown a sangfroid and firmness that appear incompatible with his nerves, but that does not surprise me at all."[39] Béraud, a veteran of many such confrontations, had also been impressed by the young writer's courage.[40] Paul Morand, a diplomat and writer who knew Proust well later in life, faulted biographers and playwrights for depicting him as weak and effeminate, saying that nothing was further from the truth: "Proust had a lot of authority, what the English call 'poise,' and, at the same time, lots of courage. He looked you right in the eye, with a somewhat defiant air, like D'Artagnan, head back. He was very courageous."[41]

Proust had earlier surprised his peers not only by successfully completing his voluntary year of military service but by trying to reenlist. The army declined to accept him because he had finished next to the bottom of his class, but he often reminisced fondly about his year in the infantry at Orléans, telling Maurice Duplay that the time had been "paradise" for him.[42] Duplay had also noticed that although Proust's body resembled a "fragile envelope, it hid great courage."[43]

After the duel, Mme Arman de Caillavet, like the others in Proust's circle who had been vilified by Lorrain, expressed her gratitude for his having defended their reputations. "Dear Marcel," she wrote, "I thank you for your sweet thought and take you to my heart for being so brave and coming back to us safe and sound from your adventure." As for Lorrain, she felt that he had gotten off lightly: "I wish the monster had come to some harm but even so it's fine of you to have attacked him, considering the universal cowardice which had thus far given that ruffian impunity."[44] How Daudet reacted to Proust's having defended their honor is not known. A few years later, looking back to the time of the duel, Proust expressed, in a letter to Lucien, his surprise that they had ever been so close: "It's odd to think that we loved each other."[45]

We have seen Proust and Hahn use *pony* as a term of endearment when addressing each other. Another common term of affection, one harder for someone who is not a native speaker of French to comprehend, is *rat*, which is generally used for a child or a woman. In half a dozen or so of the known letters to Daudet, Proust uses this word to express his affection or to say that he misses seeing his friend. The first such occurrence dates from February 1901, long after the two men had drifted apart. Proust begins the letter "Vieux rat gentil" (Nice old rat) and signs it "affectionately, Rat."[46] I see no connection between this use of *rat* and Proust's later sadistic use of the rodents in brothels as part of a bizarre and cruel sexual ritual.

Proust must have felt a burst of pride on being singled out by Mme de Caillavet for his bravery in the midst of cowardly men. He may have been remembering his own courage, as an example of one among many, when he made a note years later in a passage about homosexuals: "Insist on the fact that homosexuality has never prevented men from acting bravely, from [Julius] Caesar to [Horatio Herbert] Kitchener."[47]

Proust never did accept any insinuation that he was less than manly. In 1920 he challenged the critic Paul Souday for having used the word *feminine* to compare Proust's style to that of the duke de Saint-Simon, the seventeenth-century author whose *Mémoires* of life at the court of Louis XIV is considered a masterpiece. Souday had written that while the novelist's style did share many characteristics with Saint-Simon's, "Marcel Proust is above all a highly sensitive aesthete, somewhat morbid, almost feminine." Rattling his saber, Proust rejected the characterization: "From feminine to effeminate, there is only a step. Those who served as my seconds in duels will tell you if I am soft like men who are effeminate."[48]

Proust did make at least one attempt to reignite the flames of his love for Hahn. This came two years after their breakup, in the fall of 1898, when Proust was vacationing at Trouville. He made a day trip up the coast to Madeleine Lemaire's villa at Dieppe, where Hahn was composing a piece called "Destiny."[49] Proust enjoyed walking with Hahn and Mme Lemaire along the cliff overlooking the sea. It seemed like old times—or nearly so. On returning to Trouville, Proust found himself in a nostalgic mood, and he wrote to Hahn, saying how he missed their happy days together and proposing ways in which those moments could be revived. He suggested that they meet again halfway along the coast between Trouville and Dieppe, or if that was not possible, he could visit Hahn later in the fall, wherever he might be. Having summoned up the bittersweet memories of the days when they were intimate, he addressed Hahn as "My dear little one" and assured him that the recent silence on his part, far from being the silence that prefigures forgetfulness, was instead like the "undying embers that brood an ardent, intact love." And he had no other love. "Is it the same with you?" He ended the letter on a hopeful note: "See you soon, Marcel." Then he added a postscript evoking their happiest time together: "Does Beg-Meil tempt you at all?"[50]

Although steadfast in his devotion to Proust, Hahn did not accept his invitation to resume their passionate friendship. Unquestionably Hahn remained, in Proust's own words, inscribed in the copy of his translation of Ruskin's *Bible of Amiens*, "O my little Reynaldo, O greatest affection in life."[51] In the copy he gave Daudet, Proust, still plagued by allusions to his homosexuality, did not even dare use the word *admiration* to describe his feelings, as he did in the copies sent to

Daudet's mother and brother Léon, because he feared that "it might appear m.g. in the eyes of imbeciles."[52] *M.g.*—mauvais genre—was one their code terms for homosexual.

A decade after the letter inviting Hahn to resume their intimate relationship, Proust was absorbed in the enormous and lonely task of writing his novel. One evening in Cabourg, he lingered in the dining room of the Grand-Hôtel listening to a gypsy band. He asked the musicians whether they knew anything by Reynaldo Hahn. Proust described what happened next in a letter to Hahn: "When they started playing *Rêverie* I began to cry as I thought of my Bunibuls in the big dining-room surrounded by a score of dismayed waiters who put on long faces! The head waiter, not knowing how to commiserate with me, went to fetch a finger-bowl."[53]

Proust's insane jealousy had deprived him of Hahn's passionate love. His intention to use this malady in his novel, as he had in earlier stories, is indicated by the plot note made in the first notebook for *In Search of Lost Time*, known as *The Notebook of 1908*, a diagnosis applicable to the Narrator and his creator, each of whom was afflicted with "an incapacity for happiness." The dynamics of Proustian erotic love had been established in his adolescence and early manhood in the demands for attention and a possessiveness that had frightened and repulsed his classmates at Condorcet. His overwhelming youthful desire to be "loved, caressed, and spoiled" remained just as strong in his maturity. None of Proust's friends and lovers could tolerate for long his excessive, unreasonable demands, which he knew resulted from his great need for affection and his insecurity in being able to inspire and sustain such love. The Narrator's obsessive curiosity about Albertine's present and past becomes so enormous that it takes on cosmic proportions that can only end in frustration and disappointment:

And I realised the impossibility which love comes up against. We imagine that it has as its object a being that can be laid down in front of us, enclosed within a body. Alas, it is the extension of that being to all the points in space and time that it has occupied and will occupy. If we do not possess its contact with this or that place, this or that hour, we do not possess that being. But we cannot touch all these points.[54]

Over the years, Hahn never seemed to lose his youthful demeanor and enthusiasm. In the years following the deaths of Proust's parents — his father died in 1903, his mother two years later — Hahn's arrival at 102 boulevard Haussmann always created a stir. Although he alone of all Proust's friends had the privilege of coming unannounced at any hour, the entire household usually knew immediately that he had entered the apartment. He first stopped in the living room, where he played the grand piano for a few minutes before rushing into Proust's room. Céline Cottin, Proust's housekeeper at the time, always used to say, on hearing Hahn come through the door: "It's the wind!" To which the sedentary writer, brightening at the news, replied, "The hurricane!"[55]

Proust always described Hahn as the person "I love most in the world" and "another me."[56] He may have had Hahn in mind when the Narrator gives this definition of love, on realizing how close he and Albertine have become: "Was she not, after all (she in whose being there now existed an idea of me so habitual and familiar that, next to her aunt, I was perhaps the person whom she distinguished least from herself) . . . ?"[57] In 1912 Proust wrote to Hahn, who had gone to Bucharest to give a lecture. Though so far away, he still felt his friend's presence within him: "You are so mixed up now with my thoughts, my sleep, my reading that writing to you seems as irksome as writing to myself."[58]

Daudet remained a constant, if at times distant and absent, friend. Like Hahn, he was among the first to recognize and appreciate Proust's genius. Years later, on the publication of *Swann's Way*, Proust sent Daudet an affectionate letter, explaining that "you are absent from this book: you are too much a part of my heart for me to ever be able to depict you objectively; you will never be a 'character,' you are the best part of the author. But when I think that so many years of my life have been spent on 'Lucien's Way' . . . then the words

'Time Lost' assume for me many different meanings, very sad ones, but very beautiful ones also. May we one day 'regain' it again."[59]

Hahn and Daudet were, as far as we know, the only men Proust chose as lovers who were also his social equals. Two years after Proust's breakup with Hahn, he became infatuated with Count Bertrand de Fénelon, a strikingly handsome blond with blue eyes, who became the primary model for the blond Marquis Robert de Saint-Loup in the novel. This unrequited love for a man who seemed to like only women made Proust ill for a time.[60]

For the remainder of his life, Proust chose as his sexual partners young men from the servant or working classes, those who exchanged sex for money either as domestics or in male brothels, as he, like his great homosexual character Charlus, continued to seek beauty in all its forms. The discovery of new forms of masculine beauty was an important element in making Proust consider his stint in the military to be "paradise."

In 1889, his year of service, the minister of war had decreed that this last crop of volunteers be dispersed through all the companies and have the same obligations as the recruits from the lower classes. This meant that although Proust was allowed to live among cadets of his own social background, he would train with young men from modest families.[61] These "peasant comrades," as he called them, made a highly favorable impression, as seen in a short piece written at the time. "Memory's Genre Paintings" depicts such youths caught at some ordinary moment in their lives. Proust had been particularly struck by the soldiers' physical beauty combined with a simplicity to which he was unaccustomed: "The rural character of my peasant comrades whose bodies had remained more beautiful and more agile, their minds more original, their hearts more spontaneous, their characters more natural than those of the young men I had known before, or those I knew afterwards. . . ."[62]

Years later, when he began making the preliminary sketches for *In Search of Lost Time*, Proust jotted down in the margins of *The Notebook of 1908* the addresses of such men, whose names now have no meaning. This is, as Proust reminds us in *Time Regained*, an inevitable effect of the unstoppable nature of time: "A book is a huge cemetery in which on the majority of tombs the names are effaced and can no longer be read. Sometimes on the other hand we remember a name well enough but do not know whether anything of the individual who bore it survives in our pages."[63]

CHAPTER FIVE

A Nun of Speed

On August 5, 1907, Proust left Paris for the seaside resort of Cabourg, a trip that marked a rebirth for him after two years of intense grief and illness following his mother's death. A month before his arrival, Cabourg had inaugurated the large and sumptuous Grand-Hôtel, one of the most modern on the Normandy coast. The new amenities included a service offering chauffeured cars for hire. Jacques Bizet, now a medical school dropout, served as the director of one of the first car-rental agencies, Taximètres Unic, which made automobiles available to vacationers in Cabourg in the summer and in Monaco during the winter. It was through Taximètres Unic that Proust met two young chauffeurs, Odilon Albaret and Alfred Agostinelli, who were to play crucial roles in his life, roles that ultimately changed the course of the novel.

For the first of Proust's many excursions in the region, he hired Agostinelli and his new red taxi to drive him to Caen, famous for its medieval churches. Agostinelli, whose father was Italian, had grown up in Monaco. At nineteen, although slightly plump with rounded cheeks, he was an attractive, athletic youth with thick dark hair and fair skin. His habitual shyness disguised a daredevil nature that revealed itself in his passion for the new machines of speed, the automobile and the airplane. Although Proust immediately admired Agostinelli's skills as a driver and resourcefulness as a servant, he did not fall in love with the young man until six years later, when Agostinelli reappeared in his life in desperate need of employment.

The stay in Cabourg brought about a dramatic change in Proust, which he described in a letter to a friend: "The pure air joined with a deadly dose of caffeine" allowed him "to go out every day in a closed car."[1] Riding across the Normandy countryside with Agostinelli in his red taxi was, the novelist said, like being shot out of a cannon.[2]

Proust found the 1907 trip to Cabourg so invigorating and so pleasant that he returned to the Grand-Hôtel every summer until 1914, when he made the last difficult trip with his housekeeper Céleste Albaret and Ernest Forssgren, a Swedish valet who served him briefly. Ultimately, he transposed Cabourg and its new beachfront hotel into Normandy's most famous literary landscape: Balbec, with its hotel and environs, first described in *Within a Budding Grove*. At Balbec the Narrator meets some of the novel's key characters: Robert de Saint-Loup, the haughty baron de Charlus, arguably literature's most famous homosexual, and Albertine, who will become the Narrator's great love and whose athleticism—she is "a passionate lover of every form of sport"—may have been inspired, at least in part, by the fearless young chauffeur Agostinelli.[3]

When Proust left Cabourg in late September 1907, Agostinelli drove him back to Paris, with stops in Lisieux and Évreux, where he intended to visit the medieval churches. His passion for Gothic architecture had not waned since the publication a few years earlier of his translations of John Ruskin's *The Bible of Amiens* and parts of *Sesame and Lilies*. His excursions had another purpose as well: he hoped to find a rural setting for an unspecified literary project, perhaps a novella. To avoid distraction he had decided not to accept an offer of hospitality from friends. The duke and duchess of Clermont-Tonnerre, whose country manor was at Glisolles, not far from Évreux, had invited Proust to stay with them, but he chose instead to spend four days in Évreux, which might serve as the "provincial Balzacian town" for the story he wanted to write.[4] In order to make certain that he was not disturbed, the wildly extravagant Proust rented two entire floors of the Hôtel Moderne.[5]

Proust must have thought twice before declining the invitation to stay at Glisolles, because Mme de Clermont-Tonnerre, née Élisabeth de Gramont, was one of the most intriguing society hostesses he knew. Like so many of his future characters, she was a lesbian. Unusually frank about sexual matters, she and Proust enjoyed tête-à-têtes in which they shared scandalous tidbits about their acquaintances. Once Céleste Albaret, sent to take a message to the duchess, "found her surrounded by a pack of women." When she described the scene to Proust, "he laughed at first, then said he admired the Duchess for her intelligence and sensibility." Proust had been amused, of course, by Céleste's discovering the lady basking in a milieu that revealed her true sexuality and by his housekeeper's naïveté, which blinded her to the reality of the situation. Some years later, after divorcing the duke—a "brute," according to Proust—Élisabeth "became notorious as one of the so-called 'amazons,' women artists and writers of postwar Paris who defied sexual convention."[6] She even betrayed her class by later becoming a communist sympathizer.[7]

While Proust was in Évreux, Agostinelli drove him out to Glisolles one evening to visit M. and Mme de Clermont-Tonnerre. To counter his incessant asthma attacks, Proust had consumed seventeen cups of coffee before leaving the hotel, apparently the number he calculated to contain the required dosage of caffeine.[8] Mme de Clermont-Tonnerre, who was spending a quiet evening with her husband, suddenly heard what she thought was the sound of tires on the gravel in the driveway—an impression she conveyed to the duke, who remarked, incredulous, "You're crazy!"[9] But she was right; it was Agostinelli's red taxi that she had heard come to a sudden stop.

Proust lingered to chat with his hosts until late in the evening. When it was time to leave, he was shaking so severely from all the coffee he had consumed that he could barely walk. The duke took Proust by the arm and guided his "tottering, caffeine-weakened steps down the nocturnal staircase." When the writer politely declined an invitation to return the next day, the duchess protested, "But you won't see my roses!" "Show them to me this evening," Proust replied. The clever Agostinelli parked the car in front of the rose garden and shone the headlights on the bushes, whose flowers appeared like "beauties who had been awakened from their sleep."

Shortly after his return from Cabourg, Proust finished the article about the motoring trips with Agostinelli for *Le Figaro*.[10] "Impressions de route en automobile" describes the trip to Caen, where, as the taxi sped toward its destination, Proust had observed the rapidly shifting positions of the steeples of two of the town's churches, Saint-Étienne and Saint-Pierre. He later used this part of the newspaper article, with a few changes, as a text the young Narrator writes when he has a similar experience observing, near Combray, the steeples of Martinville from a fast-moving carriage.[11]

In the article for *Le Figaro*, Proust also recounted that because he and Agostinelli arrived at Lisieux after nightfall, he despaired of being able to see the cathedral façade described by Ruskin. Using the same method of illumination that had "awakened" the duchess's roses, the "ingenious" Agostinelli trained the car's headlights on the cathedral's portals, whose statues suddenly leaped out of the darkness.

Proust may not have yet fallen in love with Agostinelli, but he had begun transposing the dashing young Italian into a creature of sexual ambiguity. In the newspaper article, the author likened him to a "nun of speed" because his motoring attire, consisting of boots, a long hooded coat, and goggles—all of which nearly covered Agostinelli's body—made him look like a woman. A photograph taken by Jacques-Henri Lartigue in 1919 of his family's driver validates Proust's description of Agostinelli. The sexual identity of Lartigue's chauffeur is virtually indiscernible beneath all the motoring paraphernalia, which does indeed suggest a modernized, leather version of a nun's habit.

If the chauffeur's outfit made Agostinelli look like a nun, similar apparel in the novel also gives Albertine an androgynous or Amazon look, "swift-moving and bent over the mythological wheel of her bicycle, strapped on rainy days inside the warrior tunic of her waterproof which moulded her breasts, her head turbaned and dressed with snakes . . . she spread terror through the streets of Balbec." Agostinelli probably inspired this vision of Albertine as well as the Narrator's regret of not having embraced Albertine in her rain gear, a regret remindful of the misery, expressed in many letters to friends, that Proust later suffered from his unrequited love for Agostinelli: "Never had I caressed the waterproofed Albertine of the rainy days; I wanted to ask her to take off that armour, in order to experience with her the love of the tented field, the fraternity of travel."[12]

After Agostinelli's death years later, Proust interpreted as ominous a passage from "Impressions de route en automobile," referring to the risks of being a driver: "May the steering wheel of the young chauffeur who is driving me remain always the symbol of his talent rather than the augury of his martyrdom!"[13] Agostinelli's love affair with the machines of speed and his association with Proust did ultimately lead to tragedy.

The article on the motor trips appeared in *Le Figaro* on November 19, 1907. Among the congratulatory notes friends sent, one in particular surprised and delighted Proust. "Can you imagine," he wrote Mme Straus, "which was the prettiest letter." It was "the one from Agostinelli," to whom Proust's valet, Nicolas Cottin, had sent a copy of the article.[14] This was a hint of what Proust was later to learn, when he fell in love with Agostinelli, about what he called the chauffeur's intellectual gifts.

Before leaving for Cabourg in the summer of 1908, Proust finally saw to his wardrobe. The playwright Henry Bernstein, appalled by Proust's shabby clothes, had recently offended him by saying that he was not dressed well enough to accompany him to a brothel. Paris's leading playwright, Bernstein was also known among his companions for his sexual exploits. Although Bernstein kept a handsome young man sequestered, an arrangement which made Proust jealous, the playwright's friends admired him chiefly for the ardor with which he made love to the women he pursued, whether his mistress of the moment, society ladies who found him irresistible, or the prostitutes he routinely hired. Paul Morand records that on some evenings after the opera, "Bernstein had the taxi drivers fuck his mistress X, or when Mme Y hosted a grand dinner party, he arranged to have someone slip her a note in the middle of the dinner: 'Leave your guests, I await you in a car below. Come join me.' "[15] Bernstein particularly enjoyed taking fashionable women, such as Lady de Grey, to Le Chabanais, a luxurious brothel, where one found the most beautiful and refined whores in Paris. Here he entertained regularly, providing his guests with a fine supper, while having the pretty *filles de joie* strike lewd poses for the ladies.[16] As for the sequestered youth, Morand's private diary provides only a few intriguing details: he was twenty-five and very beautiful, his name began with the letter L, he was deaf. When Proust queried Morand about him, it was clear that the novelist envisaged the man as a "kind of Albertine," who becomes the Narrator's "captive" in the part of the novel called *La Prisonnière*.

At Cabourg, a more elegantly attired Proust hired Agostinelli to drive him out to visit many of his Paris friends, who owned or rented villas in the surrounding countryside. At Trouville, Proust was delighted to find Robert de Billy, an old acquaintance, among the summer guests at Horace Finaly's villa, les Frémonts. Now a diplomat, Billy had been a close friend since their university days. Proust knew the villa well from summer vacations many years earlier. It was here that Jacques-Émile Blanche had first sketched the twenty-year-old Proust in pencil, before painting the full-length portrait in oil that was featured in the 1893 Champ de Mars salon.[17]

Les Frémonts reminded Proust of his flirtations with Finaly's pretty sister Mary, one of several girls on whom he apparently had crushes during his late teens and early twenties. He loved her green eyes and, while gazing amorously into them, recited to her lines from his favorite collection of poems, Charles Baudelaire's *Les Fleurs du mal*. One verse seemed particularly appropriate for Mary: "J'aime de vos longs yeux la lumière verdâtre!" ("How I love the greenish light of your long eyes!"). After quoting the poem, Proust hummed Gabriel Fauré's musical setting for the piece.[18] Mary's reaction to Proust's serenading is not known, but it seems unlikely that she took it too seriously.

Sometime during the summer, Proust made a list of the six episodes for his novel drafted during the first half of the year, under the heading "Pages written."[19] Among these we find the good night–kiss scene, in which the child Narrator, unable to sleep, forces his mother to make "concessions" and spend the night in his room. This incident, the primal matter out of which grew all Proustian narration, had first been used in the early story "A Young Girl's Confession," which also included an early version of what became the profanation scene in *Swann's Way*, in which a parent (the composer Vinteuil) dies of a broken heart because of his daughter's scandalous love affair.

In 1906, Proust had sketched out in a letter to Hahn a sadistic play that he intended to write with René Peter. The drama centered on a man and a wife who adore each other; the husband is said to bear for his wife an "immense affection, saintly, pure (but of course not chaste)." The man is, however, a sadist, and has "liaisons with whores with whom he enjoys soiling his own good sentiments." He does so through another profanation ritual, for which he is remorseful "five minutes later," that consists of having the whores join him in speaking ill of his wife. Apparently, he is extremely careless and indulges in these licentious games at home, where, one day, his wife catches him in the act. She leaves her husband, who "begs her to return." Her rejection of his pleas causes him such despair that he kills himself.[20]

In the summer of 1908 Proust made a notebook entry indicating the probable source for the projected play: "the little monster . . . Robin." The note refers to a scandalous incident involving Dr. Albert

Robin and his mistress, the beautiful courtesan Liane de Pougy. While stressing that Dr. Robin remained, in all other respects, a fine, devoted family man, Proust noted that when making love to Liane, Robin could achieve satisfaction only by calling his son "the little monster." In another version of this story, related to Proust by Élisabeth de Clermont-Tonnerre in one of their gossipy exchanges, it was jealousy and anger over the doctor's refusal to leave his wife that drove Liane de Pougy to force him, during intercourse, to refer to his wife and son as "the monster and the little monster."[21] The latter version is in keeping with the key Proustian theme of the evil forces of jealousy, resulting from egotism, that inevitably destroy love.

Proust never developed the outline of this play, but his return to the topic, as indicated by the notebook entry, proves his abiding interest in the theme of cruel behavior toward those who most deserve our affection. The Robin-Pougy ritual and a similar incident in the early story "A Young Girl's Confession" ultimately led him to create the sadistic lesbian ritual between Mlle Vinteuil and her lover in *Swann's Way*.

When Proust was ready to leave Cabourg, he hired Agostinelli to drive him to the Hôtel des Réservoirs at Versailles and remain in his service for the duration of his stay. His decision to return to the hotel, where he had retreated to grieve his mother's death a few years earlier, may have been influenced by the presence of Hahn, who had come there to finish composing *La Fête chez Thérèse,* a ballet for the Paris Opéra. During rare breaks from work, Hahn came to Proust's room to sit by his bed. Even in the company of others, the effervescent, chain-smoking Hahn—he even sang with a cigarette dangling from his lips—could not resist composing, while Proust, his valet Cottin, and Agostinelli played dominoes. Proust, who required absolute solitude and silence when at work, expressed his amazement that Hahn could concentrate and compose in the midst of such noise and babble.[22] It was apparently at this time that Proust developed the habit of playing such games as dominoes and checkers with male servants. These pastimes kept young men nearby when he wanted company and offered the opportunity to hear gossip about what was going on in the hotel, a curiosity that allowed him to create many revealing and amusing scenes about the peccadilloes of masters and their servants.

Shortly before arriving in Versailles, Proust had learned that Georges de Lauris had suffered serious injuries in an automobile accident. Believing that the duties of friendship required him to call on the recuperating marquis, Proust made several attempts to visit him in Paris. Twice Agostinelli drove his employer to Lauris's apartment in Paris. Each time Proust got no further than the entrance to the building because his asthma made it impossible for him to mount the three flights of stairs to reach his friend's bedside, which forced him to communicate by letter his concerns and hopes for a speedy recovery.

Writing to Lauris to express the "mixture of grief and humiliation" that the "impotence" of his "friendship" caused him to feel on being unable to climb the stairs, Proust attempted to picture Georges's body in order to give thanks for his having survived the collision intact: "Each of your limbs so miraculously spared, your beautiful, gentle hands which from time to time, when I express a doubt about your friendship, seek mine in a gesture of persuasive eloquence." By the end of Proust's hymn of anatomical adoration, Lauris's body had become the Eucharist: "It seems to me that I have too exclusively loved your mind and your heart hitherto and that now I would experience a pure and exalting joy, like the Christian who eats the bread and drinks the wine and sings *Venite adoremus*, in reciting in your presence the litany of your ankles and the praises of your wrists."

Then, realizing that he had let himself get carried away in his praise of masculine beauty, Proust immediately tried to explain himself: "Alas, people have always been so cruel and uncomprehending about me, that these are things which I scarcely dare to say" because of misinterpretations that were certain to "spring up in others' thoughts." He remained confident that Lauris, who knew him so well, would be able to "grasp" with his "infallible intelligence the palpable reality of what I am" and "understand how purely moral and reverently paternal is what I say to you."[23]

Did Proust insert the last sentence in case the letter fell into the hands of others—a prospect he always feared when writing about intimate matters? Did the disclaimer also serve as a private joke between the two men? This may well be the case since Morand's recently published diary reveals that Lauris was also homosexual.[24] Was Proust aware of this, or had he misjudged Lauris's sexuality, as he apparently had in the case of their mutual friend Bertrand de Fénelon? Lauris's marriage in 1910 at least gave the marquis the appearance of heterosexuality or certified his bisexuality for those who knew of his homosexual practices. Marriage proves nothing, of course, one way or the other, about one's sexual proclivities. Indeed, Proust's most notorious homosexual character, Charlus, is a widower, who steadfastly maintains that homosexuals make the best husbands, in part because they do not make excessive sexual demands on wives who did not marry for love.[25]

CHAPTER SIX

Where Fair Strangers Abound

I knew that I was going to find myself in one of those very places where fair

strangers must abound; a beach offers them in no less profusion than a ball-

room, and I looked forward to strolling up and down outside the hotel.

During the 1908–9 summer vacations, Proust became friends with young men whose middle-class families owned or rented villas in or near Cabourg. Among those he met were two engineers, Pierre Parent and Max Daireaux, both in their mid-twenties. He entered Parent's name several times in his notebook, jotting down traits or dialogue eventually used for certain aspects of his fictional Saint-Loup and Albertine.[1] Since Proust viewed most individuals as androgynous, he had no hesitation in distributing traits from the young men between his male and female characters, especially these two, whose sexuality is ambiguous. Daireaux, twenty-four, was the younger brother of boys Proust had met two decades earlier at Neuilly tennis parties.[2]

Perhaps his most interesting new acquaintance was twenty-two-year-old Albert Nahmias fils, destined to be, like his father, a financial journalist. The well-to-do family resided in a Paris mansion on the elegant avenue Montaigne; their summer home was the Villa

Bertha at Cabourg. Young Nahmias was to become an intimate friend of Proust's and play an important role in the early production of *Swann's Way*.

At Cabourg, Proust surrounded himself, whenever possible, with these men in the flower of youth. He observed in his notebook the "desire to love that floats among persons who know each other," a desire that he no doubt felt more strongly than did the young men.[3] Part of the entertainment that Proust provided for the youths included reading poems to them by Anna de Noailles. One selection had a particularly appropriate title: "Les Adolescents."[4] Later, back in Paris, Proust occasionally convened some of the youths, treating them to evenings at the theater and meals in fine restaurants.

In *Within a Budding Grove,* Proust transformed the masculine features of these active and attractive young men into "the feminine, marine and sportive grace of the girls whom" his hero first sees "against the horizon of the waves."[5] The little band of girls in bloom rule the beach at Balbec, bewitching the Narrator, who finds them irresistible as a variegated bouquet of young women in flower.[6] Proust's delightful, exuberant descriptions of the adolescent girls cavorting on the beach and boardwalk in front of the Grand-Hôtel are hymns to the athleticism of the young men he met at Cabourg, whose beauty, grace, and suppleness intoxicated him.

The Narrator observes that the social class to which the girls belong has evolved to the point where "thanks either to its growing wealth and leisure, or to new sporting habits, now prevalent even among certain elements of the working class, and a physical culture to which had not yet been added the culture of the mind," it produces "naturally, and in abundance, fine bodies, fine legs, fine hips, wholesome, serene faces, with an air of agility and guile." He sees in these youths "noble and calm models of human beauty . . . outlined against the sea, like statues exposed to the sunlight on a Grecian shore." Furthermore, the constantly shifting beauty of these youths presents an enticing variety of delightful forms and features. Proust makes this distinction between a mature woman and the girls on the beach:

Certainly the attentions that a woman pays us can still, so long as we are in love with her, endue with fresh charms the hours that we spend in her company. But she is not then for us a series of different women. Her gaiety remains external to an unchanging face. Whereas adolescence precedes this complete solidification, and hence we feel, in the company of young girls, the refreshing sense that is afforded us by the spectacle of forms undergoing an incessant process of change, a play of unstable forces which recalls the perpetual re-creation of the primordial elements of nature which we contemplate when we stand before the sea.[7]

Proust plants the seeds for his hero's disappointment in love by endowing him with the same unreasonable expectations that doomed the author's love affair with Reynaldo Hahn. As the youthful Narrator falls in love with each of the girls in turn, he feels that he must know everything about her and possess her life, past and present, completely: "And it was consequently her whole life that filled me with desire; a sorrowful desire because I felt that it was not to be fulfilled, but an exhilarating one because, what had hitherto been my life [had] ceased of a sudden to be my whole life, being no more now than a small part of the space stretching out before me which I was burning to cover and which was composed of the lives of these girls." He naïvely believes that such desire offered him "that prolongation, that possible multiplication of oneself, which is happiness."[8]

The convalescing Proust drew strength and inspiration from the vibrant company of the athletic, desirable young men with whom he fell in love as a group, just as does the Narrator with the girls at Balbec: "I loved none of them, loving them all, and yet the possibility of meeting them was in my daily life the sole element of delight, alone aroused in me those hopes for which one would break down every obstacle, hopes ending often in fury if I had not seen them." Watching them, studying them, pursuing them in their rapid processions up and down the beach constitutes a "passionate astronomy."[9] From this cluster of stars emerges Albertine, destined to be the Narrator's great love.

When Proust decided to create the fictional counterpart of Cabourg, with its band of seaside girls, he consulted Nahmias, who had spent many summers at Cabourg, about what sort of clothes young ladies wore to dine out while at the seashore. He also questioned him about the various nicknames of the little train that served the coastal resorts for use in the sections of the novel relating to the Narrator's two stays at Balbec.[10] One can presume that the protagonist is speaking for Proust when he states that the company of these youths made him aware, as he approached the age of forty, that what he really "loved was youth."[11]

Around this time, 1908–9, in Proust's letters to his young friends there are references to obscene poems that he has written about the girls of Cabourg or about obscene books that he has read and is willing to lend. In May 1909 he wrote a letter to Max Daireaux and inquired: "Did you receive the letter in which I sent you some idiotic and obscene verses about Cabourg?" And he worried that these "horrors" might have strayed into the wrong hands.[12] These licentious verses sent to Max Daireaux are presumably the ones referred to again by Proust in another letter sent in mid-August: "I tremble on thinking about the letters which you may not have received in which I told you a thousand obscene things about the ladies of Cabourg."

For the most part, Proust's references to the obscene books he was reading—and the poems he was writing—lack precision; we don't know exactly which books he has in mind, except for a letter, not to one of the young men but to Georges de Lauris, which specifically mentions "two clandestine Verlaines, obscene and stupid." These were pornographic poems written in the first person, presumably personal on Verlaine's part, about his carnal knowledge of women and men: "Femmes" and "Hombres."[13] Is it possible that Proust's poems about Cabourg were pastiches of Verlaine's "Femmes"? Had he been testing Daireaux by seeing how he reacted to pornographic books? Proust goes on to say that he has "two other books which are merely 'improper' (and not very improper) and which might entertain you for half an hour if you don't know them: *Seven Letters to*

Stendhal and *H.B.* by Mérimée." He apparently had reason to wonder about Lauris's melancholy, which he attributed to his friend's lack of sexual contacts: "Georges, if your innocence is at last beginning to weigh on you I can quite understand that you wouldn't want to bring cocottes to your house, but it's said that . . ." Here the published version of the letter breaks off, leaving one to wonder whether the passage was censored. As for his own tastes, Proust claimed to "only like (at the moment I don't like anything, as you can imagine) young girls, as though life weren't complicated enough as it is. You will tell me that marriage was invented for such contingencies, but then she ceases to be a girl, you can only have a girl once. I understand Bluebeard, he was a man who liked young girls."[14]

The sort of seductions that Proust has in mind—was he only kidding?—seem to be those of minors, against which there were, of course, laws. In this regard, there is a related passage in which the Narrator, in despair because Albertine has left him, invites a "little poor girl" into his apartment, has her sit on his knee for a while, and gives her a five hundred–franc note for her docility. Twice the police call upon him to investigate because the "parents of the little girl whom I had brought into the house for an hour had decided to bring a charge against me for abduction of a minor."[15]

The Narrator steadfastly maintains his innocence. He had invited her home because she "looked so sweet-natured that I asked her whether she would care to come home with me, as I might have taken home a dog with faithful eyes. She seemed pleased at the suggestion. When I got home, I held her for some time on my knee, but very soon her presence, by making me feel too keenly Albertine's absence, became intolerable. And I asked her to go away, after giving her a five-hundred franc note."[16]

When the girl's parents lodge a complaint, the police bring the Narrator in for questioning:

> At the Sûreté, I found the girl's parents, who insulted me and with the words "We'd rather starve" handed me back the five hundred

francs which I did not want to take, and the head of the Sûreté who, setting himself the inimitable example of the judicial facility in repartee, seized upon a word in each sentence that I uttered for the purpose of concocting a witty and crushing retort. My innocence of the alleged crime was never taken into consideration, for that was the sole hypothesis which nobody was willing to accept for an instant. Nevertheless the difficulty of proving the charge enabled me to escape with this castigation, which was extremely violent for as long as the parents were in the room. But as soon as they had gone, the head of the Sûreté, who had a weakness for little girls, changed his tone and admonished me as man to man: "Next time, you must be more careful. Good God, you can't pick them up as easily as that, or you'll get into trouble. Anyhow, you'll find dozens of little girls who are better-looking than that one, and far cheaper. It was a perfectly ridiculous amount to pay." I was so certain that he would fail to understand me if I attempted to tell him the truth that without saying a word I took advantage of his permission to withdraw.

The Narrator remains under a cloud of suspicion and has reason to believe that his house has been placed under police surveillance. He continues to proclaim the innocent nature of the strong urges he feels to have a little girl sit in his lap as a comfort for Albertine's having left. The incident is a curious one and may reflect Proust's own fear of being caught with underage boys, whom he may have lured to his apartment under the pretext of running errands for him or providing other legitimate services. As we shall see, Proust recruited waiters from the Ritz for sexual trysts, and he may not always have been certain that they had reached the age of consent.

The attitude of the public at large and the moral and legal issues relative to homosexuality occupied Proust's thoughts throughout 1908. That year a sex scandal erupted in Germany involving allegations of homosexuality at the highest levels of Kaiser Wilhelm II's court. Prince Philipp Eulenburg, the suave, cultivated former ambassador to Vienna and the kaiser's closest friend, was accused by

Maximilian Harden, the muckraking, nationalistic editor of the bellicose weekly newspaper *Die Zukunft*, of having peopled the kaiser's
inner circle with homosexuals.[17] A dismissed minister who had kept
secret files of the private lives of his associates at court sought revenge
by releasing the damaging documents to Harden. Harden and his
colleagues believed that Eulenburg and his associates were pacifists
and Francophiles whose influence on the kaiser thwarted Harden's
own ambitions. Harden's charges resulted in a series of libel trials that
ended in Eulenburg's disgrace and arrest. Not since the Wilde trial
had homosexuality been the focus of so much public attention.

Proust followed the Eulenburg trials through the press and through
his contacts with French diplomats who knew the German court. In a
letter of November 9 he asked Robert de Billy what he thought about
"this homosexuality trial? I think they've hit out rather at random,
although it's absolutely true about some of them, notably the Prince,
but some of the details are very comic."[18] For Proust, whose thoughts
often centered on sexual ambiguity and homosexuality, the plight of
Eulenburg and others accused of acts considered perverse provided
another occasion to ponder same-sex love and society's persecution of
such behavior. There is no doubt as to whose side Proust took. In a
letter to Hahn, he criticized the German ambassador to France, Prince
von Radolin, for having failed to show sufficient sympathy for Eulenburg's plight.[19]

From a diplomatic point of view, the French in their glee over the
embarrassing scandal at the kaiser's court failed to appreciate that the
disgrace of Eulenburg and other "catamites" could only work to
France's disadvantage as Germany grew more bellicose. In Paris one
heard references made to the "German vice," and Berlin was nicknamed *Sodome-sur-Spree*. In the places where French homosexuals
gathered, "Parlez-vous allemand?" (Do you speak German?) became
the password for those seeking partners.[20]

At some point in late 1907 or early 1908, perhaps inspired by the
German trials, Proust began to consider writing an essay about homosexuality.[21] He also began to relive the trials and downfall of the Irish

poet, novelist, and playwright Oscar Wilde, whose visit to Paris in the late fall of 1891 had been the great event of that season's literary salons. Wilde, who had published his first and only novel, *The Picture of Dorian Gray,* a year earlier, had yet to write *Salomé* or the sparkling light comedies on which his literary fame rests today. But his reputation in France, where his novel was not yet known, derived from his poems and fairy tales, as well as from his wit and eccentricities. Although Wilde's hosts may have been at pains to explain the precise nature of his accomplishments, they did not doubt that his gifts were authentic and certain to lead him to greatness and renown. Wilde possessed qualities the French had always held in high esteem: those of a dazzling conversationalist and a sharp, brilliant wit. During his Paris visit, Wilde remarked to Enrique Gómez Carrillo, a young Guatemalan diplomat whom he met at the Café d'Harcourt: "I have put all my talent into my works. I have put all my genius into my life."[22] And this Irishman had mastered the language of Racine and Molière, acquiring a prodigious vocabulary and eloquent style; fluent French— even if badly pronounced—poured from his large, voluptuous lips. Wilde relished being the new Paris sensation. Like Proust, whom he was soon to meet, Wilde thoroughly enjoyed society, finding "in it both the satisfaction of his vanity and an inexhaustible source of fatuity."[23]

In spite of all the amusements offered by the City of Light, Wilde soon undertook a serious work. Inspired by French art, especially Gustave Moreau's paintings and Stéphane Mallarmé's verses, he began to write, in French, his play *Salomé.* He explained to Gómez that the story of the veiled dancer and the Christian martyr appealed to his decadent side: "I flee from what is moral as from what is impoverished. I have the same sickness as Des Esseintes."[24] Joris-Karl Huysmans created this famous character with the strange sounding name in his novel *À rebours* (1884). Des Esseintes is a decadent hyperaesthete largely inspired by Count Robert de Montesquiou—after whom Proust was to model a character destined to become even more notorious: the homosexual baron de Charlus.

Wilde, too, seemed larger than life, with his decadent side very much on display to his Paris hosts, who observed his addiction to absinthe and opium-tainted cigarettes. Marcel Schwob sketched in his journal the Irishman's exaggerated features: "A big man, with a large pasty face, red cheeks, an ironic eye, bad and protrusive teeth, a vicious childlike mouth with lips soft with milk ready to suck some more."[25] When André Gide met Wilde, he saw an altogether different person, whose overpowering "beauty" captivated him. Gide's diary entry for January 1, 1892, speaks of Wilde's disconcerting effect on him: "Wilde has done me, I think, nothing but harm. With him, I have forgotten how to think."[26] For his part, Wilde found many aspects of Gide's character appalling, especially those that resulted from his strict religious upbringing. Wilde diagnosed Gide's problem, telling him that his lips were "too straight, the lips of someone who has never lied. I must teach you to lie, so your lips will be beautiful and curved like those on an antique mask."[27] The previous summer, Wilde had discovered such a pair of lips on the face of a young English noble-man, Lord Alfred Douglas. Being in love with Bosie, as he called Douglas, the smooth, flamboyant Wilde had no interest in being pursued by the awkward, austere Gide. But Gide, after the transform-ing encounter with the fascinating and frank Irishman, did begin to be more open about his own homosexuality, as he set about to liberate himself from the restraints of his highly conservative family.

Sometime that fall in Paris, Wilde supposedly met the twenty-year-old Marcel Proust. According to Mme Arthur Baignères's grandsons, it was in her drawing room that Jacques-Émile Blanche introduced the two writers. This account provides few details, not all of them ac-curate, about the meeting and the subsequent visit Wilde supposedly paid Proust. At Mme Baignères's, Wilde was touched by the "enthusi-asm for English literature evinced by Proust, by the intelligence re-vealed by his questions about Ruskin and George Eliot . . . and willingly accepted his invitation to dinner at the Boulevard Hauss-mann."[28] Proust's love of English and American letters is well docu-mented: "It's odd," he later wrote, "how in every genre, however different, from George Eliot to Hardy, from Stevenson to Emerson, there's no other literature that has a power over me comparable to English and American literature. Germany, Italy, quite often France, leave me indifferent. But two pages of *The Mill on the Floss* are enough to make me cry."[29]

According to the Baignèreses' account, when Wilde arrived at the apartment, Proust was running late for some reason, and the visitor was shown into the drawing room, where he met Proust's parents. Apparently, the solid bourgeois appearance of Dr. and Mme Proust frightened the bohemian in Wilde, causing his "courage to fail" him; he hid in the bathroom, which is where Proust found him when he returned home, out of breath. Wilde explained the circumstances to Proust and took his leave, "Goodbye, dear M. Proust, goodbye." Proust's mother told him that before retreating to the bathroom, Wilde had looked around the drawing room and commented, "How ugly your house is."[30]

Is this account true? Two inaccuracies indicate that the story is probably apocryphal. In 1891 Proust had not yet read John Ruskin, none of whose works had been translated into French, a task to which Proust was to apply himself a decade later; nor did he reside at 102 boulevard Haussmann, an address that would not be his until fifteen years later, after the deaths of both his parents and of Oscar Wilde. The same remark about an ugly house is uttered by Charlus when he calls upon the Narrator, but the same insulting comment about the Proust apartment and the furnishings had been voiced in real life by another visitor, considered by many to be the arbiter of Parisian taste: Count Robert de Montesquiou, the primary model for Charlus. Wilde was certainly capable of such impertinence, but it is more likely that Montesquiou inspired Charlus's insulting remark. If Proust did meet Wilde, it seems odd that the remarkable encounter left no traces in Proust's letters and notes. Robert de Billy suggested that it was Wilde who selected the dove-gray tie that Proust wore for his portrait in oil by Jacques-Émile Blanche.[31] But again there is no confirmation of this in the known documents or in Blanche's memoirs, *Mes Modèles,* about his famous subjects, who include not only Proust but also Henry James, Jean Cocteau, and André Gide. Nor does Blanche mention having introduced Proust and Wilde, something that he probably would have remembered, given the subsequent great celebrity of the two writers.

If the visit did take place, Proust had the occasion to observe, if only briefly, the man to whom he later alluded in his novel as a martyr to society's prejudices, a man who had yielded to homosexual temptation and whose petulance and pride led to the greatest downfall and humiliation ever suffered by a prominent writer in the modern era. There is no record of Proust's reaction to the trial and sentencing of Oscar Wilde in 1895. So famous was the case that when Proust published *Sodom and Gomorrah*, two decades after Wilde's death in Paris—where he had exiled himself, ruined, anonymous, and ill— there was no need to name the victim. Everyone knew who the "poet" was. Proust placed the allusion to Wilde's reversal of fortune near the beginning of his sermon on homosexuality in the sentence said to be the longest in literature: "Their [homosexuals'] honour precarious, their liberty provisional, lasting only until the discovery of their crime; their position unstable, like that of the poet one day fêted in every drawing-room and applauded in every theatre in London, and the next driven from every lodging, unable to find a pillow upon which to lay his head . . ."[32]

Whether Proust met Wilde or not, it is clear that in 1908 the Eulenburg trials in Germany revived his memories of the tragic events of Wilde's life, all of which heightened Proust's own preoccupation with homosexuality and made him determined to write about it. He now returned to the subject that he had first treated, but only briefly, many years earlier in "Before the Night," the story featuring a lesbian who commits suicide in order to avoid a scandal over her sexual orientation. By the time Proust finished *In Search of Lost Time*, he had made homosexuality a dominant theme of his ambitious novel.

The events leading to Wilde's conviction and imprisonment are well known, but it may be useful to summarize them here, given

Proust's concentration on homosexual scandals during the period in which he clearly began the various writing projects that led to his novel. In the spring of 1895, while Wilde's latest play, *The Importance of Being Earnest*, enjoyed a highly successful run at Saint James's Theatre, he was found guilty of "gross indecency" and given the harsh sentence of two years at hard labor. Wilde's troubles had begun when he brought a libel suit against John Sholto Douglas, Marquess of Queensberry, who had accused him of being a sodomite and having a bad influence on his son Lord Alfred Douglas. Wilde had made little attempt to hide his sexual preferences. In 1893 the French poet Henri de Régnier had visited him in London and seen how the playwright flaunted his homosexuality, which Régnier later described to Edmond de Goncourt: "Yes, he admits his pederasty. He once said: 'I've been married three times in my life, once with a woman and twice with men!' "[33]

In the months leading up to the libel suit and trials, Wilde had hired young males, usually unemployed or gentleman's servants down on their luck, who were willing to sell themselves for sex. He later claimed special privilege and a degree of self-exoneration as an artist free to explore the more sordid aspects of life while risking danger: "People thought it dreadful of me to have entertained at dinner the evil things of life, and to have found pleasure in their company. But then, from the point of view through which I, as an artist in life, approach them, they were delightful, suggestive and stimulating. It was like feasting with panthers; the danger was half the excitement."[34] The artist in life had been devoured, not by panthers, but by the criminalization of homosexuality and the British justice system.

Proust may well have known about an earlier homosexual scandal in London: the Cleveland Street affair preceded by six years the downfall of Oscar Wilde. In 1889 the police raided a male brothel frequented by prominent members of the aristocracy, such as Lord Arthur Somerset, superintendent of Prince Edward's stables, and the Earl of Euston, eldest son of the Earl of Grafton.[35] Many of the prostitutes arrested in the Cleveland Street raid were telegraph boys working in the brothel to supplement their legitimate earnings.[36] Lord Somerset, setting an example that Wilde's friends later urged him to follow, avoided prosecution by fleeing England to reside in France and Italy.[37]

Given Proust's keen interest in what he considered the persecution of homosexuals, it seems highly probable that he had heard about the London telegraph boys. Another indication of this may be Proust's eagerness, in 1908, to interview a telegraph boy who had once delivered messages to him from Louis d'Albufera. In March, Proust wrote Albu, as he called him, and asked:

> Am I dreaming or used you to send letters round to me by the hand of a young telegraph operator? . . . If so you could be of service to me because for something I'm writing I need to get to know a telegraph operator. You will tell me that all I need to do is talk to the one who brings me telegrams, but first of all no one writes to me any more, and secondly in my neighbourhood they're all children incapable of giving the slightest bit of information. But in any case information is not the thing I need; what I want above all is to see a telegraph operator exercising his functions, to get an "impression" of his life.[38]

That spring we find Proust particularly interested in two young people of different classes and sexes: the telegraph operator and an aristocratic girl, Mlle de Goyon, said to be exceptionally beautiful and very distinguished. Proust began to spin fantasies in his head about them both, neither of whom can be readily identified as the direct source of a character in the novel, but his curiosity about the girl may be taken as additional proof that an important role for an adolescent female existed from the conception of the novel and well before Proust fell in love with Agostinelli, although neither Gilberte nor Albertine belong to the aristocracy.

In asking Albufera about the telegraph boy, Proust had again made himself an easy target for malicious friends who enjoyed teasing him about being homosexual. Albufera provided the boy's name, Louis Maheux, and joked that he had never had intimate relations with him, implying that this might be Proust's motive for seeking out the young man. Thanking Albufera for supplying the name, Proust said the joke "was unnecessary and the idea would never have entered my head." He continued in a tone of barely controlled anger: "I'm not so stupid, if I were that sort of scum, to go out of my way to let the boy know my name, enable him to have me put in prison, tell you all about it, etc." Then, his temper cooling a bit, he admitted: "Perhaps I'm going on a bit about your joke."[39]

In April, Proust announced to Albufera that he was "about to embark on a very important piece of work." But the many things that he wanted to write about made it nearly impossible to focus on one topic or genre. This dilemma became clear in early May, when Proust sent Albufera one of the most important letters that we have regarding the writer's literary preoccupations during this time when all the material that was to coalesce and form *In Search of Lost Time* was gestating in his mind. He also informed Albufera that Louis Maheux had contacted him about the interview, but that the two had not yet been able to agree upon a meeting time. Since then, he had heard nothing from the telegraph boy, which did not seem to concern Proust a great deal. "In any case I'm not sure I won't abandon my Parisian novel."[40] Then Proust, who knew that Mlle de Goyon and Albufera were related, asked whether he had

by any chance—something that's always so interesting—any family photograph albums? If you could lend me one for a few hours (especially if Mlle de Goyon was in it) I should be delighted. It's true that I should be even more delighted if you came here and could tell me the names. By the same token, do you have your genealogy in a few lines? It's again because of what I'm working on that all this would interest me. For I have in hand:

a study on the nobility
a Parisian novel
an essay on Sainte-Beuve and Flaubert
an essay on women

an essay on pederasty (not easy to publish)

a study of stained-glass windows

a study on tombstones

a study on the novel

These are the topics that interested Proust most in the 1907–9 period, when he began the first drafts of his novel. Seven of the eight items are called essays or studies, but the single title "Parisian novel" eventually absorbed all the others.[41] These drafts contain, not surprisingly, many of the same elements as *Jean Santeuil* and the early stories: the child's nervous dependency on his mother, obsessive jealousy, snobbery in the world of high society, and the transcendent nature of the arts, especially literature and music.

Immediately after Proust posted the letter containing the list of topics, Louis Maheux came by for an interview. After he left, Proust sent Albufera his impressions: the boy appeared to be "very nice, very intelligent," and had provided some information of interest, about which, alas, Proust gave no specifics. But he seemed somewhat disappointed that the boy proved too genteel, and, most astounding of all: "He resembles Bertrand de Fénelon, except that he's much better dressed. Speaking of telegraphists he said to me, 'They're rather the Grenelle type than the rue Saint-Dominique.' Rue Saint-Dominique in his mind meant *his* type. He would be a perfect model for a picture of society mores." Grenelle was a working-class district of Paris, the rue Saint-Dominique one of the most fashionable streets in the old aristocratic faubourg Saint-Germain.[42] Apparently, Proust found Maheux more amusing than enlightening. Snobbery, he already knew, was not restricted to the upper classes. Had he, like Charlus in the novel, hoped to find in the young man a tougher or even sadistic side? In any case, the male brothel Proust describes in his novel is frequented primarily by members of the aristocracy, whose sexual needs are met by boys from the working class and soldiers on leave.

Proust continued writing drafts for the essay on homosexuality, uncertain as to its final form. Discouraged by the negative reaction to "the forbidden article" by Robert Dreyfus, an old friend who was now an editor at *Le Figaro,* Proust considered writing a novella about homosexuals. He explained to Dreyfus why he had finally abandoned the idea of drawing directly from the trials of Wilde and Eulenburg: he judged it an error to make

> an artistic project depend on notions which are themselves anecdotal and too directly drawn from life not to partake of its contingency and unreality. All of which, moreover, presented thus, seems not so much false as banal and deserving of some stinging slap in the face from outraged existence (like Oscar Wilde saying that the greatest sorrow he had ever known was the death of Lucien de Rubempré in Balzac, and learning shortly afterwards, through his trial, that there are sorrows which are still more real). But you know that such banal aestheticism cannot be my artistic philosophy.[43]

This remark from Wilde about the death of the handsome Lucien de Rubempré is quoted in the novel by Charlus, who cannot remember the name of its author, only that he was a "man of taste":

> It's so beautiful—the scene where Carlos Herrera asks the name of the château he is driving past, and it turns out to be Rastignac, the home of the young man he used to love; and then the abbé falling into a reverie which Swann once called, and very aptly, the *Tristesse d'Olympio* of pederasty. And the death of Lucien! I forget who the man of taste was who, when he was asked what event in his life had grieved him most, replied: "The death of Lucien de Rubempré in *Splendeurs et Misères.*"[44]

The sentiment expressed, and one that Charlus certainly understood and admired, is the regret that the abbé Carlos Herrara (alias Vautrin) never expressed his unrequited love for Lucien. This dilemma is a very common one for closeted homosexuals, for those who bear the burden of the love, as Bosie said, that dare not speak its name.

As the 1908 texts evolved from seven essays to a single work of fiction of unprecedented scale, Proust, remembering the examples of Wilde and Eulenburg, characterized homosexuals in the opening pages of *Sodom and Gomorrah* as belonging, like Jews, to "an accursed race." The comparison is based on the long and unjust persecution to which both "races" have been subjected. The Dreyfus case had served as a recent and potent example of the anti-Semitism that was rampant in France during the years when Proust was maturing as a writer and as an observer of society. His compassion for his characters was evident as early as "Before the Night" and *Jean Santeuil:* "We cannot approach the most perverse people without recognizing them as human beings."[45] Proust's characters come to life because he loved them enough, in spite of their failings, to see the redemptive features of each.

Since Proust was half Jewish and homosexual, he has often been criticized for having made the Narrator Gentile and heterosexual. I agree with Harold Bloom that these criticisms are unjust, that Proust's characterization of the Narrator depended entirely on aesthetic considerations and was not determined by misplaced guilt or denial of his Jewish heritage and sexual orientation:

> Proust knew precisely what he was doing: Swann and Marcel are contrasts to the homosexual Charlus and the bisexual Saint-Loup. The torments of love and jealousy transcend gender and sexual orientation, and it would spoil the novel's mythology of the Cities of the Plain if the Narrator could not distance himself from homosexuals and Jews alike. . . . Proust rightly judged that the Narrator would be most effective if he could assume a dispassionate stance regarding the mythology that raises the narrative into a cosmological poem, Dantesque as well as Shakespearean. Balzac, Stendhal, Flaubert are left behind in Proust's leap into a vision that compounds Sodom and Gomorrah, Jerusalem, and Eden: three abandoned paradises. The Narrator, as a Gentile heterosexual, is more persuasive as a seer of this new mythology.[46]

As Proust gathered information for the homosexual episodes, he recalled his shock on learning of Wilde's harsh sentence, which struck him not only as cruel and unjust but hypocritical. He knew many prominent Parisian men who hired male prostitutes just as Wilde had done. In France, as in Britain, wealthy people employed a large retinue of servants. Homosexuals often recruited valets and drivers for their looks and willingness to render services quite different from the usual job requirements. Most homosexuals understood the need for discretion, and officials were willing to look the other way. A trial like the one that had destroyed Wilde was unthinkable in Paris, where, as we have seen, there were no laws criminalizing homosexuality. If anyone cast doubt publicly on a gentleman's virility, the demands of honor could be quickly satisfied by a duel. Proust, who had begun to write about homosexual love in stories like "Before the Night," was to make society's unfair treatment of homosexuals a major theme in his novel.

An August 1909 letter to the publisher Alfred Vallette reveals that Proust had completed a first draft of *In Search of Lost Time,* with its conclusion but still lacking many key episodes that constitute the novel as we know it today. Proust had made the innovative and courageous decision to make homosexuality an important part of his narrative. He still used as his working title the leftover one from his essay attacking the eminent nineteenth-century literary critic Charles Augustin Sainte-Beuve, as he explained to Vallette, in this letter that he labeled "Confidential and fairly urgent":

> I am finishing a book which in spite of its provisional title: *Contre Sainte-Beuve, souvenir d'une matinée,* is a genuine novel and an extremely indecent one in places. One of the principal characters is a homosexual. And this I count on you to keep strictly secret. If the fact were known before the book appeared, a number of devoted and apprehensive friends would ask me to abandon it. Moreover I fancy it contains some new things (forgive me!) and I shouldn't like to be robbed by others.

The letter went on to explain the presence of Sainte-Beuve's name, eventually abandoned in the definitive text, of course. What Proust

Jacques Bizet, a schoolmate on whom Proust had a crush. Private Collection

Daniel Halévy, another schoolmate with whom Proust exchanged notes about homosexuality and literature. Private Collection

Reynaldo Hahn, composer and musician and the great love of Proust's life. Paul Nadar /
Arch. Phot. / Coll. MAP © CMN, Paris

Marie Benardaky, with whom Proust flirted during his adolescence and who became one of the models for Gilberte in *In Search of Lost Time*.

Proust at the feet of Jeanne Pouquet. Although Pouquet was engaged to his friend Gaston de Caillavet, Proust liked to remain on the sidelines, where he wooed her at what he called the "court of love." Photo: Bibliothèque nationale de France, Paris

Proust, Robert de Flers, and Lucien Daudet. Proust and Daudet were intimate friends for a brief period. Photo: Bibliothèque nationale de France, Paris

Bertrand de Fénelon, the dashing, handsome young count with whom Proust became infatuated. Fénelon was the primary model for Robert de Saint-Loup in the novel.

Jean Lorrain, the journalist whose printed insinuations that Proust and Lucien Daudet were lovers provoked a duel. Photo: Réunion des Musées Nationaux / Art Resource, N.Y.

Louisa de Mornand, the actress and mistress of
Proust's friend Marquis Louis d'Albufera. Some
biographers believe that Proust was her lover. Paul
Nadar / Arch. Phot. / Coll. MAP © CMN, Paris

Odilon Albaret and Alfred Agostinelli in a hired automobile. Photo: Bibliothèque nationale de France, Paris

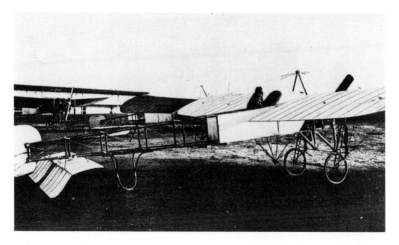

Alfred Agostinelli in his airplane.

The Lartigue family chauffeur in his motoring attire. A similar costume worn by Alfred Agostinelli inspired Proust to call him a "nun of speed." Photo: Jacques-Henri Lartigue © Ministère de la Culture-France / AAJHL

Paul Morand, the diplomat and writer, who became a friend and confidant of Proust's during the war years.

Albert Le Cuziat, a homosexual who began his career as a valet and later operated male brothels visited by Proust, thus inspiring Jupien's brothel in the novel. Photo: Bibliothèque nationale de France, Paris

Proust's drawing of a woman as an erect phallus from a manuscript notebook. Photo: Bibliothèque nationale de France, Paris

said next proves that he had written the novel's conclusion, which resolves the novel's main themes and states Proust's artistic credo: "The name of Sainte-Beuve is not there by chance. The book does indeed end with a long conversation about Sainte-Beuve and about aesthetics . . . and once people have finished the book they will see (I hope) that the whole novel is simply the implementation of the artistic principles expressed in this final part, a sort of preface placed at the end." The purpose of the letter was to test the waters by alerting Vallette to the "obscene" but original nature of the work while reassuring him that "many parts of the book are perfectly proper, even pure." But the publisher must understand, should he be interested, that removing the "indecent" part was out of the question: "the suppression of the obscene sections would upset me considerably." He offered to send Vallette some sample pages and guaranteed him that in the entire manuscript "there isn't a hint of *pornography*."[47] Vallette showed no interest in what Proust had written.

It is impossible to say what role, if any, was played by the "obscene books" that Proust kept referring to in his letters of this time. We know, of course, that Verlaine's "Hombres" gives pornographic descriptions of homosexual couplings and that "Femmes" depicts heterosexuality, but the exploits of the girls of Cabourg depicted in Proust's obscene poems are unknown. Perhaps he was exploring the limits not only of sexual expression but of propriety as well. Charlus's scatological outbursts may well have been like those of Montesquiou, as readers of the novel who knew the real-life model have said, but they are also typical of Proust. For example, Proust wrote to an acquaintance in the last year of his life: "I am beginning to say a little less often: 'I will drown you in an ocean of shit.' "[48] The letter provides no context for such verbal violence. Had he resigned himself to his status as a permanent invalid? Had Proust lately been given free expression to scatological outbursts? Or was it perhaps a "return to a very infantile anal stage, which also characterized his sexuality"?[49]

After the publication of *Swann's Way,* Proust explained to Gide—

as he had to potential publishers—his conception of Charlus, infatuated with virility because, without knowing it, he was a woman. Charlus was, Proust readily conceded, not the only homosexual type but one that had not been portrayed in literature. He paraphrased for Gide a remark by the Narrator, who, once he sees Charlus for what he is, became convinced that sexuality was the key difference between Charlus and his brother the duc de Guermantes: "It's because of his homosexuality that M. de Charlus understands so many things which are a closed book to his brother, . . . that he is so much more subtle and sensitive."[50]

Gide in his reply expressed his admiration for Charlus but contended that Proust had "contributed to the habitual confusion between the homosexual and the invert."[51] For Gide, a man in love with another man carried on a noble tradition that dated back to the ancient Greeks, whereas a man like Charlus, who wanted to be a woman for another man, represented a decadent variety of homosexuals.

According to Gide, Proust felt compelled, in a conversation years later, in the spring of 1921, to justify the absence from *Sodom and Gomorrah* of handsome, virile homosexuals like those to be idealized by Gide in *Corydon*. He confessed that in order to depict the attractive features of the girls at Balbec, he had drawn upon memories of his own homosexual experience. Since he had given all the young men's tender, graceful, and charming attributes to the girls in his book, there remained nothing for his homosexual portraits but "mean and grotesque qualities."[52]

Proust, who was as capable as anyone of contradicting himself, flatly denied in a letter to Jean Schlumberger, a year after the avowal reported by Gide, that his girls were boys in disguise. Schlumberger had written in a review for *Le Figaro*, "As ever, this artist makes free use of everything he observes, lending one the experiences of another, placing a head on shoulders where it doesn't belong, turning an adolescent boy into a young girl, a dowager into an old gentleman." The indignant author objected:

I found the transpositions of gender you attribute to me—without premeditation, I'm sure—particularly hurtful after everything that has been said. Your paragraph is perfectly logical, and contains no hint of spite. But coming on top of so many absurd remarks about my young girls being young men in disguise, it looks as if you are giving the blessing of your infallible mind and great talent to an absurd hypothesis.[53]

Proust might better have defended his depiction of male homosexuals by citing to Gide the example of the handsome, dashing Robert de Saint-Loup, a virile homosexual who dies a hero's death while leading his troops into battle during World War I. Perhaps Proust did not want to reveal this important plot element of *Time Regained*.[54] Although he had anticipated Gide's reaction and was grateful to him for keeping it private, Proust felt that it had been too harsh. He defended his depiction of his homosexual characters in a letter to the critic Jacques Boulenger, acknowledging that *Sodom and Gomorrah* had "angered many homosexuals." He deeply regretted this, but "it's not my fault if M. de Charlus is an old gentleman, I could not suddenly give him the appearance of a Sicilian Shepherd such as one finds in Taormina." Proust later told Boulenger that Gide was "a very difficult man" to whom he should not even have mentioned *Sodom and Gomorrah*, since it had caused their friendship "to cool."[55]

In *Time Regained*, Robert de Saint-Loup's virility is starkly contrasted with Charlus's effeminacy: Saint-Loup's "life had not coarsened him or slowed him down, as had happened with M. de Charlus; on the contrary, working in him an inverse change, it had given him, in a degree in which he had never had it before . . . the grace and the ease of a cavalry officer."[56]

In homosexuals like Saint-Loup the ideal of virility is false because

they do not want to admit to themselves that physical desire lies at the root of sentiments to which they ascribe another origin. M. de Charlus had detested effeminacy. Saint-Loup admired the courage of young men, the intoxication of cavalry charges, the intellectual and moral nobility of friendships between man and man, entirely pure friendships, in which each is prepared to sacrifice his life for the other. War, which turns capital cities, where only women remain, into an abomination for homosexuals, is at the same time a story of passionate adventure for homosexuals if they are intelligent enough to concoct dream figures, and not intelligent enough to see through them, to recognise their origin, to pass judgment on themselves. . . . For Saint-Loup . . . war was the very ideal which he imagined himself to be pursuing in his desire . . . an ideal which he could serve in common with those whom he preferred to all others, in a purely masculine order of chivalry, far from women, where he would be able to risk his life to save his orderly and die inspiring a fanatical love in his men. . . . I admire Saint-Loup, for asking to be sent to the point of greatest danger, infinitely more than I do M. de Charlus for refusing to wear brightly coloured cravats.[57]

Proust stated in a 1917 letter to Jacques Truelle that he did not find homosexuals "immoral, but I do have periods, especially when I am somewhat sad, when their mannerisms and their ways irritate me immensely." A year earlier, he had written to Gaston Gallimard, his publisher, to say that he meant his depiction of homosexuality to be bereft of any "immoral intention," that he had attempted simply to convey "the most complete and explicit realism."[58]

Since Proust stated more than once his belief that there is no moral distinction between heterosexual and homosexual love and the heterosexual Narrator adopts at least a neutral position, one can safely assume that the occasional use in such passages of the word *vice*, usually attenuated by a parenthetical remark, is a concession to the prevailing public and scientific opinions regarding homosexuality.[59] This seems a fair conclusion, especially given Proust's belief that prejudices have eliminated all conventional homosexuality. Other passages reveal Proust's belief that homosexuality was determined not only by neurotic conditions but also by heredity, a tenet that also encouraged his tolerant attitude.[60] Current research investigating the mysteries of sexuality and sexual orientation is yielding some results that appear to indicate a genetic component in determining one's sexual preferences.

Gide, who soon adopted the stance of a more militant homosexual, had by 1910 written but not yet published *Corydon*, his proselytizing work on male homosexuality. The relatively mild reception of Proust's *Sodom and Gomorrah*, depicting a homosexual encounter and an unprecedented variety of homosexual types, encouraged Gide to proceed with the publication of *Corydon* in 1924.[61]

Paul Morand not only was among those who believed that Proust had given all the desirable qualities to girls, he also maintained that it was obvious to him that the young girls by the sea are really boys in disguise. Morand agrees with his friend and Proust biographer Maurice Bardèche that Proust went through a period in late adolescence and early manhood when he found girls and young women fascinating. In his succinct appraisal, Morand writes: "Proust was in love with women without desiring them."[62] But he insists that anyone who knows women at all will see immediately "how false everything is in Proust's girls from Albertine to Andrée." He gives as an example the Narrator's claim that he enjoyed, in a single season, the favors of fourteen girls.[63] "In 1905, that was unthinkable." Morand does not tell us whether the possession of fourteen boys in a single season was thinkable at the time, but such is the implication. One wonders whether Morand, on reading Proust's passages about the Narrator's fascination with the seaside girls, is not suffering from the disadvantage of having known Proust and his homosexual friends too well. At one point, Morand quotes the writer and critic Benjamin Crémieux, another acquaintance of Proust's, and one who worried about the distortions that might result from having been too close to the creator of *In Search of Lost Time:* "To take the true measure of Proust's achievement, it is perhaps a great advantage not to have known him."[64]

The "great reproach," Morand maintains, "that one can level at the 'heroines' of homosexual writers" such as Proust is that they do not come across as women because they are "men disguised as women." Morand excuses Proust and his contemporary Julien Green, to a large degree, because they were following "a convention of the time," but he maintains nonetheless that the reader is not fooled and quickly "tires of having to make adjustments."[65] In *Le Passé défini*, Jean Cocteau expresses the same view: that all Proust's girls are boys in disguise.

These categorical remarks overlook Odette and her daughter Gilberte, to mention only two characters whose genuine femininity has never been questioned. Perhaps this is because Gilberte is based on girls that Proust played and flirted with during his high school years, the sisters Marie and Nelly Benardaky and later Jeanne Pouquet, whose daughter Proust used as the model for Mlle de Saint-Loup, the child of Gilberte and Saint-Loup. That these girls are the first models for Gilberte is beyond dispute, since Proust describes Marie and Nelly under their real names in drafts for *Jean Santeuil*.[66]

Morand met Proust in 1916, long past the time when the author had engaged in flirtations with girls like Marie Benardaky and Mary Finaly and courtesans like Laure Hayman and the actress Louisa de Mornand. Morand's complaint about the adjustments readers of books by homosexual authors must make regarding the sexuality of female characters echoes a common problem for gay readers, who experience it from the other end of the sexual spectrum. Proust's own sympathy lay with the homosexual reader of his era, who could find very few books that portrayed same-sex love. Gay readers cannot easily assimilate the literature produced by a society that condemns homosexuality and either makes discussion of it taboo or discourages works that adequately reflect the feelings and experiences of homosexuals. On overhearing Charlus reciting lines from poems by Alfred de Musset to Morel, the Narrator observes: "M. de Charlus, who usually gave a more masculine style to his love-making, also had his tender moments. Moreover, during his childhood, in order to be able to feel and understand the words of the poets, he had been obliged to imagine them as being addressed not to faithless beauties but to young men."[67] Heterosexual love scenes or pornography may delay but cannot prevent a homosexual youth's discovery of the true object of his desire:

> The boy who has been reading erotic poetry or looking at obscene pictures, if he then presses his body against a schoolfellow's, imagines himself only to be communing with him in an identical desire for a woman. How should he suppose that he is not like everybody else when he recognises the substance of what he feels in reading Mme de La Fayette, Racine, Baudelaire, Walter Scott, at a time when he is still too little capable of observing himself to take into account what he has added from his own store to the picture, and to realise that if the sentiment be the same the object differs, that what he desires is Rob Roy and not Diana Vernon?[68]

In our era of equal rights and greater—though certainly not universal—acceptance of homosexuality, such "conventions" are no longer required in literature and the arts. Indeed, books, films, and television programs with homosexual characters have become commonplace. We have become more "Proustian" in another sense as well: We live in a culture in which everyone is, if our films and popular magazines reflect our true feelings, in love with youth. Perhaps it was ever thus.

During the 1910–12 period, when Proust was hard at work writing *In Search of Lost Time*, Albert Nahmias began to serve as his unofficial financial adviser, usually with disastrous results, and—with much better results—as his assistant in preparing the manuscript copy of *Swann's Way*. Proust refused to blame his "little Albert" for his unwitting role in the rapid decline of the author's fortune.

Dr. Henri Mondor, who had examined Nahmias, told Philip Kolb that the young man was homosexual. Jean-Yves Tadié observes that "bisexual" would be more accurate, since Nahmias married twice. Years later, when asked whether he was the model for Albertine, Nahmias replied: "There were several of us."[69] Even if Nahmias's bisexuality is established, it is impossible to say when he began having sex with men or whether Proust knew about his dual nature. Proust apparently never guessed the truth about Bertrand de Fénelon, a blind spot that contradicts a number of the writer's maxims about what is now called "gaydar," the ability of homosexuals to recognize one another almost immediately: "Every vice, like every profession, requires and develops a special knowledge which we are never loath to display. The invert sniffs out inverts."[70] And elsewhere: "Members of the same profession recognise each other instinctively; so do those with the same vice."[71] Proust also describes those whose sexuality alters over time, as apparently was the case of Fénelon and also that of the fictional characters Saint-Loup and Morel. Such conversions do take place, as indicated in this maxim: "No one can tell at first that he is an invert, or a poet, or a snob, or a scoundrel."[72] Morand also subscribes to the belief in the infallibility of "gaydar," although it was he who recorded that Proust had failed to recognize Fénelon's bisexuality.[73]

It is uncertain when Proust learned, apparently to his astonishment, that Fénelon had begun having affairs with men. When Proust met Fénelon in 1901, the future diplomat had as his mistress the pretty blonde actress Louise Montaud, whose stage name was Louisa de Mornand. A notation that Proust made in *The Notebook of 1908*, which contains the first notes for the future novel, indicates that Fénelon was also the "lover" of Louisa's sister, Suzanne Montaud, another aspiring actress who played at the Bouffes under the stage name Jane Moriane.[74]

The alleged sexual evolution of Fénelon is another link to the character modeled on him: Robert de Saint-Loup. When we first meet Saint-Loup in *Within a Budding Grove*, he is the passionate, jealous lover of the actress Rachel, modeled primarily on her real-life counterpart Mornand. Not only that, Saint-Loup appears to be an exceptionally virile man who detests homosexuals. The first hint of Saint-Loup's potential homosexuality lies in his remarkable masculine beauty. After an afternoon visit to the theater to see Rachel, Saint-Loup strikes a man who, finding him irresistible, had dared to approach him on the street in the daytime. The Narrator comments:

> My friend could not get over the audacity of this "clique" who no longer even waited for the shades of night to venture forth, and spoke of the proposition that had been made to him with the same indignation as the newspapers use in reporting an armed assault and robbery in broad daylight in the centre of Paris. And yet the recipient of his blows was excusable in one respect, for the trend of the downward slope brings desire so rapidly to the point of enjoyment that beauty in itself appears to imply consent. And that Saint-Loup was beautiful was beyond dispute.[75]

One of the criticisms frequently leveled at Proust's novel is the high percentage of characters who are homosexual or bisexual. When one looks carefully at the important characters, one is struck by the rarity of those who are exclusively homosexual. Apparently, Mlle Vinteuil alone fits this category; at least, we lack any evidence to the contrary. Charlus's statistics on the percentage of male homosexuals in the general population shock his listeners, even though the numbers include bisexual as well as homosexual experience: "As things are, the average rate of sanctity, if you see any sanctity in that sort of thing, is somewhere between three and four out of ten."[76]

In the summer of 1922 Proust expressed his surprise to critic Jacques Boulenger that society ladies had not been shocked by *Sodom and Gomorrah*. Perhaps this was because "they haven't understood what they've read," or because they realized that the actual number of homosexuals was greater in real life than in his novel. He eagerly pointed out how many "normal" characters his book contains: "Perhaps . . . [society ladies] see that the proportion of those tainted by 'shameful vices' in society is marginally greater than in my books, where at least people like Cottard, Elstir, Bergotte, Norpois, etc., etc. maintain the tradition of what used to be deemed 'normal.' "[77]

Proust's beloved confidante Mme Straus was one society lady who had certainly understood, without being in the least shocked, his revelations regarding sexuality. This was, to a large degree, because she had heard him expound his ideas in person, as she recalled in congratulating him on the publication of *Sodom and Gomorrah:* "I am not at all scandalized by the subject. In fact, we used to discuss all this when you came to visit late in the evening."[78]

There was no one whose conversation he relished more than Mme Straus's and with whom he was more eager to share gossip. Years earlier he had delighted her by recording for her pleasure the unintentionally obscene remarks made by another society lady, Mme de Saint-Paul. Warning Mme Straus that what followed was not "very proper but then we're both invalids," he reported that the lady in question had been overheard saying to a society hostess: "My dear, say what you like, Madeleine likes good cooking. I prefer to give you good music. . . . Madeleine likes it in her mouth, but I prefer it in my ear. Each to her taste, my dear, it's a free country, after all."[79]

Paul Morand, who knew both Bertrand de Fénelon and Proust, writes in his memoir that the novelist "invented nothing" by making Saint-Loup bisexual. Morand is quite confident that Fénelon is the model and says that Proust, having failed to detect his friend's true sexual nature, had obtained the information about his friend's bisexuality from the best sources: "The ravishing blond young man with blue eyes, the darling of the ladies of 1900, who served as a model for Saint-Loup, was indeed to end in heresy, or more precisely to use the jargon of the time, 'bimetallism.' "[80]

Morand's diary reveals that Proust knew another handsome young blond—and notorious womanizer in his youth—who later became homosexual. Count Boni de Castellane had married the American railway heiress Anna Gould, whose fortune he used to build such sumptuous residences as the Palais Rose and give lavish parties that became legendary. One of the count's most spectacular fêtes, to which he invited a mere three thousand guests, took place in the Bois de

Boulogne, which had been hung with eighty thousand Venetian lanterns for the event.[81] Proust told Morand that Castellane became a homosexual after the age of fifty. Since Castellane had been known as one of the "big seducers of women" at the turn of the century, he was, Morand writes, "a recruit of note, which made the fairies very proud." Morand's remarks make it clear that Proust's social circles were fluid enough to include male friends who were heterosexual as well. In addition to himself, Morand lists such friends as "Antoine Bibesco, Jacques Porel [son of the celebrated actress Réjane], Louis d'Albufera, etc."[82]

In the novel Proust takes a rather dim view of sexual experimentation, although many of his characters apparently try it. We remember that so far as sexual ethics are concerned, Proust believed that one must, above all, remain true to one's own nature, "for every individual follows the line of his own pleasure, and if he is not too depraved, seeks it in a sex complementary to his own. And for the invert vice begins, not when he enters into relations (for there are all sorts of reasons that may enjoin these), but when he takes his pleasure with women."[83]

As we have seen, Proust's identification of a variety of sexual types caused him to object to the term *homosexual,* preferring instead *invert,* because he believes that a man who makes love to another man is doing so with a creature different from himself. In some cultures, for example, a man who performs as the active partner in anal intercourse does not consider himself to be homosexual. In large measure the "beauty" of the Charlus-Jupien encounter derives from the discovery by the two men of their missing and complementary halves: "This scene was not, however, positively comic; it was stamped with a strangeness, or if you like a naturalness, the beauty of which steadily increased." And Jupien is "the man predestined to exist in order that [men like Charlus] may have their share of sensual pleasure on this earth: the man who cares only for elderly gentlemen." All this is complicated and may strike the reader, at times, as highly fanciful, but this is how Proust imagines love. The variety of sexual types that Proust depicts in his novel illustrates the complex dynamics of erotic attraction in the universe.[84]

Proust's own androgynous nature is seen not only in the characters he created but also in the sensual yearnings that he blatantly expressed in letters and poems he sent to young men during his high school days. As an adult he sometimes conveyed the same sentiments to young men whose discretion he trusted, as in a letter to Albert Nahmias, where we find Proust wishing to "change my sex, my face and my age, take on the looks of a young and pretty girl in order to embrace you with all my heart."[85] It was clear to those who observed Proust and Nahmias together that the two men were very close. Not surprisingly, rumors sprouted that they were lovers.[86] A similar situation arose with an attractive blond youth named Marcel Plantevignes. Proust paid so much attention to him that rumors began again. Proust found out that some gossip on the boardwalk had warned Plantevignes to stay away from him and that the young man had listened to this insinuation of his homosexuality without refuting it. The youth's failure to deny the rumor infuriated Proust, who challenged his father to a duel because Plantevignes was too young to be called out. This situation set off a series of complicated negotiations involving Vicomte Charles d'Alton, president of the Cabourg Golf-Club, and others eager to defuse the situation and reestablish peace and harmony. The letter that Proust wrote young Plantevignes on hearing of the gossip's accusation has the same tone and expresses the same sentiment that Charlus later uses to scold the Narrator for having let slip the opportunity to become his protégé.[87] As we shall see, Proust rebuked Albert Nahmias in a similar manner.

Once Proust scolded Nahmias over a matter relating to his work on the manuscript. Then, sensing that he had been too harsh, Proust softened and tried to picture the young man's face: "Dear Albert, I wish I were less tired so that I could tell you how fond of you I am: near to my heart and even my eyes, for as I write I seem to see . . . the smiling eyes of your good days, and that distension, that swelling of the nostrils which with you is a sign of benevolence and also, when it occurs, a great embellishment."[88] Realizing the value of Nahmias's editorial assistance, not to mention the appeal of the embellished nostrils, Proust quickly forgave him.

❋

As often as not love is no more than the association of the image of a girl (whom otherwise we should soon have found intolerable) with the heart-beats inseparable from an endless wait in vain and her failure to turn up at the end of it.[89]

Not long after his arrival at the Grand-Hôtel at Cabourg in August 1912, Proust accepted an invitation from Charles d'Alton to attend the golf club's annual dinner and ball, which many considered the highlight of the summer social season in Normandy. On the day of the ball, Proust dressed and went out on the boardwalk where, between six and seven, he was to meet Nahmias, due back from Deauville. Proust waited for a long time, but the young man never came.

Infuriated at Nahmias for standing him up, Proust returned to the hotel. When his jealousy was aroused, Proust often exhibited a possessiveness as domineering and as irrational as those of Swann and the Narrator in their worst moments. Now the writer directed his anger at the thoughtless youth by beginning a long, scathing letter, telling him that a small event like his failure to keep their rendezvous could assume a great importance for someone in poor health and that he had naturally assumed that Nahmias would rush back from Deauville to be on time. Had their roles been reversed, Proust would have hurried to be there "dead or alive."[90]

Proust had made the worst possible choice of words. Nahmias, who by now knew Proust well, had in fact rushed back from Deauville, a decision that proved disastrous. During the drive to keep his appointment with the novelist, Nahmias's car hit a little girl, killing her. Unaware of these tragic events, Proust put his letter aside to attend the gala dinner. After the party, still seething with rage over Nahmias's absence, Proust resumed writing the letter and finished his indictment of the young man's thoughtlessness. To shame Nahmias further, Proust mentioned distinguished older writers who had gone out of their way to accommodate him, such as Alphonse Daudet, who "at the height of his fame and ill health, when he could scarcely scribble a line without weeping with the pain it caused him all over his body," had written him twice one evening before he was to dine with the Daudets, merely to inquire where he would prefer to be placed at table.[91]

In rebuking Nahmias, Proust used language like that employed by Swann and Charlus when enraged. The "very deep and genuine feelings of friendship" he had for Nahmias forced him to observe that his young friend was "not perfectible. You are not even made of stone, which can be sculpted when it is lucky enough to come across a sculptor (and you might well meet greater sculptors than I, though I would have done it with tenderness), you are made of water, commonplace, impalpable, colourless, fluid water, eternally insubstantial, endlessly flowing away." Swann uses similar and equally demeaning imagery to chastise Odette in an analogous situation: "You are a formless water that will trickle down any slope that offers itself, a fish devoid of memory, incapable of thought, which all its life long in its aquarium will continue to dash itself a hundred times a day against the glass wall, always mistaking it for water." A remark made toward the end of the letter hints that Proust had already conceived the famous scene in which Swann's oldest friend, the duchesse de Guermantes, running late for a dinner party, does not have time to listen to him, although he has, at her insistence, just revealed to her that he has a terminal illness and will soon die. "One day," Proust wrote Nahmias, "I shall describe those characters who, even from a vulgar point of view, will never understand the elegance, when one is dressed and ready for a ball, of forgoing it in order to keep a friend company."[92]

We hear echoes of such Proustian venom in another passage, where Charlus berates the Narrator for having failed an early test to live up to the baron's initial favorable opinion of him: "You may say that you chanced upon a first-rate friendship, and that you botched it."[93] Such outbursts were often based on Proust's own tantrums: his demolition of Bertrand de Fénelon's hat became the Narrator's destruction of a hat belonging to Charlus, who had made an offer similar to the one Proust proposed to Nahmias of sculpting him into a better person.[94] At Deauville, that evening when Nahmias did not show up, much more was at stake than a new hat. When Proust learned that Nahmias's car, in the rush to be on time, had killed a child, he felt ashamed.

CHAPTER SEVEN

Lovesick

In the spring of 1913 Alfred Agostinelli, at the age of twenty-five, fell on hard times and appealed to Proust for work. Since the novelist had already engaged Odilon Albaret as his regular driver, he offered Agostinelli the position of secretary, albeit with reservations about his qualifications, to aid in preparing the typescript of *Swann's Way:* "I suggested [to Agostinelli] without much confidence, that he might type my book. It was then that I discovered him, and he and his wife [Anna] became an integral part of my life."[1]

Agostinelli, whose resourcefulness and intelligence Proust had noticed on earlier occasions, had by now lost most of his adolescent plumpness and become serious about pursuing a career in the new, exciting, and dangerous field of aviation. Bicycles and motorcars had always fascinated him; now, like many daring young men of his generation, he became passionately interested in the ultimate machine of speed: the airplane. He was determined to become a pilot in spite of the expenses and risks involved. Among his friends, Agostinelli had the reputation of a fearless daredevil.[2] Although his recent financial setbacks had forced him to appeal to Proust for employment, he intended to remain at boulevard Haussmann only until he could save enough money to pay for flying lessons. He could not have anticipated that Proust would fall in love with him, making it easy to acquire the funds needed to become a pilot but difficult to abandon the lovesick writer.

Anna Agostinelli has been described as ugly and unpleasant. The normally discrete and indulgent Odilon Albaret, frequently exasperated by the woman's capricious and volatile nature, called her "the flying louse."[3] Why a handsome young man like Agostinelli should desire her puzzled Proust, who found her not only unattractive but disagreeable.[4] Proust may have claimed to be perplexed about the attraction Anna held for Agostinelli, but he was being disingenuous. In his novel, he demonstrates again and again the highly subjective nature of love. The servant Françoise provides the coarsest example in a bit of doggerel verse: "Qui du cul d'un chien s'amourose / Il lui paraît une rose" (Whoever falls in love with a dog's ass mistakes it for a rose).[5]

According to Proust, Anna was insanely jealous and would have killed Agostinelli had she been aware of his many infidelities with other women.[6] Since Agostinelli kept his trysts secret from her, but not from Proust, who could be relentless in his interrogations, the author alone experienced terrible pangs of jealousy. But Proust suffered most of all from the impossible longings that he felt for the youthful, athletic man, the full extent of which was to be exposed by tragedy.

Proust showered Agostinelli with money in spite of the huge financial losses he continued to suffer in his stock market speculations. In letters to friends and publishers, he cautioned them not to mention money matters when writing or telephoning. He did not want his servants to know—out of pride, perhaps, but also out of prudence—that he was paying to have his novel published. While extremely generous to the Agostinellis, he certainly did not want them to know anything about his finances, apparently for fear they might demand even more of him. As for his servants, Nicolas and Céline Cottin, they needed to be kept in the dark not only for the sake of propriety but also because they would be devoured by jealousy if they learned the extent of his largesse toward his new secretary.

In letters to friends Proust alluded obliquely to the kind of suffering that he experienced when in love. He told Mme Straus how "very, very unwell" he had been. Referring to his feelings for Agostinelli, he said that he had "a great many other worries too," troubles that "might be a little less painful if I told them to you. And they are sufficiently general, sufficiently human, to interest you perhaps." He did not confide in her, however, and quickly turned to the safe topic of music and his love of Beethoven. In a subsequent letter lamenting his woes, he said that music was his sole "consolation . . . when I'm not too sad to listen to it." He had even purchased a pianola, but, alas, the piano roll suppliers did not have the music he most wanted to hear: "Beethoven's sublime XIVth quartet doesn't appear among the rolls."[7]

It is highly likely that Agostinelli pumped the pianola pedals for Proust, as does Albertine for the Narrator in *The Captive*. For the scene where she is described as an "angel musician," pumping the pedals to play Rameau and Borodin, Proust borrowed imagery that he had used to depict Agostinelli in "Impressions de route en automobile" and Bertrand de Fénelon in a draft of *Jean Santeuil*. This androgynous shift thus endows Albertine with qualities taken from two of the young men of whom Proust was enamored. In the story for *Le Figaro* about his motoring days in Normandy, he compared Agostinelli steering the wheel while manipulating the gears of the car to the patron saint of music, Saint Cecilia, at the organ. Elements of the description of Albertine's legs as she pumps the pianola can be found in an earlier and admiring description of Bertrand de Fénelon's legs in *Jean Santeuil*, where Fénelon is easily recognizable under the name "Bertrand de Réveillon." The scene of the fictional Bertrand running along the banquette and clambering over tables in a restau-

rant to reach Jean more quickly is based on a real incident that occurred when Fénelon performed a similar gymnastic to bring the
shivering Proust a coat. Proust uses the scene again when Saint-Loup
renders a similar service to the Narrator, thus restoring Bertrand's
legs to his male fictional counterpart.[8]

Agostinelli may have had occasion to resume, temporarily, his old
post as chauffeur. In early spring, Odilon Albaret returned home on
an important mission. On March 27, 1913, Proust sent a telegram to
Albaret, who was far away in his native village of Auxillac, in Lozère,
a rugged mountainous region in southern France. Proust wanted to
congratulate his driver on an event that proved to be of greater importance to the novelist than he could have ever imagined. Odilon, aged
thirty-one, received Proust's wire just as he set out to the church to
marry a young woman named Céleste Gineste. With the outbreak of
war a little over a year later, when all the young able-bodied men were
mobilized, thus depriving Proust of his male servants, Céleste was to
become his housekeeper, a role that she made famous.

Odilon soon returned to Paris with his twenty-one-year-old bride,
who, never before having left her native village, was to have diffi-
culties in adapting to the big city so far from home.[9] The Albarets
took a new, modest apartment in Levallois-Péret, on the outskirts of
Paris. Nearby was a cafe that stayed open late at night and had a
telephone, two requirements for Odilon, who, once his wife grew
accustomed to Paris, was to remain on call at night, awaiting the
summons from Proust.[10]

Swann's Way was scheduled for fall publication, but Proust still
had not made the final revisions, a task made even more difficult by
Agostinelli's troubling presence. In a letter to Robert de Louis, a
literary friend whose judgment he respected, the nervous author worried over Louis's warning about the risks of publishing an unusually
long volume. Then he discreetly referred to his lovesickness over
Agostinelli: "I am very ill and what's more I have a lot of sorrow."[11]

In late July 1913, Proust left for the Grand-Hôtel at Cabourg with
Agostinelli, Anna, and Cottin. He was to have little time to enjoy his

room overlooking the sea. On August 4, barely a week after his arrival, he and Agostinelli set out for nearby Houlgate to call on several friends who had rented villas in or near the seaside town. En route, Proust abruptly decided to return to Paris, without informing anyone at the hotel.

We know little about this strange episode. Proust realized that his sudden change of plans would puzzle his acquaintances, especially since he was returning for no good reason and at a time when persons of means fled the sweltering city to cool and amuse themselves in various vacation spots. In letters to male friends, Proust, who always dreaded new insinuations regarding his homosexuality, invented a camouflage story to explain his precipitous return to Paris. Georges de Lauris received this explanation: "On leaving for Cabourg, I had left behind a person whom I rarely saw in Paris but whom at least I know to be there, and at Cabourg I felt far away and anxious." So, although he had decided at once to return to Paris, he kept postponing the departure from Cabourg. Afterward, he and Agostinelli had "set off to do some shopping in Houlgate, where he thought I looked so sad that he told me I ought to stop hesitating and catch the Paris train at Trouville without going back to the hotel." Proust did not mention Agostinelli's name to Lauris, but referred to the man accompanying him as "my secretary," presumably because Lauris already knew that the person in question was Agostinelli and also because he had covered himself by hinting that he was in love with someone back in Paris.[12] Lauris is no more likely to have been fooled than were any of the others to whom Proust explained his motives.

A letter sent to Charles d'Alton provides a somewhat fuller account of Proust's return to the capital, including the presence of Agostinelli, but makes no mention of the mysterious person he so urgently needed to see in Paris.[13] Proust prudently asked Alton not to tell anyone that Agostinelli was in his employ as a secretary.

Proust also informed Albert Nahmias about his arrival in Paris, saying that he intended to stay only a day or two before traveling elsewhere. Then he quickly dismissed the idea of additional trips, saying that his severe weight loss made another trip too dangerous for his health. Proust, who often used postscripts to express the true purpose of a letter, added one to warn Nahmias to keep silent about Agostinelli: "People are so stupid they might see in it (as they did in our friendship) something homosexual. That would make no difference to me, but I would be distressed to place this boy in a bad light." Then, almost as an afterthought, or perhaps to show that his heterosexual urgings were still functioning properly, he mentioned that, while dining alone at Larue's, he had spotted a friend of Nahmias's with a ravishing blonde.[14]

Not long afterward, André Gide made an indiscreet remark about Proust's sexuality. Still worried about such gossip, Proust wrote Jacques Copeau, one of Gide's colleagues at the *Nouvelle Revue Française,* and expressed his unhappiness about remarks attributed to their mutual friend. Perhaps he intended for Copeau to pass along the thinly veiled threat: "If Gide knew how many stories about Turkish baths, Arab youths from the [Paris] world's fair, and boat captains on the Calais-Dover runs that have been related to me by another of your collaborators, etc., and which I have tried to refute in exchanges with his best friends, perhaps he would be more circumspect in speaking about me."[15]

Gide had the reputation of being a pedophile, a predilection that he shared with the hero of his novel *L'Immoraliste.* Gide and Camille Saint-Saëns, to name only two, might be cited as pioneers in the travel-for-gay-sex industry. Gide often went to North Africa in order to seduce Arab boys. Morand reveals that Jean Cocteau once surprised Gide by entering his hotel room in Marseille to find the "young elevator operator kneeling in front of him [Gide]. 'He's sewing a button on for me,' said Gide." Cocteau was not fooled, of course, and regaled his friends with the story, while "imitating the stingy, pinched lips of Gide" muttering, "He's sewing a button on for me."[16]

The lovesick Proust told Lucien Daudet that his weight loss had alarmed his doctor, who ordered him to rest whenever possible and avoid writing letters because he needed "to regain thirty kilos (!)" A few days later Daudet received another letter repeating the cover story used for the precipitous return from Cabourg; this version may lend some credibility to Proust's reasons for returning because it mentions a woman (unnamed) with whom the author claimed to be in love. The other letters had simply referred to a "person." One wonders why such a precaution, if that is what he intended, would be needed with Daudet, who knew him so intimately. "To think that in love, when we love and are not loved in return (the form in which I usually experience this emotion), we make endless calculations to try to persuade ourselves that it hasn't been physically possible for the woman to write to us yet, however much she may want to."[17] The hasty return from Cabourg remains veiled in Proustian mystery.

Perhaps being constantly in Agostinelli's company in Cabourg reminded Proust too forcefully of the impossible nature of the love he felt for the young man. In *Sodom and Gomorrah*, Proust writes of the frustrated desire of homosexuals to find a straight lover because they "are enamoured of precisely the type of man who has nothing feminine about him, who is not an invert and consequently cannot love them in return; with the result that their desire would be forever unappeased did not their money procure for them real men."[18]

We can speculate that the canceled vacation and sudden return to Paris and the hints of going to Italy meant that Proust was beginning to think of separating himself from Agostinelli in order to put an end to a maddening situation. In *The Fugitive* there is a clue that this may have been the case. Suddenly aware that the future held no promise of happiness for him, the Narrator decides not to remain in Balbec with Albertine: "I had been in despair at Balbec when I saw the day break and realised that none of the days to come could ever be a happy one for me."[19] The cause of the Narrator's anguish is the revelation that Albertine had been a close friend of Mlle Vinteuil's. Convinced that she is a lesbian, he believes that she can never love him, and he wonders how he can possibly compete with women for her favors. A life with Albertine, he is convinced, would bring him nothing but frustration and jealousy.

Proust had faced a similar dilemma a decade earlier when traveling with Bertrand de Fénelon in Holland, when he feared, rightly, that his love for Bertrand, whom he considered "perfection on earth," must remain forever unrequited. He had sent Reynaldo Hahn a drawing of Dordrecht and a poem expressing his lovesick woes: "Dordrecht endroit si beau / Tombeau / De mes illusions chéries" (Dordrecht, a place so beautiful, tomb of my cherished illusions).[20] Miserable and fearful of making Fénelon unhappy by his own despondency, Proust sent him away to tour Holland on his own while setting off himself in another direction to do likewise. Then he wrote his mother from the Hôtel de l'Europe in Amsterdam to explain the decision to journey alone and his plans to meet Fénelon again for the return trip to Paris:

> Today to Haarlem to see the Frans Hals, I've been alone here since yesterday. I am in so disastrous an emotional state that I was afraid of poisoning poor Fénelon with my dreariness, and I've given him a breathing spell, far from my sighs. I'll see him again at The Hague, but I shall . . . return to Paris either Sunday or Monday, overjoyed to embrace my little Mama and little Papa after so long an absence.[21]

In describing the Narrator's impossible desire for Albertine—impossible because his jealous demands and emotional expectations exceed all rational bounds—Proust labels such love "reciprocal torture."[22] One can also see a parallel to the situation with Agostinelli in the Narrator's determination to end his misery and break with Albertine by asking her to move out of his apartment. Living in the same apartment with Agostinelli—so desirable but always beyond reach—had created a situation that neither man found tolerable. But Proust, like his fictional counterpart, was too enthralled to make the break.

The certainty that his lifelong ambition to publish a novel was about to be realized brought no relief. Proust's thoughts remained centered to a remarkable degree on his unrequited love for Agostinelli, which made him miserable. Years earlier, laboring in vain to complete *Jean Santeuil*, Proust had written in the preface notes that the book contained the "very essence of my life."[23] Now finally on the verge of publishing the first part of a book that was to fulfill this promise, he felt little joy or satisfaction. He complained to his friends of enduring relentless "mental sorrows, material problems, physical suffering, and literary nuisances."[24] Nearly every letter he wrote during this period bemoans his severe thinness and profound unhappiness. As always, he kept the source of his melancholy secret, which only added to his frustration.

The suffering and weight loss due to his lovelorn misery has its fictional counterparts in the Narrator's self-torture stemming from his jealousy over Albertine. Proust had decided long ago to transpose his life's experience into the novel. In life and art, the loss of actual physical substance is compensated by the knowledge of self and comprehension of the human condition that become the body of work. Thus love's labor and its travails are not lost but lead to creation. For Bergotte, whose career as a novelist is behind him, "The bulk of his thought had long since passed from his brain into his books. He had grown thin, as though they had been extracted from him by a surgical operation."[25] Likewise, the Narrator is willing to sacrifice his life to give birth to the book that he carries within himself:

> Let us accept the physical injury which is done to us for the sake of the spiritual knowledge which grief brings; let us submit to the disintegration of our body, since each new fragment which breaks away from it returns in a luminous and significant form to add itself to our work, to complete it at the price of sufferings of which others more richly endowed have no need, to make our work at least more solid as our life crumbles away beneath the corrosive action of our emotions.[26]

Nineteen thirteen is known in French aviation history as the Glorious Year. French flyers flew nonstop from Nancy to Cairo, and on September 23 Roland Garros became the first aviator to fly across the Mediterranean Sea. A new speed record of 126 mph was set, and pilots reached altitudes of twenty thousand feet. Aerodromes opened at Issy, just south of Paris, and a little farther west at Buc, a little town near Versailles. These new airfields drew crowds of the curious, the idle rich, and daring young men like Agostinelli, who saw a new frontier opening up before them and rushed to fly the new machines and make their fortunes.

Proust tried to dissuade Agostinelli from taking flying lessons, but his objections were undermined by the determination of Anna, who thought that she and her husband would become fabulously wealthy if he learned to pilot an airplane.[27] Proust had warned the young flyer: "If ever you have the misfortune to have an aeroplane accident, you can tell your wife that she will find me neither a protector nor a friend and will never get a sou from me."[28] Yet the doting writer's generosity made it possible for Agostinelli to take flying lessons at nearby Buc, where Garros had opened an aviation school. Since Agostinelli's economic woes had forced him to sell his car, Proust paid Albaret to drive the apprentice pilot to and from the airfield.[29]

Agostinelli grew increasingly restless that autumn under Proust's constant surveillance. How could a man who dreamed of flying—man's oldest dream of absolute freedom—content himself with the sedentary life of a secretary charged with typing a manuscript of such length and complexity, all under the lovesick gaze of his benefactor? At some point he must have spoken to Proust about returning to his native Mediterranean coast, where he could earn a pilot's license at one of the new aviation schools near Monte Carlo. Proust, desperate to keep the young man near him no matter what the cost, may have hinted at buying Agostinelli a Rolls-Royce if he wanted to resume his job as a driver, and even an airplane for a career as a pilot.

In October 1913, a month before the publication of *Swann's Way*, Proust's heavy losses on the stock market forced him to sell all his shares of Royal Dutch Petroleum in order to pay his rent. Still profoundly unhappy, he began making unrealistic plans to leave Paris and even France; perhaps he would go to Florence, which he had always dreamed of visiting.[30] He had recently written to Jean-Louis Vaudoyer to ask whether he knew of a "quiet, isolated house in Italy, no matter where, I should like to go away." One can only smile at

Proust's notion of economizing: the house he was thinking of renting, he explained to Vaudoyer, was one of the most splendid Renaissance palaces in Italy, the Palazzo Farnese, which had been completely restored and rented to a rich American. Perhaps his friend could find out whether the palace was indeed available: "You don't happen to know if that Farnese palace . . . is to let? Alas, at the moment when my book is appearing, I'm thinking of something utterly different."[31]

Such extravagance seems foolish given Proust's precarious financial condition, but by now he was completely demoralized. He confided to a literary friend that he lacked the energy and will to recopy the last two volumes of his novel even though they were "completely finished." Thanking Anna de Noailles for a letter sent after the publication of *Swann's Way,* he said that his book "enjoyed no success." Were it to succeed, he would take no joy in it because he was "too sad at present." He had not been this dispirited since the period following his mother's death. Even an admiring letter from the poet Francis Jammes comparing him to Shakespeare and Balzac had failed to lift his spirits.[32]

Had the idea of fleeing to Italy been conceived as a way to break with Agostinelli, or at least to avoid him, a repetition of the tactic used years earlier when he was hopelessly in love with Bertrand de Fénelon? Or had he intended for Agostinelli to accompany him on the voyage south? Or was the trip to hasten his recovery from Agostinelli's anticipated departure? Having become an expert on the nature of unrequited love did not enable Proust to cure himself of it.

CHAPTER EIGHT

Grieving and Forgetting

In the late fall of 1913 the relationship between Proust and Agostinelli finally reached the breaking point, but, not surprisingly, it was Agostinelli who made the decisive move. On December 1, Alfred and Anna fled 102 boulevard Haussmann and headed for Monte Carlo, where Agostinelli's father, Eugène, lived.[1] Céleste Albaret believed that Anna was largely responsible for the sudden departure of the Agostinellis because she did not like living in Paris and was eager to return to the Riviera.

Distressed and angry, Proust appealed immediately to Nahmias for help, sending him a letter containing a "strange question." Had he ever used private detectives to have anyone followed, and, if so, could he give Proust their names and addresses? Stressing the urgency of the situation, Proust asked him to call "not to talk" about the matter "openly on the telephone, but I could perhaps question you cryptically about an address."[2]

Mad with impatience and jealousy, Proust began to live scenes from a cheap detective novel: He hired a private eye in Monte Carlo to keep him informed of the whereabouts of Agostinelli and his father, then dispatched Nahmias to the Riviera with instructions to bribe Eugène Agostinelli to persuade his son to return to Paris. Proust knew that Alfred would categorically reject any overtures and offers made directly to him. Nor would the young man agree to come back if he knew that Proust had paid his father. Thus it was imperative that Nahmias keep the negotiations secret.

For a period of five days Proust and his emissary exchanged long, cryptic telegrams under assumed names and elaborate cover stories: one maintained the fiction that Nahmias had gone to the coast on a mission for his own father; another involved an alleged major, secret stock market speculation. On December 3 Proust telegraphed Nahmias, under the young man's real name, at the Hôtel Royal in Nice. The wire provided the Monte Carlo address of Eugène Agostinelli, who ran a hotel at 19 rue des Moneghetti. Proust ordered Nahmias to act quickly because his source had informed him that Eugène was to leave the following morning for Marseilles. Nahmias was to offer a hefty monthly payment to the father for persuading Agostinelli to return immediately to Paris, without being told why, and to remain there until April. Above all, Nahmias must remember not to offer the money directly to Agostinelli (not named in Proust's wire) because he would certainly refuse it. And Nahmias must forcefully deny any suggestions on Agostinelli's part that incentives of any sort had been offered to his father. Proust signed the telegram "Max Werth." The importance of the April date is unclear; perhaps he believed that Agostinelli might agree to a temporary return, thus allowing Proust to regain some control over the situation.

It is true that love makes fools of us all, but never have we seen Proust so naïve as he was in pursuit of the fugitive Agostinelli. Perhaps he enjoyed to some degree the role of the suspicious, jealous older man tracking down the elusive beloved. The cloak-and-dagger routine ended abruptly when it became apparent that Nahmias's mission had failed and that Agostinelli intended to remain on the Riviera.[3]

This episode is the direct inspiration for the flight of Albertine in *The Fugitive*, when Robert de Saint-Loup is dispatched on a similar mission yielding the same results. A letter from the Narrator to Albertine ends with a postscript in which he denies sending Saint-Loup to bribe her aunt, Mme Bontemps, in exchange for the girl's return. Proust, who had instructed Nahmias to make a similar denial, was as mendacious in his dealings with Agostinelli as are the Narrator and Swann with the women they pursue. In the novel Proust inserts a bit of humor into the Narrator's denial, a sentiment absent from the real-life episode: "It's pure Sherlock Holmes. What do you take me for?" Of his desperation to win her back at any costs, the Narrator says, "Living apart from her seemed to me worse than death." The errors made in attempting to secure her return result from the immense suffering caused by her flight: "When the pain is too acute, we dash headlong into the blunder that consists in writing to, in sending somebody to intercede with . . . in proving that we cannot do without, the woman we love."[4]

While one can enumerate certain facets that Albertine owes to Agostinelli and to others of Proust's male friends, it is important to remember that her major function as a character was outlined in a note in *The Notebook of 1908*, long before Proust fell in love with Agostinelli. Another and perhaps the most irrefutable proof that a character like Albertine was to play a major role in the plot is her ultimate link to the Mlle Vinteuil episode, an episode that Proust regarded as key to his story, and one written well before Agostinelli took up residence in his apartment. Before publication he had resisted the advice of trusted writers like Louis de Robert, who had urged him to delete the scene because of its scandalous nature: "I obey a general truth which forbids me to appeal to sympathetic souls any more than to antipathetic ones; the approval of sadists will distress me as a man when my book appears, but it cannot alter the terms in which I probe the truth and which are not determined by my personal whim."[5] In a letter written many years later to the novelist François Mauriac, Proust explained that if he had heeded the advice of those who wanted him to remove the scene "by tearing down the column with the obscene capital," he "would have brought down the entire vault" of his cathedral-novel.[6]

Proust persevered in his goal of securing Agostinelli's return, continuing to correspond with him. In early May 1914 he contacted his financial adviser, Lionel Hauser, with the urgent request to sell enough of his Royal Dutch shares to raise roughly 10,000 francs. Hauser phoned and left a message with Nicolas, reminding Proust that he had already sold his Royal Dutch shares. Mortified, Proust apologized, then arranged the sale of some additional stocks so that he had enough money in hand for the final attempt to lure Agostinelli back to Paris.[7] By month's end, Proust was to dangle before his former secretary one of the most generous offers ever made to a runaway for his return.

On May 28 Proust ordered, as gifts for Agostinelli, an airplane and a Rolls-Royce.[8] Two days later he wrote a long letter to his former secretary, telling him that he had spent 27,000 francs to purchase an airplane for him. In 1914, a Rolls cost 26,200 francs, nearly as much as an airplane. Proust began by thanking Agostinelli for his recent letter, from which he quoted a line that he later attributed to Albertine: "Thank you very much for your letter—one sentence was *ravishing* (crepuscular etc.)—and for your preliminary telegram which was an additional kindness."[9] Apparently Agostinelli had sent Proust a wire and a letter, whose contents are unknown, as replies to letters from the novelist. Proust's letter of May 30 refers to a very recent one that he had sent to Agostinelli, asking him to cancel the order for the airplane and another unnamed gift—most likely a Rolls-Royce. The exact nature of the game Proust was playing is unclear and must remain so, given the letters missing from the exchanges between the two men. Perhaps Proust thought that Agostinelli would not have the will to resist the magnificent gifts of the machines that he loved—machines that might well make his fortune—if he had to cancel the order for them himself.[10]

Should Proust decide to keep the airplane, he told Agostinelli in the May 30 letter, he intended to have verses by Stéphane Mallarmé that the young aviator admired inscribed on the fuselage: "You know: it's the poem you loved even though you found it obscure, which begins: *Le vierge le vivace et le bel Aujourd'hui.* Alas, 'today' is neither 'virgin' nor 'vivacious' nor 'beautiful.'"[11] Knowing how much Agostinelli loved sports, Proust had enclosed with the letter an article on *Swann's Way* from a sports newspaper.[12] As always in such circumstances, he asked Agostinelli to return this letter, making certain that the envelope was well sealed; he then chided his young friend for having so far failed to follow these instructions.[13]

The article Proust sent Agostinelli, published on May 3, 1914, in *Le Sport belge,* was by playwright Henry Bernstein, who had been particularly moved by the novel's evocations of Auteuil and the Bois de Boulogne. Addressing his readers, Bernstein wrote "You must have certainly read *Swann's Way,* the book by Marcel Proust . . . that takes its place among the greatest. It concludes" with a passage about the Narrator's "return to the Bois de Boulogne" wherein he develops a theory of "memory, full of poetry and genius" that is both "gripping and sublime." Proust knew that his secretary would take pride in having contributed to a work being heralded in Paris as brimming with poetry and genius. The young aviator had seemed particularly intrigued by the character of Charles Swann.

Early that spring, in a bizarre homage to his benefactor, Agostinelli had enrolled, under the name Marcel Swann, at the aviation school run by the Garbero brothers at La Grimaudière, near Antibes. Could Proust have explained to Agostinelli that Charles Swann is a kind of surrogate father to the Narrator, who later says that "the raw material of my experience, which would also be the raw material of my book, came to me from Swann"?[14] The Narrator hints once that if his name were the same as the author's, it would be Marcel.[15] Agostinelli's use of a pseudonym is strange because one assumes that he would want his pilot's license to be in his own name. Was he playing "Max Werth's" game and using an alias in an attempt to keep his whereabouts hidden from Proust? Did he fear the wrath of the jealous, jilted writer? Did Proust make novelistic use of his own anger and frustration in the pursuit of Agostinelli to depict Morel's great fear of the scorned—and, as it is revealed after his death, murderous—Charlus?[16]

Agostinelli progressed rapidly during his two months of pilot training. On Saturday, May 30, the very day that Proust sent his offer of regal gifts, Agostinelli went to the airfield for his lesson. Around five o'clock in the afternoon he took off in a monoplane for his second solo flight. Anna and Émile, Agostinelli's younger brother, also in pilot training, watched the flyer go through his maneuvers. Elated by his success, Agostinelli, ignoring the warnings of chief pilot Joseph Garbero, left the designated flying area and headed out over the Bay of Angels. Attempting a turn, the inexperienced pilot forgot to increase his altitude, and the right wing skimmed the water, pulling the plane into the sea as his wife and brother watched in horror.

Once Agostinelli recovered from the shock of finding himself unexpectedly plunged into the water, he noticed that the plane, although three-fourths submerged, was floating. Standing atop the pilot's seat, the desperate Agostinelli waved and screamed for help. Those on shore quickly launched a boat and began rowing frantically toward the downed aviator. But suddenly the aircraft sank beneath the waves, taking Agostinelli with it. He was known to be a good swimmer, and his friends were later puzzled that he seemed to disappear without a struggle.[17] Some said that sharks had been spotted nearby, while others claimed that the plane went down in an area known for its swift currents. Search boats plied the waters in the bay until darkness forced them back to port.

Proust learned of the tragedy that evening when he received a telegram from the bereaved Anna.[18] On Sunday morning a boat found the sunken plane, but the body had been swept away. The family provided the newspapers a description of Agostinelli's clothes: a khaki one-piece flying suit, a brown rubber helmet, gray shirt, black pants, black shoes, and a signet ring with the initials AA.[19] In addition to the heavy clothing, Agostinelli had on his person all his money, a considerable sum of about five or six thousand francs, the remainder of what he had saved from Proust's generous salary. Agostinelli's father and brother realized that if the body were found, all the money would go to Anna as the pilot's legal wife. They sent a telegram to the Prince of Monaco, revealing that she was only Agostinelli's mistress.[20]

The family dispatched Agostinelli's half-brother Jean Vittoré to Paris, where a profoundly aggrieved Proust wept in his arms. Vittoré had come to entreat the novelist to hire divers to search for the body.[21] The divers, who would have to come from faraway Toulon, wanted five thousand francs for their trouble. Proust did not attempt to engage the men since his "debt settlements alone" would "entirely absorb" the cash that Hauser had raised for him.[22] Eight days after the accident, fishermen found Agostinelli's body.

On June 1 the *Nouvelle Revue Française* published excerpts from the forthcoming volume describing the Narrator's first stay at Balbec. Proust continued to receive packets of proofs, but was far too upset to work.[23] Soon Anna and Émile arrived on his doorstep. After Agostinelli's funeral, they had come running back to Paris, confident that he would help them in spite of his earlier warnings to Anna that she would never receive a penny from him if Agostinelli died in a plane crash.

As was his nature in such circumstances, Proust relented and did what he could to help. He tried to remedy Anna and Émile's financial plight by finding them employment, enlisting, on their behalf, the aid of such friends as the lawyer Émile Straus. He even wrote a letter to the Prince de Monaco to inquire whether Anna could inherit anything from Agostinelli even though he now knew that she was not legally his widow. He told Émile Straus that Anna deserved to be designated Agostinelli's rightful heir: the young man had "lived for her alone and would have left her everything he had."[24]

In appealing to his friends to help the Agostinellis, Proust stressed his former secretary's intellectual gifts.[25] In a letter to André Gide, Proust spoke of his great sorrow over "the death of a young man whom I loved probably more than all my male friends since it has made me so unhappy." He maintained that although the unnamed youth came from humble origins, he was extremely intelligent and wrote letters like "those of a great writer." It was only after falling in love with him that Proust discovered in him "those qualities that were so marvellously incompatible with everything else he was—discovered them with amazement, though they added nothing to my affection for him: I simply took pleasure in making him aware of them. But he died before he realized what he was, before he even became it entirely."[26] Proust doubted that Gide or anyone else would ever see the sequel to *Swann's Way*. Since the death of his "poor friend," he had not had the strength to open a single one of the packages of proofs that arrived daily from the printers.[27]

In the weeks following Agostinelli's death, Anna tried several times to commit suicide, and Proust feared that if her situation grew desperate enough, she might actually succeed.[28] He himself was not immune to death wishes. He later confided to Lucien Daudet that in the days following the accident he had longed to die: "After having put up so well with being ill without feeling sorry for myself, I found myself hoping, with all my heart, every time I got into a taxi that an oncoming bus would run me down."[29] The Narrator, considering Albertine's death, ponders his own demise, if he should die before writing his book: "By losing my life I should not have lost very much; I should have lost only an empty form, the empty frame of a work of art."[30]

Not only had Proust lost someone he loved passionately, but he felt responsible for Agostinelli's death. Had he not lavished money on his secretary, "Marcel Swann" probably could not have afforded to relocate in Antibes and enroll in the aviation school. And while he had tried at first to discourage Agostinelli from becoming a pilot, he knew that he later took advantage of the young man's passion for flying by giving him money for the lessons in a futile attempt to keep him on a leash.[31]

The increased importance that Albertine's role in the novel assumed after Agostinelli's death greatly altered the dimensions, but not the substance, of the work. As we have seen, Proust had anticipated such a character in the earliest stages of the manuscript, long before becoming infatuated with Agostinelli, but the name Albertine does appear for the first time in drafts written in 1913, when Proust began adapting elements of his relationship with Agostinelli to flesh out the girl in whom he was to concentrate all that remained for him to say about love, jealousy, death, memory, oblivion, and the relationship of suffering to the role of art.[32] Proust later told his publisher, Gaston Gallimard, that he considered his pages on "Albertine's death" and on the process of "forgetting" and recovery the best that he had ever written.[33]

Although not mentioned by name, Agostinelli, of all the young men Proust loved, has by far the largest presence in the novel, having inspired several incidents involving Albertine. Among these episodes are the offers of a Rolls-Royce and a yacht to the fugitive girl, as well as a thirty thousand–franc bribe for her aunt to persuade her to return to the Narrator. Subsequently she dies in a horseback-riding accident, for which the protagonist blames himself: "From my prison she had escaped to go and kill herself on a horse which but for me she would not have owned."[34]

In *The Notebook of 1908*, begun well before Agostinelli moved into the writer's apartment, Proust had sketched the Narrator's relationship with a female character in a single sentence whose final words summarize the experience of all Proustian lovers: "In the second part of the novel the girl will be financially ruined and I will keep her without seeking to possess her due to an incapacity for happiness."[35] This sentence, like many of Proust's utterances, before and after he met Agostinelli, can be read as eerily prophetic. The writer believed that all his efforts to find contentment in reciprocated love were doomed to failure due to his "incapacity for happiness." All his amorous relationships, especially the vital, early ones with Reynaldo Hahn and Lucien Daudet, had convinced him of this. Disillusionment with erotic love will be the Narrator's fate as well, but the theme will ultimately be linked to his quest to become a writer, the only role—he finally realizes—that brings him true joy.

Proust does not subscribe to the belief that "absence makes the heart grow fonder." He has his own theory that he calls the "general law of oblivion." The absent or the dead are quickly forgotten, not because we are indifferent or callous but because living simply demands that we recover and move on. Ultimately his love for Agostinelli, like the Narrator's for Albertine, must be forgotten: "I had finally ceased to love Albertine. So that this love . . . had ended . . . by succumbing, like my love for Gilberte, to the general law of oblivion."[36]

In late 1917, when Paul Morand prepared to depart for a posting at the French embassy in Rome, Proust sent him a letter in which he referred to the recently published excerpts from the forthcoming volume *The Guermantes Way*. In this letter, as is not infrequently the case, we see Proust identifying with his Narrator, who finds it impossible to remain faithful to the memory of the dead or the merely absent: "If you [Morand] read in the *N.R.F.* the pages in which I show how I finally reconcile myself to the departure of my friends, though the idea that I will so reconcile myself is precisely what saddens me most, you will understand my state of mind when I realize that soon I shall see you no more, and that a day will come when, a new 'self' having formed, I shall no longer miss you."[37]

A half-century later, when Morand lost his beloved wife, Hélène, he found that Proust "had spoken true." Morand's journal entry for May 8, 1975, reads: "Oblivion is a form of this awful erosion known as habit. This morning, I posed my lips on the urn containing Hélène's ashes without weeping." He then recalled Proust's 1917 letter about how helpless one remains before the destructive forces of time that obliterate even the memories of those we hold dearest: "It's not because you're leaving for Rome [that makes me sad], it's because I know that I am going to forget you." This line of Proust's becomes something of a motif in Morand's journal.[38] Morand must also have remembered that Proust reprises this theme in *The Fugitive*, where it becomes even more dominant, when the Narrator discovers himself in the process of forgetting Albertine: "It is not because other people are dead that our affection for them fades; it is because we ourselves are dying. . . . My new self, while it grew up in the shadow of the old, had often heard the other speak of Albertine; through that other self, through the stories it gathered from it, it thought that it knew her, it found her lovable, it loved her; but it was only a love at second hand."[39]

This view is consistent with Proust's theory of personality, of the multiple selves we each possess, the shifting sentiments, the ebb and flow of emotions: all in keeping with the phenomenon of the "Intermittencies of the Heart," which Proust had long intended to use as the general title of his novel before finally choosing *In Search of Lost Time*. Not long after Agostinelli's death, the novelist had identified the various stages of the grieving and forgetting process, which he described in a letter to Hahn. Proust had expected the September 1914 trip to Cabourg, so filled with memories of Agostinelli, to worsen the pain of his loss. Proust then proclaimed his love for Agostinelli before comparing it to his love for Hahn, who remained his most trusted and intimate friend:

I really loved Alfred. It isn't enough to say I loved him, I adored him. And I don't know why I write that in the past tense, for I love him still. But in the last analysis, in feelings of grief there is an element of the involuntary and an element of duty which sustains the involuntary part and ensures its durability. This sense of duty doesn't exist in the case of Alfred, who behaved very badly towards me; I give him the regrets that I cannot help but give him; I don't feel bound to him by a duty of the sort that binds me to you, that would bind me to you even if I owed you a thousand times less, even if I loved you a thousand times less.[40]

The bad behavior must refer to Agostinelli's leaving Proust since, as we have seen, the novelist did everything in his power to persuade the fugitive to return. The letter to Hahn continues with what is perhaps a reference to Ernest Forssgren, the young Swede who had accompanied Proust to Cabourg as his valet: "So if I had a few weeks of relative inconstancy at Cabourg, don't condemn me as fickle but blame the person who was incapable of deserving fidelity."[41] The inconstancy may be a reference to Proust's attempt to seduce Forssgren. According to Forssgren, Proust had given him a volume of Oscar Wilde's *De profundis* to read in order to gauge his reaction to homosexuality.[42] The person undeserving of fidelity is obviously Agostinelli. The Narrator experiences a similar moment of recovery from Albertine's death and uses a musical analogy to describe it: "The memory of Albertine had become so fragmentary that it no longer caused me any sadness and was no more now than a transition to fresh desires, like a chord which announces a change of key."[43] After returning to Paris, to Proust's "great joy," the pain over the loss of Agostinelli resumed, although somewhat attenuated:

> But I also realize with sadness that, however acute, it is perhaps less excruciating than a month or two ago. It isn't because others have died that grief diminishes, but because one dies oneself. And one needs a great deal of vitality to maintain and keep alive and intact the "self" of several weeks ago. His friend hasn't forgotten poor Alfred. But he has joined him in death and his successor, the "self" of today, loves Alfred but only knew him from the accounts of the other. It's an affection at one remove.[44]

We are not to blame for this scheme of things, according to Proust, any more than we are for falling in love in the first place. These conditions—indifference followed by oblivion—are the products of our fundamental nature. Ah, but the memories of those we loved and the happy days we spent together can be enshrined in a novel. The Narrator discovers that this task, so long delayed, is "the whole purpose of my life and perhaps of art itself." He is tempted to believe that art can grant a sort of immortality, that art is the imperishable fruit of suffering and sacrifice:

The cruel law of art is that people die and we ourselves die after exhausting every form of suffering, so that over our heads may grow the grass not of oblivion but of eternal life, the vigorous and luxuriant growth of a true work of art, and so that thither, gaily and without a thought for those who are sleeping beneath them, future generations may come to enjoy their *déjeuner sur l'herbe*.[45]

The Narrator quickly concludes, however, that in the long run even our works are destined to perish because future generations will be indifferent to them: "No doubt my book too, like my fleshly being, would in the end one day die. But death is a thing that we must resign ourselves to. We accept the thought that in ten years we ourselves, in a hundred years our books, will have ceased to exist. Eternal duration is promised no more to men's works than to men."[46]

Clive Bell, in his book on Proust, finds much to admire in such an attitude: Proust "is never vulgar, never sentimental. And if he avoided those messy pits into which most modern creators—Dickens, Hugo, Balzac, Dostoievsky—have fallen, that may have been because a philosopher was ever at hand to remind him, that the one wholly good gift the gods have given man is death."[47]

Proust did not, however, completely consign Agostinelli to the dustbin of oblivion. With the approach of the first anniversary of his death, Proust wrote to an old family friend, Mme Anatole Catusse, at her villa in Nice, where she had decided to seek refuge during the war, and asked her to send forty francs' worth of flowers to be placed on the young man's tomb. He urged her not to spend much time selecting something tasteful because the intention would be lost on the Agostinellis. At Alfred's funeral the family had been disappointed because the magnificent four hundred–franc bouquet sent by the bereaved author contained real flowers instead of plastic ones. In a letter to Mme Jean Vittoré, Agostinelli's sister-in-law, Proust maintained that the war alone prevented him from making a melancholy pilgrimage south to visit Agostinelli's grave. Here, perhaps because he is addressing a member of Agostinelli's family, he vividly evokes the memory of the young man and mourns his loss: Even "all the war deaths" have done nothing to "weaken in me the memory, so sad and so tender, that I have of Alfred. I think of him constantly and my friendship and sorrow have only grown deeper and deeper. Certainly, I miss his company terribly, I so loved his appearance and his heart!" The sentiment seems genuine enough, especially as Proust also declared to Clément de Maugny, who had no idea who Agostinelli was, that a year had passed since he had lost a friend, who, "with my mother, my father, is the person I loved most."[48] In any event, each year on the anniversary of Agostinelli's death Proust arranged for flowers to be placed on his tombstone.

During the war, Proust heard several times from Émile, Agostinelli's younger brother, whom he continued to aid. He had given the threadbare Émile, now a chauffeur like his late brother, what remained of Dr. Proust's clothes. On Proust's recommendation, the Edmond Rostands had hired Émile as a driver. Rostand, famous for his play *Cyrano de Bergerac,* had a son Maurice, an effeminate homosexual, who had become a friend of Proust's and a great admirer of *Swann's Way.*

Although Proust rarely saw Émile, he maintained contact with him in hopes of learning more about Agostinelli's life between the time he fled Paris and the months in Antibes leading up to his death. He had also reminded Maurice Rostand to question Émile about Agostinelli's activities and to seek any information about him that his brother might have learned from the other pilots at the aviation school. In case Rostand suspected his motives, or perhaps out of fear that someone else might read the letter, Proust explained that such details intrigued him as a novelist and might allow him to imagine a kind of "Balzacian reconstitution."[49] In other words, he was simply collecting realistic details for a novel. Not long after Agostinelli's death, Proust had visited the airfield at Buc to question aviators who had learned to fly in Nice.[50] According to Proust, such curiosity about a deceased beloved's activities and possible betrayals constitutes an intermediate stage on the way to the inevitable indifference. His persistent interrogations of those who knew Agostinelli match the Narrator's tireless investigations into Albertine's past after her death:

> My jealous curiosity as to what Albertine might have done was unbounded. I suborned any number of women from whom I learned nothing. If this curiosity was so tenacious, it was because people do not die for us immediately, but remain bathed in a sort of aura of life which bears no relation to true immortality but through which they continue to occupy our thoughts in the same way as when they were alive. It is as though they were traveling abroad. . . . I continued to sacrifice everything to the cruel satisfaction of this transient curiosity, although I knew in advance that my enforced separation from Albertine, by the fact of her death, would lead me to the same indifference as had resulted from my voluntary separation from Gilberte.[51]

Surviving traces of real people in fictional characters—bits that are rendered appropriately obscure—inspire the Narrator to observe, while contemplating the novel he intends to write, that "a book is a huge cemetery in which on the majority of the tombs the names are effaced and can no longer be read."[52] "On the majority" implies, of course, that not all the names have been obscured by the author or rubbed off by the corrosive effects of time. The name Agostinelli is among those that remain discernible in the beguiling traits of the fictional, fugitive girl named Albertine. As for Bertrand de Fénelon, fictionalized to some degree as Saint-Loup, he was among the rare friends who received a special tribute in one of several instances when Proust knowingly blurs the lines between fiction and autobiography to pay tribute to a man he had loved and who was killed early in the war: "My dearest friend the best, bravest, most intelligent of men, whom no one who knew him could forget: Bertrand de Fénelon."[53] After all, lucidity about our common fate is not enough to discourage us in our efforts to defeat time.

In *Time Regained,* as Proust resumes, orchestrates, develops, and resolves the grand themes of his novel, he returns to the idea of grief. The Narrator, now obsessed with the destructive chemistry of time, recalls why the body of a beloved contains the power to harm us until death and time do their work, leaving us at last with only memories that can be enshrined in the pages of a book:

> And it is because they contain thus within themselves the hours of the past that human bodies have the power to hurt so terribly those who love them, because they contain the memories of so many joys and desires already effaced for them, but still cruel for the lover who contemplates and prolongs in the dimension of Time the beloved body of which he is jealous, so jealous that he may even wish for its destruction. For after death Time withdraws from the body, and the memories, so indifferent, grown so pale, are effaced in her who no longer exists, as they soon will be in the lover whom for a while they continue to torment but in whom before long they will perish, once the desire that owed its inspiration to a living body is no longer there to sustain them. Profound Albertine, whom I saw sleeping and who was dead.[54]

CHAPTER NINE

The Night Prowler

For what fault have you most toleration?

For the private life of geniuses.

By 1917 Proust had come to depend on two primary sources of information for which he paid. Each informant was a specialist, highly knowledgeable in his own domain: Olivier Dabescat and Albert Le Cuziat. Dabescat, as the maître d'hôtel of the Ritz, served the world's wealthy elite; Le Cuziat operated the Ballon d'Alsace, a male brothel and Turkish bath for men who wished to remain anonymous. Some of these men, like Proust, were clients of both Dabescat and Le Cuziat. Proust used the brothel to spy on its habitués and to obtain information for his novel. Le Cuziat's tenure as a servant in some of Paris's grandest houses and his fascination with history made him the source of knowledge on topics that greatly interested Proust: genealogy and etiquette. As we shall see, Le Cuziat had an important link to Ernest Forssgren and may well have been the person who pointed the jobless Swede in Proust's direction in 1914.

During the war years, Proust often went late at night to dine alone at the Ritz where he could "ruminate and rest."[1] Dabescat kept Proust "informed of such details as who dined with whom, what dress Madame so-and-so wore, and what sort of etiquette was observed at the various tables."[2] Dabescat also commanded the Ritz's bevy of handsome young waiters, much admired by Proust.

Dabescat willingly served the writer in a private room at any hour of the evening or early morning; this arrangement allowed Proust to engage him or other members of the staff in conversation for lengthy periods to glean information about guests and hotel personnel alike. Élisabeth de Clermont-Tonnerre often observed the novelist and the headwaiter talking for what seemed like hours at a stretch. Proust's charm and largesse worked their magic on Dabescat and his underlings, who devoted themselves to their nocturnal visitor with a thoroughness and enthusiasm that surpassed even the superb service given to ordinary guests. Not since his eight years of summer vacation at the Grand-Hôtel in Cabourg had Proust enjoyed such attention and such well-informed sources regarding the antics of Europe's wealthiest and most pampered citizens.

While being seen at the Ritz could enhance one's reputation, being caught at Le Cuziat's establishment—often the target of police raids—could land one in jail. Le Cuziat began his career, modestly enough, as a footman in the service of the Russian Prince Alexis Orloff, which, we now know, is where Ernest Forssgren met him in 1913.[3] He later served Prince Constantin Radziwill, who hid his homosexual proclivities from no one, including his wife. Céleste Albaret believed that Proust first met Le Cuziat at Prince Radziwill's.

Having become expert in the practices and needs of Paris's closeted homosexuals, the enterprising valet opened a succession of brothels and Turkish baths in the vicinity of the Church of the Madeleine, not far from 102 boulevard Haussmann. Proust did not hide from his housekeeper the nature of Le Cuziat's establishment, and the shocked Céleste took an immediate and intense dislike to the man. In her memoirs, she described him as "a bean-pole of a Breton, slovenly, fair, with cold blue eyes like a fish—eyes that matched his soul. The precariousness of his profession was in his face and his look, a hunted look, which was not surprising, seeing that . . . he often did short spells in jail."[4]

It is impossible to determine the prevalence of male brothels in Paris because, unlike legal houses of female prostitution, the clandestine male establishments were not officially registered with the police, and their employees were not subject to regular visits by the health inspectors. In 1870, the year before Proust was born, there were 145 official brothels in Paris, which seems to have been the peak. The numbers gradually declined to 59 in 1892, when Proust was twenty-one. The primary reason for the decline was the increase in clandestine brothels, which contained by about this time fifteen thousand female prostitutes.[5]

We do know that gay men could arrange for assignations with male prostitutes in female brothels.[6] In fact, Proust situates a comic scene involving the insanely jealous Charlus and the object of his affection, the bisexual violinist Charlie Morel, in such a brothel. The prince de Guermantes, who is Charlus's brother and a married homosexual, meets the violinist without knowing who he is "or being known to him either, and offered him fifty francs to spend the night with him in the brothel at Maineville; a twofold pleasure for Morel, in the remuneration received . . . and in the delight of being surrounded by women who would flaunt their tawny breasts uncovered." Charlus gets wind of the assignation and, "mad with jealousy," asks Jupien to bribe the madam "to hide them in some place where they could witness what occurred." Proust then describes how jealousy has "enriched" and revitalized the aging baron's brain:

> Love can thus be responsible for veritable geological upheavals of the mind. In that of M. de Charlus, which a few days earlier had resembled a plain so uniform that as far as the eye could reach it would have been impossible to make out an idea rising above the level surface, there had suddenly sprung into being, hard as stone, a range of

> mountains . . . as elaborately carved as if some sculptor . . . had chiselled . . . on the spot . . . vast titanic groups Fury, Jealousy, Curiosity, Envy, Hatred, Suffering, Pride, Terror and Love.

Morel has somehow learned that he is to be spied on, the prince has been "spirited away," and Charlus sees nothing through the one-way pane of glass but a "terrified, speechless" Morel "not daring to lift his glass for fear of letting it fall."[7]

After Proust's death, Céleste persistently denied the rumors that he had given Le Cuziat the funds to get his business going, but she did admit that when "Le Cuziat told M. Proust he didn't have enough money to buy furniture for his own bedroom," the writer "let him have the key to the shed and told him to take what he wanted. He only took a green half-length chaise-longue . . . and one or two other chairs and a pair of curtains."[8] In the novel the Narrator gives some of the furniture inherited from Aunt Léonie to a female brothel. When he sees the family furniture again in its new setting, he finds its profanation painful to behold:

> As soon as I saw [the pieces of furniture] again in the house where these women were putting them to their own uses, all the virtues that pervaded my aunt's room at Combray at once appeared to me, tortured by the cruel contact to which I had abandoned them in their defencelessness! Had I outraged the dead, I would not have suffered such remorse. I returned no more to visit their new mistress, for they seemed to me to be alive and to be appealing to me, like those apparently inanimate objects in a Persian fairy-tale, in which imprisoned human souls are undergoing martyrdom and pleading for deliverance.

Later he recollects that he had lost his virginity on that very sofa: "It was upon that same sofa that, many years before, I had tasted for the first time the delights of love with one of my girl cousins, with whom I had not known where to go until she somewhat rashly suggested our taking advantage of a moment in which aunt Léonie had left her room."[9]

Proust often summoned Le Cuziat to boulevard Haussmann, or, more rarely, he went to the brothel, located in the Hôtel Marigny at 11 rue de l'Arcade. Le Cuziat provided information of a scandalous nature, such as "the names of people who used to frequent the house in rue de l'Arcade—a list that included politicians and even ministers. Albert supplied details about their vices." When Proust needed more information from Le Cuziat, which sometimes involved specifics about genealogy or protocol, he sent his housekeeper with a note to summon him, always warning her, "And don't forget, Céleste . . . give him the letter personally. And whatever you do, see that he *gives it back to you*." Proust destroyed the notes because he did not want anyone to know about his relationship with Le Cuziat; above all, he wanted his visits to the brothel to remain secret: " 'I don't like to stay there too long when I go,' M. Proust used to say, 'You never know when there will be a police raid. I shouldn't like to see myself all over tomorrow's papers!' "[10] In addition to the danger of being swept up in a police raid, Proust risked blackmail should the notes fall into the wrong hands.

Proust likely transposed some of his own anxiety about being arrested at Le Cuziat's to the character Legrandin, who takes pains to hide his snobbery and his homosexuality, and whose fears of being found out are treated in a lighter, humorous vein. Legrandin has grown thin from the exertions of rushing about in order to avoid detection: "Legrandin had become slimmer and brisker. . . . This velocity of movement had its psychological reasons as well. He was in the habit of frequenting certain low haunts where he did not wish to be seen going in or coming out: he would hurl himself into them."[11]

We now know that Proust suffered, on at least one occasion, the indignity of being caught in a police raid. It happened during the night of January 11–12, 1918, at Le Cuziat's establishment in the rue de l'Arcade. In a report dated January 19, an officer Tanguy related the nature of the establishment raided the previous evening: "This hotel was brought to my attention as a meeting place for major and minor homosexuals." Like Jupien's brothel in the novel, Le Cuziat's counted among its "major" customers deputies, ministers, military officers, and men like Proust, who were members of the upper bourgeoisie. Tanguy described "the owner of the hotel, a homosexual himself," who "provided opportunities for adepts of unnatural debauchery to meet. Surveillances that I had carried out confirmed the information I had collected about the nature of the establishment. When I arrived, I found Le Cuziat in a parlor on the street level, drinking champagne with three individuals who looked like pederasts." Among those whose names Tanguy listed "between a soldier recovering from his wounds and a corporal waiting to be discharged: 'Proust, Marcel, 45 years old, private income, 102, bd Haussmann.'"[12] This new information provides another snapshot of Proust, a man utterly unknown and, apparently, of little interest, to the police inspector, a picture that confirms what we already knew about the novelist's nocturnal visits to the brothel and tells us that, at least on one occasion, Proust was caught in the trap that he had so wanted to avoid.

Two of the young men found in rooms at the hotel confessed. They were seventeen and nineteen years of age and hence below the age of consent of twenty-one. Le Cuziat confessed as well, saying that he was "adept at unnatural debauchery and did not believe that he was doing any harm by receiving homosexuals in his hotel." Le Cuziat was found guilty of two charges: selling liquor after hours, a restriction enacted due to the war, and the corruption of minors. He was fined two hundred francs and sentenced to four months in prison. After the war, due to the intervention of some of his influential clients, Le Cuziat managed to resume operations of male brothels.

As we have seen, Paul Morand knew that Proust was homosexual, brought him documents and books to read, and teased him, presumably in private, about his homosexual orientation. Judging from a 1918 letter to Morand, Proust was a good sport about such teasing and made light of it: "Do you remember that a short time ago you had offered me a letter that would have permitted me to study M. de Charlus without danger, and in manner other than in front of my mirror?"[13] Proust often used the name Charlus generically to refer to homosexuals.

In 1919 Morand went too far when he published an "Ode to Marcel Proust," in which he alluded to the novelist's nocturnal excursions and publicly embarrassed him. Morand began the poem by evoking, in free verse, the famous room lined with cork and the figure of Proust reclining in bed a "shadow born from the smoke of your fumigations, Céleste, with her accustomed rigor, yet gentle, dips me in the black juice of your room which smells of warm cork and a cold chimney." Proust cannot have been too happy with what he had read so far, but the penultimate stanza, in which Morand speculates about the novelist's late evening prowlings, infuriated him: "Proust, what routs do you attend at night to return with eyes so heavy and so lucid? What forbidden terrors have you known to come back to us so indulgent and good, while knowing the travails of the soul . . . and that love hurts so much?"[14]

In his journal, written many years later, Morand speaks about what he calls Proust's "côté rôdeur" (prowler side), an aspect neglected, he says, in books about homosexuals. Proust the night prowler and frequenter of male brothels is the pale, curious phantom that Morand dangerously evoked in his ode, and "pain," of course, has all kinds of overtones. According to Morand, all homosexuals are like "ferrets, constantly hunting, never satiated by their adventures: Gide, Montherlant, Proust, eternal prowlers, tireless sexual adventurers."[15]

Proving that he was indeed indulgent and good, Proust did not break with Morand over the poem. He did, however, give him a good scolding, saying that readers of the "Ode to Marcel Proust" might assume that he had been arrested in a raid. And, for good measure, he meted out a severe form of literary punishment to his young, indiscreet friend. He had intended to write another volume of parodies devoted entirely to Morand and his lover, the beautiful and wealthy Princess Hélène Soutzo, "your accomplice in the 'Ode.'" Proust informed the diplomat that his ode had forced him to abandon the pastiche project, saying that he could not "publish it, it being infinitely eulogistic, without looking like a coward." While acknowledging Morand's artistic right to publish the "Ode," Proust declared that the poem had exposed him "to public opprobrium" and, with no factual basis, humiliated him: "(apaches have always been sweet to me, and routs unknown)." As for Morand's "charming dedication," scribbled in Proust's personal copy, those words "will be unseen by the public and do nothing to counteract the 'Ode' wherein you cast me into this Hell reserved by Dante for his Enemies."[16] Having expressed his discontent and well-founded fears for his reputation, Proust put bitterness aside and quickly resumed his friendship with the handsome young man. Within a year, Proust contributed a preface to Morand's first book, *Tender Stocks*.

In spite of the ode and his apprehension in the raid, Proust did not abandon his practice of visiting the brothel whenever he wished. Céleste found it strange that her employer, upon returning from Le Cuziat's, used to describe to her, in rather precise detail, what he had seen through the peephole, just as nonchalantly "as if he'd come back from an evening at Count de Beaumont's or Countess Greffulhe's." When she told Proust, somewhat indignantly, that she could not understand why he would receive someone like Le Cuziat and, even worse, go to his establishment, the novelist replied rather disingenuously that he did so because he lacked imagination: "I know, Céleste. You can't imagine how much I dislike it. But I can only write things as they are, and to do that I have to see them."[17] Although we may find it difficult to believe that Proust had no imagination, there is a sentence in his notebook that indicates that he believed this to be true: "Everything [I am writing] is fiction, laboriously though, for I have no imagination."[18] Therefore, he was not being totally disingenuous when he justified his own spying and collection of gossip as nourishment for his literary imagination, which he, at least, transposed into fiction, thus protecting the real-life models—a safeguard that Morand had failed to provide on publishing his "Ode."

Le Cuziat excelled at staging erotic dramas that Proust yearned to see. He may well have inspired this portrait of Aimé, the headwaiter at the Grand-Hôtel in Balbec, whom the Narrator engages to find out whether or not Albertine had sex with the laundry girls. As a private investigator, Aimé proves to be resourceful and discreet: "He belonged to that category of working-class people who have a keen eye to their own advantage, are loyal to those they serve and indifferent to any form of morality, and of whom—because, if we pay them well, they prove themselves, in their obedience to our will, as incapable of indiscretion, lethargy or dishonesty as they are devoid of scruples—we say: 'They are excellent people.'"[19]

One afternoon Proust received a message telling him to come that evening if he wanted to see a particular spectacle that Le Cuziat had earlier described to him and which had made him intensely curious. Afterward, Céleste noticed that Proust returned home "with his hat cocked, which meant he hadn't been wasting his time." He had seen something "unimaginable," the flogging of a man, supposedly a "big industrialist who comes down from the north of France specially for that. Imagine—there he is in a room, fastened to a wall with chains and padlocks, while some wretch, picked up heaven knows where, who gets paid for it, whips him till the blood spurts out all over everything. And it is only then that the unfortunate creature experiences the heights of pleasure."

" 'And did you have to pay a lot of money to see it?' "

" 'Yes, Céleste. But I had to.' "[20]

Céleste expressed her disgust with the whole business, saying that Le Cuziat deserved to die in prison. Proust, who managed to find redeeming qualities in nearly everyone, pointed out that Le Cuziat adored his late mother and had done everything possible to make her happy.[21] His unwillingness to condemn others is an attribute he shared with the Narrator, who makes this comment about being judgmental:

> We ought never to bear a grudge against people, ought never to judge them by some memory of an unkind action, for we do not know all the good that, at other moments, their hearts may have sincerely desired and realised. And thus, even simply from the point of view of

prediction, one is mistaken. For doubtless the evil aspect which we have noted once and for all will recur; but the heart is richer than that, has many other aspects which will recur also in the same person and which we refuse to acknowledge because of his earlier bad behavior.[22]

Le Cuziat's kindness to his mother may have inspired, in part, another element of Jupien's brothel. The masochistic Charlus, engaged in a fruitless quest to find a genuinely sadistic partner, expresses his frustration and anger at Jupien when Maurice, the prostitute hired to flog him and whom Jupien had touted as a vicious murderer, turns out to be a nice young man, respectful of his family, even to the point of sending money home to his unfortunate brother.[23] Charlus's inability to find a truly sadistic partner provides comic overtones and lessens the weight of depravity that might otherwise be associated with the baron's sexual misadventures. In a letter to a prospective publisher, Proust had stressed the fact that although his subject matter was in part taboo because of Charlus's sexuality, "this elderly gentleman of a noble family reveals himself as a pederast who will be portrayed in a comic light but, without any obscene language."[24] Proust's portraits of his principal characters often do range from the ridiculous to the sublime. The elderly Charlus—in his dotage and completely dependent on Jupien to guide him through the streets and prevent the ever rapacious, but now blind, baron from attempting to seduce boys who are underage—is also likened to King Lear.[25]

Whatever else Proust may have done at Le Cuziat's, it is clear that he made that brothel the model for Jupien's establishment, financed by Charlus. In the novel, the Narrator, who bears no obvious traces of homosexuality, stumbles upon Jupien's brothel one night during the wartime blackout. While there, he observes through a peephole a sadomasochistic scene similar to the one Proust described to Céleste.[26]

Proust did not, in spite of Céleste's assertions to the contrary, tell his housekeeper everything he saw and did at Le Cuziat's establishment. A young prostitute who worked at the brothel left testimony recorded by Marcel Jouhandeau, the novelist and memorialist, who, although married, was a frequent patron of the Ballon d'Alsace.[27] According to the prostitute, on those nights when Proust came to the brothel not for gossip but to satisfy his private needs, he first peered "through a glass pane into a room" where a group of young men were "playing cards."

After choosing his partner for the evening, Proust went to an upstairs room, climbed into bed, and waited. "A quarter of an hour later," said the young man, who was often the one favored by Proust

> I knocked on the door, went in, and found Marcel already in bed with the sheet drawn up to his chin. He smiled at me. My instructions were to take off all my clothes and remain standing by the closed door while I satisfied myself under the anxious gaze of Marcel, who was doing the same. If he reached the desired conclusion, I left after having smiled at him and without having seen anything other than his face and without having touched him.

If Proust failed to achieve orgasm, "he would make a gesture for me to leave and Albert would bring two cages," each of which contained a famished rat. Le Cuziat would set the cages together and open the door. The two starving beasts would attack each other, making piercing squeaks as they clawed and bit each other, a spectacle that allowed Proust to achieve orgasm.[28]

The testimony from the anonymous prostitute quoted by Jouhandeau sounds plausible, especially for the writer's later years when he was nearly incapacitated by illnesses and self-medication, and his phobia of germs intensified, which would have made him fear physical contact with a brothel inmate. Proust's fear of contamination is well documented from his letters and from Céleste's memoirs. She attributed his phobia, in part, to his upbringing: "It mustn't be forgotten that his father was not only a famous doctor but also a specialist in hygiene. This has left M. Proust with a fear of germs which itself would have been enough to give him almost an obsession with cleanliness." Toward the end of his life, Céleste tells us, he feared shaking hands with others or even touching his own mail, which caused him to take extreme measures to protect himself:

> He began wearing gloves in bed when people came to see him whom he knew too well or not well enough to be certain about their health. And he would keep the gloves on until the people went, for fear the visitors might pass on germs when they shook hands. Someone advised him to get a box and put formol [a disinfectant] in it. Then the letters were placed in the box both before and after they were opened.[29]

Jean Cocteau, a friend who was also homosexual, knew about the caged rats, which he alleged involved the profanation of a photograph of Proust's mother. According to Cocteau's diary, he had learned about the rats from the "awful indiscretion of Gabriel (Jupien) whose establishment on the rue de l'Arcade was subsidized by Proust, as he tells us Jupien's was by Charlus." The first sentence of Cocteau's next paragraph makes this startling revelation: "The rat killed in its cage was made even more troubling by the photograph of his mother." In the margin next to this, Cocteau, who was rereading *Sodom and Gomorrah* at the time, wrote "Profaned mothers," Proust's title for a part of the novel that was never written.[30] Here is what the Narrator says about the projected passage in a statement about lascivious sons who resemble their mothers: "Besides, can one entirely separate M. de Charlus's appearance from the fact that sons, who do not always take after their fathers, even without being inverts and even though seekers after women, may consummate upon their faces the profanation of their mothers? But let us not consider here a subject that deserves a chapter to itself: the Profanation of the Mother." Cocteau's notation is the same as Proust's in *Sodome et Gomorrhe:* "Mères profanées."[31]

It is not clear from Cocteau's diary, begun in 1951, two decades after Proust's death, whether the proprietor of the male brothel whom he identifies as Gabriel told him that Proust brought the photograph of his mother to the establishment or whether this is Cocteau's supposition based on his rereading of the novel. The mingling of biog-

raphy and fiction here—Gabriel-Jupien and "profaned mothers"—
and Cocteau's interpretation of a passage from *The Guermantes Way*,
makes it impossible to say. Cocteau's journal entry regarding profaned mothers continues: "If one rereads Proust attentively as I am
rereading him, one finds again and again the theme that he attributes
to others (characters) of the sullied mother." Cocteau names the
profanation of Vinteuil, saying that the mother has become the father
here, and then the defiled mother again when "Charlus says that
Bloch would interest him perhaps if he would consent to beat his
mother"; as additional evidence he mentions the scene in which Saint-
Loup "answers with insolence and coldness" to his mother's love.
And "above all," Cocteau sees a direct link between Proust's ritual
with the rats and a passage on sleep from *The Guermantes Way* which
contains this description of a nightmare:

> nightmares with their fantastic picture-books in which our relatives
> who are dead are shown meeting with serious accidents which at the
> same time do not preclude their speedy recovery. Until then we keep
> them in a little rat-cage, in which they are smaller than white mice and,
> covered with big red spots out of each of which a feather sprouts,
> regale us with Ciceronian speeches.[32]

Cocteau concludes from all this that Proust never knew love but
"only the maniacal tortures of his lies and his jealousy." Yet one must
observe that the passage he cites is not about love or sexuality but
sleep and that the deceased trapped in the rat cage are vague "relatives" and not the mother. Cocteau's diagnosis of Proust's deprivation of love elicits pity and then admiration for the good use the
novelist made of the tortures he "endured in the rituals of the rue de
l'Arcade," torture that he ultimately "transcended" at the conclusion
of his novel, where the bitter lessons learned from vanity and cruelty
are converted into the positive forces of art.[33]

As for "Gabriel," it is impossible to identify him. Since Cocteau
placed Jupien's name next to his, one might conclude that Cocteau is
simply mistaken about Le Cuziat's given name, Albert, but that seems

unlikely. A notation a few pages later indicates that Cocteau is confusing his brothels, situating Albert (Le Cuziat's) in the rue de Madrid and Gabriel's in the rue de l'Arcade.[34] But that matters little since we know that the entrepreneurial Le Cuziat operated several different establishments.

After Proust's death, Céleste heard the disturbing rumors about the caged rats at Le Cuziat's, a story that made her scoff, as did any gossip that might discredit her hero. But Proust admitted to André Gide, whose credibility seems unquestionable, that he did engage in such practices. Gide recorded the conversation, published posthumously in his memoir *Ainsi soit-il:*

> During a memorable nighttime conversation (of which there were so few that I remember each of them well) Proust explained his preoccupation with combining the most diverse sensations and emotions in order to achieve orgasm. That was the justification for his interest in rats, among other things; in any case Proust wanted me to see it as such. Above all, I saw it as the admission of some type of psychological inadequacy.[35]

Unfortunately, Gide provides no details about "the diverse sensations" that Proust employed as a stimulus to reach orgasm. There is sufficient testimony to lend credibility to the allegation that one of Proust's methods involved the profanation of photographs. The police raid, the only official document known that describes Le Cuziat's brothel in the rue de l'Arcade, a raid that involved a thorough search of the hotel, makes no mention of caged rats or photograph albums being found on the premises. We will also see that, in spite of Morand's diary entry on the topic of rats and the photograph of Proust's mother, no direct testimony has been found so far to support the allegation that the novelist used her photograph in such a sordid situation. The absence of testimony proves nothing one way or the other, but it does seem pertinent to point out that although Mlle Vinteuil and her lover profane the photograph of her father during their lesbian love ritual, the theme of parental profanation is present in

Proust's earliest writings, long before he began to frequent male brothels. "A Young Girl's Confession," which contains the prototype of the Vinteuil scene, was written in 1894, when Proust was only twenty-three years old.

Proust's fetish for photographs—another trait shared with the Narrator—is well documented. Both men go to great lengths to acquire pictures of attractive men and women, especially ones that capture the androgynous resemblances between siblings or other relatives. The exceedingly handsome Saint-Loup resembles his aunt the duchesse de Guermantes, the Parisian beauty whom the smitten Narrator follows in the streets of Paris and whose photograph he goes to great lengths to obtain, with no success. The Narrator's obsession with photographs matches Proust's own lifelong attempts to possess photographs of those he found attractive.

Paul Morand was one of those favored by being shown the pictures: "Proust adored old photographs," which, when he had visitors, he liked to "spread out on his bed and comment upon."[36] The novelist had inherited his great uncle Louis's rich photographic collection of Paris's celebrated beauties. Known to be quite a ladies' man, Louis had kept many photographs of cocottes, actresses, singers, and dancers, who had eagerly inscribed on the pictures their affection for the man who had been so kind and "generous" to them. Among the photographs were ones of the "celebrated courtesan Laure Hayman," who had been the mistress of Proust's father, and a prized photograph of the talented American soprano Marie van Zandt. Van Zandt, who had created the title role in Léo Delibes's opera *Lakmé*, had presented Dr. Proust with an inscribed photograph of herself dressed as a man, a travesty that delighted Proust and may have inspired Elstir's sexually ambiguous portrait of Odette as Miss Sacripant. Proust never missed an opportunity to enhance his uncle's and father's collections. When he won the Goncourt Prize in 1919 for *Within a Budding Grove*, the celebrated actress Réjane sent her son Jacques Porel to ask Proust what he would like as a present to express her happiness over his achievement.[37] Without hesitation, he requested that she give him a photograph of herself dressed as the Prince de Sagan, an androgynous vision that thrilled him. The actress gladly obliged and signed the photograph, "Homage from a Prince, Admiration from an artist, Friendship from a friend."[38] Morand recalled Proust's having shown him "astonishing" pictures of "his family, Reynaldo Hahn and Lucien Daudet in their youth."[39]

Maurice Sachs's *Le Sabbat* gives the fullest description of Proust's alleged abuse of the photographs at the brothel. While the male prostitutes spat on the photographs of Proust's distinguished lady friends, such as the picture of "the princesse de C***," the young men would ask, "as instructed, 'Who's that whore?'"[40]

Sachs's book, which reads like memoirs because it is about himself and those he knew, bears the disclaiming description "roman" (novel). Not generally considered the most reliable of witnesses, Sachs was for a time a protégé of Jean Cocteau's and André Gide's; Gide influenced Proust's publisher, Gaston Gallimard, to hire Sachs in 1933. Sachs thought nothing of stealing original drawings and manuscripts from his friends, selling them, and keeping the money. Among the books he sold were autographed editions of Proust and Apollinaire. When his misdeeds were brought to light, he forged a letter from Cocteau authorizing him to sell rare papers and editions. The infuriated Gallimard fired the swindler.[41]

Jean Mouton told Morand about Proust's taste for profanation, a confirmation that Morand notes in his diary, and to which he added this parenthetical notation: "(the photograph of his mother, taken to the brothel in the rue de l'Arcade)."[42] Proust may well have taken his mother's image to the brothel for defilement, but Morand's parenthetical addition refers to George D. Painter's biography, which he was rereading at the time. Painter maintains that Proust had one of the male prostitutes spit on a photograph of his mother and cites as proof an article by Maurice Sachs written on the occasion of Albert Le Cuziat's death. Had Morand checked Painter's source he would have found that it contains nothing about the profanation of the mother's photograph.[43] In fact, Sachs does not mention Proust's mother as a victim of profanation in either *Le Sabbat* or the article cited by Painter, but he does speak of *In Search of Lost Time* as a shrine to her, a sentiment in direct contradiction to the biographer's interpretation of his own missing evidence.[44]

Céleste, always quick to defend Proust, raises a practical objection to the story of his taking the photographs to the brothel. Since Proust routinely rang for her to come to his room and hand him any item he needed that was not next to him on the bedside table, she simply refused to believe that he, with no assistance, could find the box of photographs, wrap it up, transport it to a brothel, and then return home with it. "The only thing he ever took out with him was sugar, which he had me do up in a parcel to give as a present to my sister-in-law, Adèle Larivière, when it was rationed during the war."[45] It is always possible, of course, that Proust had Céline or Nicolas Cottin wrap the photographs for him in the years preceding Céleste's arrival at 102 boulevard Haussmann.

Morand's persistent anti-Semitism is evident in his entry about Proust and the "taste for profanation." Which he finds "very Jewish," remarking that he can "still see Maurice de Rothschild, with a look of rapture on his face, caressing his statues of gothic virgins in his home on the rue de Monceau." Proust tried to cure Morand of his anti-Semitism by giving the diplomat his six-volume set of Joseph Reinach's *Histoire de l'Affaire Dreyfus*. The cure, unfortunately, proved totally ineffective.[46]

The details of the amorous relationship between Proust and the men to whom he was attracted are likely to remain unknown. Louis Gautier-Vignal, who often saw Proust during the period after Agostinelli's death and observed his poor health and dependence on others—especially Céleste—believed that all of the novelist's crushes on young men were platonic, going so far as to speculate that he was impotent.[47] Proust himself hints at his lack of sexual energy in a letter to Jacques Porel: "The neighbors in the adjoining room make love . . . every day with a frenzy which makes me jealous. When I think that in my case this sensation is weaker than that obtained from drinking a cold beer, I envy those people who can cry out in such a way."[48] His occasional broadcasting in letters to acquaintances of his lack of sexual energy forms part of the famous Proustian litany of illnesses.

Proust's apparent resignation to having seen the last of his days as an active, energetic lover may be reflected in a scene in *Sodom and Gomorrah*. On a summer's day at Balbec, while riding with Albertine on the little train that serves the coastal towns, the Narrator falls under the spell of a "glorious girl" who boards the train at one of its many stops and enters their compartment: "I could not take my eyes off her magnolia skin, her dark eyes, the bold and admirable composition of her forms." She asks permission to open the window and then to smoke; the enthralled Narrator grants both requests.[49] At the third stop, the girl "sprang from the train." The next day he asks Albertine who the girl could be and exclaims that he "should so like to see her again." Albertine, who does not know the girl, advises him not to worry: "One always sees people again." This cheery prediction does not come true: "I never saw her again," but "I never forgot her." At intervals, he finds himself, when thinking of her, "seized by a wild longing." We then come to the apparent reason for the episode: he proclaims his nostalgia for lost youth, and with it, the energy fueled by lust. Time ultimately saps our sexual energy and wreaks devastation upon youth and beauty:

> We can sometimes find a person again but we cannot abolish time. And so on until the unforeseen day, gloomy as a winter night, when one no longer seeks that girl, or any other, when to find her would actually scare one. For one no longer feels that one has attractions enough to please, or strength enough to love. Not, of course, that one is in the strict sense of the word impotent. And as for loving, one would love more than ever. But one feels that it is too big an undertaking for the little strength one has left.

Proust then gives some examples of the decrepitude of old age ("Setting one's foot on the right step is an achievement, like bringing off a somersault"), when one's energy and stamina diminish ("One can no longer face the strain of keeping up with the young"), even though the sex drive may rise ("Too bad if carnal desire increases instead of languishing!"). What to do? The easy, obvious solution is to hire a prostitute: "One procures for it [carnal desire] a woman whom one need make no effort to please, who will share one's couch for one night only and whom one will never see again."[50]

One senses in this episode, as at so many junctures in the book, that the author's longings, deprivations, and sexual inadequacy have been transferred to the Narrator. As the novel progresses, it becomes clear that Proust burdened his fictional counterpart with a number of the same illnesses, including neurasthenia, that leave the hero weakened and depressed. He is also discouraged, as he reminds us periodically, by his apparent lack of talent for his chosen vocation as a writer and his woeful lack of energy and will to work.

Proust may not have been impotent in the "strict sense of the word," but it seems clear that in the last decade or so of his life he devoted nearly all his energy to writing his novel. And what a tremendous amount of energy that must have required. He had, as his hero reminds us, once his labors finally begin, undertaken the awesome task of "transcribing a universe which had to be totally redrawn."[51] Proust created for himself an apparent handicap by consuming huge doses of stimulants to stay awake and work followed by soporifics to sleep. Morand once warned him that this practice was like driving recklessly with his feet pressing "the accelerator and the brake at the same time."[52] Proust's literary exertion left him exhausted, which is not surprising, given his peculiar regimen and excessive and self-prescribed use of drugs, all of which hindered his pursuit of desirable young men. Whether Proust was impotent, we cannot say; we do know that he continued to enjoy surrounding himself with attractive youths and may have been capable of seducing them as well.

Looking back over his love life, it seems fair to say that Proust never had a sexually fulfilling relationship with a companion whom he loved. If he did, one finds no definite trace of such affection in his letters and writings. It seems unlikely that he could have found a partner capable of satisfying his great longings or with sufficient patience to endure his endless and unreasonable demands. In the end, he became disillusioned about erotic love. The Narrator, commenting on Charles Swann's long, troubled liaison with Odette, reaches the same disheartening conclusion about "the act of physical possession (in which, paradoxically, the possessor possesses nothing)."[53]

Proust often lightens such depressing conclusions by giving us in other passages a humorous version of such plights, including some of the homosexual encounters, even those that are the most troubling because of their masochistic components. Here are only a few scenes of many that could be cited of high—and low—comedy related to sexual matters: Charlus, thwarted in his attempts to spy on Morel during his assignation with the prince de Guermantes in the brothel; Legrandin's having grown thin from rushing in and out of male brothels in order to avoid being seen; Charlus's inability to find, in wartime Paris, a genuinely brutal partner to flog him during his masochistic fantasy. And when the Narrator, after much anticipation and a failed first attempt, finally succeeds in kissing Albertine on the cheek, his sole benefit is the realization of how inadequate a kiss can be. He tells himself, as he leans over to kiss her, that " 'Now at last . . . I am going to discover the fragrance of the secret rose that blooms in Albertine's cheeks . . . where I shall at last have knowledge of it through my lips.' I told myself this because I believed that there was such a thing as knowledge acquired by the lips; I told myself that I was going to know the taste of this fleshly rose, because I had not stopped to think that man, a creature obviously less rudimentary than the sea-urchin or even the whale, nevertheless lacks a certain number of essential organs, and notably possesses none that will serve for kissing. For this absent organ he substitutes his lips, and thereby arrives perhaps at a slightly more satisfying result than if he were reduced to caressing the beloved with a horny tusk."[54]

CHAPTER TEN

The Boys from the Rit{

We fall in love for a smile, a look, a shoulder. That is enough;

then, in the long hours of hope or sorrow, we fabricate a person,

we compose a character.

By the middle of 1918, the last summer of World War I, Proust had a compelling reason for wanting to remain in Paris in spite of an antici- pated final German offensive, with the conquest of Paris as its objec- tive. He had met at the Ritz Hotel a young waiter named Henri Rochat, who had captivated him. We know about his attraction to young waiters, and how he recruited them to serve him, from an interview given many years after Proust's death by Camille Wixler, who had been a waiter at the Ritz during the war.[1] Swiss like Rochat, Wixler, who was only nineteen when he met Proust, had learned his trade at the École Hôtelière de Lausanne and come to Paris as an apprentice under Olivier Dabescat. One day Dabescat told Wixler that Proust had noticed him and wondered whether he would be willing to wait his table. The young man gladly accepted, having heard about the enormous tips that the writer gave.

The personnel at the Ritz were expected, of course, to cater to the whims of tardy diners. Waiters were forbidden to look at the clock, and if a guest wanted to stay late in the restaurant, there was always someone to serve him either a meal or coffee or cigars and liqueurs. But no one in those days expected such service around midnight, with the exception of Marcel Proust.

That first evening with Wixler as his waiter, the novelist had an unusually hearty appetite. He requested freshly roasted young chicken with potatoes and fresh vegetables, followed by a salad, for which the chef prepared a vinaigrette containing chives. Proust sometimes had vanilla ice cream for dessert if the waiter pronounced it good. Wixler must have recommended the Ritz's ices, but, since he had been *chef glacier* in his previous post, he offered to fix his own special recipe for the writer the next time. Proust asked to have his coffee served in the small salon and, warning Wixler that he drank many cups, suggested that he bring a large and very full pot.

During the meal, and afterward in the small salon, where he consumed a dozen or so demitasses of coffee and then asked for more, Proust chatted and asked questions about the personnel. He was especially curious about Wixler's compatriot Henri Rochat. Could Wixler ask whether Rochat would be willing to serve his table? Wixler "agreed to this, naturally, and instructed Rochat" on what Proust liked. Not long afterward, when Wixler asked whether Rochat was proving satisfactory, Proust answered in the affirmative, adding that he had offered the young man an occupation better suited to his abilities, an apparent reference to the position of secretary.

We have no photographs and only vague physical descriptions of Rochat. Wixler said that he was handsome, and he certainly must have been, at least according to the writer's standards. We know that he had a fair complexion and brown hair because, as we shall see, Proust contrasted Rochat's darker mane with Ernest Forssgren's blond good looks in a gossipy letter to the duchess of Clermont-Tonnerre about sexual practices generally considered perverse.

After Proust's death, an unsent note to Dabescat was found among his papers. It reads like the kind of excuse a parent writes for a child who has to miss school. Proust began by telling "cher Olivier" that he was "embarrassed" to ask him yet again for a favor on Rochat's behalf: the young man was not well and needed to see a doctor and therefore asked "permission not to come to work today." Proust enclosed two hundred francs for all the trouble he was causing the maître d'hôtel. "I believe that this will be the last time I torment you in this regard. Your devoted and grateful Marcel Proust."[2]

Wixler had recently noticed that when he and Rochat changed from street clothes into their uniforms at the Ritz, Rochat now wore handsome suits and underclothes of the finest quality. Aware that his colleague's salary at the Ritz did not permit such indulgences, Wixler asked how he could afford such expensive garments. Rochat "answered frankly and even with pride that he did so with the aid of M. Proust."

It finally dawned on Wixler that Proust was using him to procure young waiters, apparently for sexual trysts at boulevard Haussmann. The moment of illumination occurred on the first evening that Wixler delivered a takeout dinner from the Ritz to Proust's apartment.[3] Proust asked him whether he thought that a new, very young waiter by the name of Vanelli would come to see him. Suddenly suspicious of the writer's motives, Wixler replied that Vanelli was not the type to accept such a proposition, no matter how large the tips. Proust had a different opinion, however, and instructed Wixler to put it to the young man bluntly. Wixler was astounded when Vanelli asked to be introduced to Proust, even before he had the chance to broach the subject. He reported Vanelli's eagerness to Proust, who said that he would come to the Ritz that night. While Wixler served the novelist dinner, he left the important task of serving the coffee to Vanelli. Vanelli went home with Proust and in no time became his favorite. According to Wixler, this was shortly before Rochat sailed for South America in June 1921.

Wixler's information about Rochat seems accurate: Proust did hire him as his secretary, rapidly grew weary of him as a companion, and eventually found him a post in faraway Buenos Aires. Regarding Vanelli, the situation is less clear. If the waiter of such tender years did succeed Rochat as Proust's "favorite," he did so without leaving any traces in the documents and memoirs that we have.

Around the time that Proust met Rochat, he described for Lucien Daudet an evening at the Ritz when the openly gay Count Antoine Sala and his friends, who usually occupied a table in the dining room, were absent; this made the service exceptionally good, "since the waiters did not have to flee towards the kitchen except to serve the dishes" or "run outside to the Place Vendôme."[4] Proust apparently excluded himself from those who interfered with the smooth service at the Ritz, since his own courting of the waiters usually took place at such a late hour that other customers were not inconvenienced by his interrogations and discreet flirtations.

Paul Morand provides the first detailed portrait that I have found of Proust the seducer of young men. Henri Bardac, a close friend of Morand's and Proust's—indeed it was Bardac who arranged for Morand to meet the novelist—told Morand about Proust's favorite stratagem for enticing bellhops. Proust would ring for the bellboy and then begin washing his hands. When the boy entered the room, Proust, who was leaning over the sink, would say to him, "My friend, I have a tip for you, but I can't give it to you because my hands are wet; please get it out of my pants pocket."[5]

Maurice Duplay once caught Proust in a compromising position with a handsome young actor when he arrived in the novelist's apartment unannounced. "I had visibly disturbed them. The young stranger jumped up awkwardly, causing some papers to slide off the desk, his face crimson." Duplay noted the youth's regular features and thick black hair parted in the middle. "Marcel, who had made a quick recovery" from Duplay's surprise entrance, "made the introductions."[6] Unfortunately, this is all the information that Duplay gives; there is no hint of the approximate date of his intrusion.

By late summer 1918, shortly after he met Rochat, Proust began to exhibit the same lovesick symptoms found in the prewar letters when he was falling in love with Agostinelli. In mid-September, Proust wrote Hauser that for two months he had suffered great heartaches.

To Blanche he spoke of a "great mental suffering of which I shall certainly die and which is poisoning my life." He informed Mme Straus that his health was "rather less poor" but that he had "embarked on sentimental things without resolution, without joy," which were "perpetual sources of fatigue, suffering, and absurd expenditures."[7] He never, of course, revealed to these friends that the object of his affection and the source of his "sentimental" joys and woes was a waiter at the Ritz.

Céleste agrees that Proust recruited Rochat at the Ritz but, being naïve or perhaps overly protective, insists that her employer took the young man as an act of charity and because he was touched by Rochat's ambition to become a painter. Proust used to say to her, somewhat disdainfully, whenever the young man was busy at his easel: "He thinks he's painting." Her description of Rochat as "surly and silent" is close, as we shall see, to Proust's own characterization of him.[8]

Paul Morand, who claims to have known Proust's "lovers" from the servant class, says they were all alike: "From Le Cuziat to Rochat, all Proust's lovers were boring and bored boys, weak, nondescript, who remained imprisoned until they couldn't put up with Proust's jealousy anymore. *All of them liked women* (hence the frequency of lesbian affairs in the novel)."[9]

As for class distinctions, Proust claimed to make none. In a 1913 letter to the hostess and art lover Misia Sert, he had answered her "stupid" question about whether or not he was "a snob." He told her that "if among the very rare friends who still, out of habit, stop to see" how he is doing, "there happens to be a duke or a prince, they are more than offset by other friends of whom one is a valet [Le Cuziat] and the other a chauffeur [Agostinelli] and whom I treat better [than the nobles]. All of them are just as worthy. The valets are better educated than the dukes and speak a much prettier French, but they are more punctilious regarding etiquette and, being less simple, are more sensitive." He ended his praise of the servants by adding that "the chauffeur is more distinguished."[10]

This egalitarian attitude is given to the Narrator's mother, grand-mother, and the protagonist himself:

> I had never made any distinction between working people, the middle classes and the nobility, and I should have been equally ready to make any of them my friends. With a certain preference for working people, and after them for the nobility, not because I liked them better but because I knew that one could expect greater courtesy from them towards working people than one finds among the middle classes.[11]

Before publishing *Swann's Way*, Proust told Mme Straus that he wanted to "reach a wider audience" by writing for "the sort of people who buy a badly printed volume before catching a train."[12] Proust sums up his view of social rank and intellectual capacity in the novel: "The classes of the intellect take no account of birth."[13]

The novel's haughtiest aristocrat, Charlus, takes great risks, not unlike Proust's earlier nemesis, the frequently battered Jean Lorrain, while pursuing sexual adventures. The baron justifies his behavior by explaining that he seeks a certain ideal masculine beauty, which may manifest itself in men of all social ranks and morals or complete lack thereof: "I, who have had so many ups and downs in my life, who have known all manner of people, thieves as well as kings, and indeed, I must confess, with a slight preference for the thieves, I who have pursued beauty in all its forms . . ."[14]

Did it really matter whether Rochat and Proust's other presumed lovers from the servant class were truly as dull and unappealing as Morand claims, given the subjective nature of love and desire? The diplomat did not see the young men with Proust's eyes. And if Proust gazed at them with impossible yearnings, he did so without illusion. While considering Albertine's intellectual gifts, the Narrator says this about love and the eyes of the beholder:

> There could be no denying that I had known people whose intel-ligence was greater. But the infinitude of love, or its egoism, brings it

about that the people whom we love are those whose intellectual and moral physiognomy is least objectively defined in our eyes; we alter them incessantly to suit our desire and fears, we do not separate them from ourselves, they are simply a vast, vague arena in which to exteriorise our emotions.[15]

In the second half of his life, when Proust apparently chose his lovers exclusively from the servant class, Rochat and the others met the requirements of subjective and illusory love, providing the vast, vague arena in which Proust exteriorized his emotions. In his idle hours, he never sought the company of his intellectual and artistic peers. He explained his attitude regarding this in a letter to Sydney Schiff: "I do my intellectual work within myself, and once among my fellow men, it doesn't much matter to me whether they are intelligent as long as they are kind, sincere, etc."[16]

Proust and his Narrator suffer from an "incapacity for happiness." The author's lifelong habit of observing others and himself, of imagining himself to be other than he was, of inventing situations in which he might be happy, of creating in his mind painful dramas in which friends and lovers betrayed and shunned him, of analyzing the behavior of people in society in all their pretentious and vain actions—all this had prepared him for the task of inventing a rich, complex fictional world. He explained as much to a young writer, Emmanuel Berl, with whom he began to correspond when Berl was a soldier in the trenches during the war:

It is my fate to be incapable of deriving profit from anyone but myself. This is not to try to justify the absurd life I lead (not entirely of my own volition). But I am myself only when alone, and I profit from others only to the extent that they enable me to make discoveries within myself, either by making me suffer (hence rather through love than through friendship) or by their absurdities (which I don't like to see in a friend) which I don't mock but which help me to understand human character.[17]

Céleste, not surprisingly, refuted the rumors that Rochat and Proust were lovers by pointing out that the floor plan of Proust's apartment made secret trysts between Proust and his protégé impossible, which seems to beg the question. The writer's room, she observes, was at one end of the apartment, Rochat's at the other. Between them, there was a living room and a sitting room to cross. Her own room "opened onto the hall and was a sort of combined cockpit and listening post commanding the whole apartment. No one coming and going could have escaped me."[18]

Sometime in late 1918 or early 1919, Rochat accepted the position as Proust's secretary, although he, like Agostinelli before him, had no qualifications for such work. Rochat was taciturn and uneducated, at least in writing and speaking French; his pronunciation and spelling of his adopted language were poor, although he wrote in a fine hand. Perhaps his ability to trace beautiful letters convinced him that he had a talent for painting.

Proust's associates must have wondered what he could possibly see in Henri Rochat. Such infatuations always puzzle one's friends, who are at a loss, of course, to see the object of affection through the eyes of the beloved. Beauty, as we saw in Françoise's doggerel verse, resides in the eye of the beholder. Once in love, one cannot resist pursuing the illusion to which one's friends are blind, a circumstance that leaves them totally perplexed, if not horrified, at the lover's apparently ridiculous behavior. Such plights allow Proust to show his fine sense of humor:

> People whose own hearts are not directly involved always regard unfortunate entanglements, disastrous marriages as though one were free to choose whom one loves, and do not take into account the exquisite mirage which love projects and which envelops so entirely and so uniquely the person with whom one is in love that the "folly" a man commits by marrying his cook or the mistress of his best friend is as a rule the only poetical action that he performs in the course of his existence.[19]

Proust had written in a similar comic vein about the reaction of the duchesse de Guermantes (then known as Mme des Laumes) to Swann's love for Odette:

> "Poor Swann," said Mme des Laumes that night to her husband, "he's as charming as ever, but he does look so dreadfully unhappy. You'll see for yourself, as he has promised to dine with us one of these days. I do feel it's absurd that a man of his intelligence should let himself suffer for a woman of that sort, and one who isn't even interesting, for they tell me she's an absolute idiot!" she added with the wisdom invariably shown by people who, not being in love themselves, feel that a clever man should only be unhappy about a person who is worth his while; which is rather like being astonished that anyone should condescend to die of cholera at the bidding of so insignificant a creature as the comma bacillus.[20]

The subjective nature of love is so evident and so prevalent that the Narrator sums it up in a humorous one-liner: "Let us leave pretty women to men with no imagination."[21] Using humor again to depict love as a superb folly, he maintains that what we often mistake for a reciprocated feeling of affection is merely the ricochet of our own love bouncing back at us, making us fall even more in love with our own illusions:

> When we are in love, our love is too big a thing for us to be able altogether to contain it within ourselves. It radiates towards the loved one, finds there a surface which arrests it, forcing it to return to its starting-point, and it is this repercussion of our own feeling which we call the other's feelings and which charms us more then than on its outward journey because we do not recognize it as having originated in ourselves.[22]

Cohabitation with Rochat quickly led to complications. Once ensconced in Proust's apartment, he immediately developed a taste for luxury and must have been rather demanding in having his expensive whims fulfilled. As the Narrator observes, "In love it often happens that gratitude, the desire to give pleasure, makes us generous beyond the limits of what hope and self-interest had foreseen."[23] Proust's letters leave no doubt as to the young man's talent for running up bills. Rochat clearly liked jewels, although we don't know whether he wore them, as did Prince Constantin Radziwill's footmen, or simply admired them in private, seeing them as beautiful objects that also represented solid investments. Rochat appears to have wanted the jewels for himself, because there is no mention of his having given any of them to his fiancée, his engagement to whom, Proust told a friend in a letter, was kept secret. When Proust began catering to Rochat's wishes, he rapidly depleted an emergency fund of twenty thousand francs he had reserved to flee Paris should the Germans advance too close to the capital in their expected final offensive. Then he had to borrow another ten thousand, just to keep his companion happy.[24] Rochat attached himself to Proust with all the tenacity of a barnacle on a rock. He stayed in the writer's service for approximately two and a half years, during which time he cost his protector a lot of money—money that Proust was forced to borrow or raise by selling off his few remaining investments.

Proust's letters to his friends indicate that Rochat had become the writer's first protracted infatuation since the ill-fated Agostinelli. Still, although the waiter's stay in Proust's apartment lasted many times longer than Agostinelli's, it proved much less consequential for the novel. Rochat did apparently contribute several minor traits to Albertine, including her ambition to become a painter. The jealous Narrator, having persuaded Albertine to take up residence in his apartment, sees her as a captive, "sitting now in my room, now in her own, engaged in some work of design or engraving."[25] The loose "captivity" in which he keeps the girl is similar to that of Rochat, who, as Céleste recalled, once Proust had tired of his company and saw that he was of little use as a secretary, "stayed in his room daubing at his painting or else he went out. We hardly saw him. M. Proust said: 'As far as work goes, he tires rather than helps me.'"[26] Céleste watched as charity became pity, the writer's attitude—confirmed by his letters—

vacillating between wanting to get rid of Rochat and being too tender-hearted to throw him out into the street.

In spite of Proust's illnesses and the mounting piles of proof for the forthcoming volumes, he kept a fairly busy social calendar that spring of 1919. He met Harold Nicolson, the British diplomat and delegate to the Paris Peace Conference, at the March dinner celebrating the engagement of Proust's friend the Romanian Prince Antoine Bibesco to Elizabeth Asquith, daughter of the British prime minister. If Proust knew the story of Nicolson's marriage, he would certainly have found it intriguing. Nicolson and the novelist Vita Sackville-West formed a devoted if unusual couple; each was bisexual and had agreed to tolerate the other's extramarital flings. Sackville-West's most famous love affair was to be with Virginia Woolf. (The Nicolsons' son Nigel later recounted his parents' unusual arrangement in *Portrait of a Marriage*.) Proust wrote Antoine Bibesco that he found Nicolson "exquisite and incredibly intelligent!"[27] Nicolson later saw Proust at two dinners at the Ritz, both of which he recorded in the diary he kept during the difficult negotiations at the peace conference.[28]

The second dinner took place at the end of April on an unusually chilly and stormy day. Among those present were the painter Jean de Gaigneron and Gladys Deacon, an American beauty who was to marry Winston Churchill's cousin, Charles Spencer Churchill, the duke of Marlborough. Nicolson thought that Gladys looked "very attic" and Proust "very Hebrew." During the dinner, the two men discussed homosexuality. As we see in the scant notes from Nicolson's diary, Proust was uncharacteristically tongue-tied on the subject and made a poor impression: "We discuss inversion. Whether it is a matter of glands or nerves. He says it is a matter of habit. I say, 'surely not.' He says, 'No—that was silly of me—what I meant was that it was a matter of delicacy.' He is not very intelligent on the subject."[29]

Alas, Nicolson gives us no further details about what either man said on a topic that both knew intimately. Did the presence of a lady inhibit Proust from saying more about a favorite subject? Normally, he, like Charlus, never tired of talking about homosexuality.

Morand's homosexual friends, including Proust and other distinguished writers, exasperated him by their preoccupation with the topic, which he saw as one of their chief characteristics: "All homosexuals are so obsessed, in this sense, that even when they are famous writers, they lose all sense of proportion: Proust, Montherlant, Gide, [Roger] Peyrefitte, etc. Even when they are not talking about it, they talk about it!"[30]

Self-knowledge and, along with it, the ability to poke fun at the foibles we all share are among Proust's strongest attributes. He depicts his obsessive interest in homosexuality in Charlus, whose knowledge on the topic is so extensive that he is said to merit a theoretical chair of homosexuality at the Sorbonne: " 'Decidedly, Baron [Charlus],' said Brichot, 'should the University Council ever think of founding a Chair of Homosexuality, I shall see that your name is the first to be submitted.' " Although clearly jocular, Brichot's remarks show that Proust appreciated the importance that homosexuality was to assume later in the century as a major social and political issue and thus anticipated the creation by universities of departments of gay and lesbian studies. This passage may also be taken as an indication that Proust was sensitive to Paul Morand's satiety on hearing him and others expound endlessly on the subject:

> The insistence with which M. de Charlus kept reverting to this topic—into which his mind, constantly exercised in the same direction, had indeed acquired a certain penetration—was in a rather complex way distinctly trying. He was as boring as a specialist who can see nothing outside his own subject, as irritating as an initiate who prides himself on the secrets which he possesses and is burning to divulge, as repellent as those people who, whenever their own weaknesses are in question, blossom and expatiate without noticing that they are giving offence, as obsessed as a maniac and as uncontrollably imprudent as a criminal.[31]

Proust no doubt would have enjoyed swapping stories with Nicolson, indulging in the kind of gossip that delighted him, a characteristic fully embodied by Charlus, who revels in making scandalous revelations about other characters. Sexual relations, explicit or alleged, between Proust's characters often have the madcap nature of a bedroom farce. The baron even hints that he and Charles Swann may have been lovers; that he, Charlus, slept with Odette because he had "thought her charming in her boyish get-up one evening when she played the role of the androgynous Miss Sacripant"; that Odette "used to force me to get up the most dreadful orgies for her, with five or six men"; that in the course of an argument Odette once tried to kill Swann and fired a revolver at him and nearly hit Charlus instead.[32] Had there been fewer people at the dinner with Nicolson, Proust might have dared to regale him with tales of the sadistic scenes he had witnessed at Le Cuziat's brothel.

On May 1, 1919, Proust wrote to his American friend Walter Berry and listed all the preoccupations that kept him from even thinking about his precarious financial situation. These included the impending and dreaded move from 102 boulevard Haussmann—a move made necessary by his aunt's sale of the building to a banking firm—work on his novel, bad health, and "the end of an unhappy love affair."[33] His affection for Rochat may have been waning, but the young man's sojourn with Proust was far from over.

During the nearly three years when Rochat resided in his apartment, Proust occasionally invited a male friend, a critic, or a budding writer, such as Paul Morand or François Mauriac, to dine at his bedside. These intimate dinner parties, usually consisting of only two or three guests, due to the cramped quarters and Céleste's nearly nonexistent culinary skills, often included Rochat. Proust assured guests in his invitations that his secretary "will not trouble us because he never says anything."[34]

Céleste recalled that even when Proust "had a guest, he stayed in bed," but he did, for the occasion, put on "fresh pajamas." After clearing "the little table where the tray was usually left," she "laid a cloth and set a single place for the visitor. M. Proust used to decide on the menu, which was always much the same—I think he adapted it to my ability. Usually it was fillets of sole, chicken, and an ice from Poire-Blanche's. Sometimes there was just chicken and ice, or fruit."[35]

In the course of these intimate but festive late-evening suppers, Proust usually drank only water but offered his visitors champagne or, as a memento of Cabourg-Balbec, bubbly cider from Normandy. When the cork was pulled, the warm, sparkling cider sent a "geyser" of froth to the ceiling.[36] Mauriac, who spent one such evening with Proust and the exceptionally quiet Rochat in February 1921, recorded his impressions of the "strange supper at ten in the evening" served next to Proust's bed, on which a "coat served as a blanket."[37] Although Proust was the author whom Mauriac had most wanted to meet, he was unprepared for the conditions he found on his first and only visit to rue Hamelin. His journal entry describes, with more than a hint of anti-Semitism, the depressing atmosphere and Proust's sordid appearance: "linen not beyond reproach, the odor of this apartment, his Jewish head with its beard of ten days, a return to ancestral filth."

While Mauriac and Rochat supped, Proust stared at his new acquaintance from behind a "wax mask" of which "only the hair seemed alive." On their first, brief meeting at a large social gathering, Mauriac had been intimidated by the steadiness of Proust's gaze, even though "the pupils" of his "nocturnal eyes" appeared "dilated by the use of drugs." Mauriac neglected to record any of the supper conversation, but he did note, without naming him, Rochat's presence: "H* . . . this boy who was to leave not long afterward for South America, where Proust had found a position for him." Mauriac can have had no illusions about the nature of the relationship between the sedentary author and this "boy." He left the apartment convinced that Proust was on the verge of becoming moribund, already "more than half-engaged in nonbeing," like an "enormous, proliferating mushroom that feeds upon its own substance, its opus: *Time Regained*."

Mauriac's vegetative analogy does not do justice to the tremendous amount of work that Proust was to accomplish during his remaining months—and with almost no assistance. Proust had long since stopped looking for ways in which Rochat might prove useful in preparing copy for the novel. Proust had asked him early on to read aloud the proofs of *The Guermantes Way* so that the writer could hear his own words and make any necessary corrections or revisions. Alas, Rochat proved inadequate to the task, mispronouncing words so frequently that Proust mistook what he heard and made unnecessary "corrections" that became new errors.[38] The practice of using Rochat as a reader had to be abandoned. From time to time, an exhausted Proust dictated some of his less personal letters to the young man.

Rochat did occasionally prove useful in merely practical matters. When Proust received an invitation to the opera from Misia Sert, he accepted and asked whether he could bring along his Swiss secretary. By then, Proust was living on rue Hamelin, where he had taken an apartment in a building with no elevator. In case he suffered an asthma attack, he would need the young man's strong arms to help him climb back up the winding staircase to his apartment on the sixth floor. Anticipating any objections Misia might have to rubbing elbows with someone of the servant class, he assured her that in the darkness of the taxi she would not mind at all being with someone who did not belong "to her world" and who furthermore is "someone whom all my friends know."[39]

Jean Cocteau was one of those friends who knew Rochat. Without naming him in his memoirs, Cocteau gives a description that matches what we know about the young man, though he calls him a bellhop rather than a waiter, a not terribly important error. Rochat was "a stupid bellhop whom he [Proust] housed and encouraged to paint. Proust got Walter Berry to purchase his canvases." Cocteau's version of Rochat's departure does not, however, coincide with the known details of his long residence in Proust's apartment. Rochat "complained that the windows were never open and the rupture came when he finally flung open a window with a bang. (One finds this scene in the novel.) He used to say to me. 'This place is suffocating.' I've forgotten whether he left or Céleste threw him out."[40] The sudden, unannounced departure matches Agostinelli's, not Rochat's.

Cocteau may be correct in attributing to Rochat the obscene expression that the Narrator overhears Albertine muttering about her intention "me faire casser le pot," a highly vulgar term for passive anal intercourse. Accusing Proust of being "naïve," Cocteau contends that "a woman, and even less a girl (and one who likes women), cannot utter such a phrase. On the other hand, it is exactly in the style of his bellboy." This and other remarks in his memoirs place Cocteau in the camp of those who believed that all Proust's girls in the novel are really boys in disguise.[41]

The bellboy is clearly Rochat—or mainly Rochat, for Cocteau seems to be conflating two or three men in his recollections. In any case, there are several inaccuracies in his account. Had Céleste had the authority to evict anyone without Proust's approval, she would have gotten rid of Ernest Forssgren and Henri Rochat at the earliest possible moment. We recall that Agostinelli and Anna left like fugitives before Céleste became Proust's housekeeper. There is one caveat to bear in mind while reading Cocteau's pages on Proust: He never makes any distinction at all between Proust and the Narrator; in fact, he never uses the term *Narrator*, only *Proust*, to refer to the protagonist of the novel. Perhaps we should not blame Cocteau too much for this confusion. When Proust wrote to friends, he nearly always spoke of the Narrator as "I." He did not portray the Narrator as himself— that is, as the real Marcel Proust—but when speaking about his book to others, he often assumed his hero's voice. As Proust lived more and more in the world he invented, he came to embody the Narrator rather than the other way around. Cocteau was clearly one of those who suffered, as Benjamin Crémieux had warned, from having known the author too well. In fact, as one reads what Cocteau wrote about Proust throughout *Le Passé défini*, one begins to suspect that he was settling old scores. Cocteau and Proust had at least one lover in common: Lucien Daudet. We know this from a letter Proust sent Reynaldo Hahn: "The *utmost* intimacy . . . reigns between Lucien and Cocteau, who went to stay with him in the country."[42]

In his memoirs, Cocteau quotes Daudet as saying that Proust "has no heart. 'No, no,' Lucien told me (and he really loved Marcel), 'No, my dear Jean, Marcel is a genius, but he is an atrocious insect. One day you will understand.'" Cocteau wrote these pages during the 1950s, when he felt that his own work was being neglected. Oddly enough, he credits Proust's success as a writer to his having found a great English translator. Following Daudet's insect quotation, Cocteau reveals a motive for his vendetta against Proust: "I didn't believe Lucien. I had, however, been astonished, when Marcel became famous, to see him abandon all his former friends and associate only with the N.R.F. group and critics (the infamous Souday among others—a true swine) to whom he offered Gargantuan meals at the Ritz."[43]

Cocteau is exaggerating. Proust became famous when he received the Goncourt Prize, France's most prestigious literary award, in December 1919 for *Within a Budding Grove*. Proust's letters show that he did not abandon his former friends; he and Cocteau had never been particularly close. Proust may well have been a monster, an insect, a sadist, and all the rest, and he did court members of the *Nouvelle Revue Française* editorial board and important critics who were judging his work, but in the light of Proust's accomplishments, Cocteau's diatribes against him stand out sharply as petty jealousy.

On May 31, 1919, Proust left his apartment at 102 boulevard Haussmann, where he had conceived and written most of *In Search of Lost Time*, to take up temporary residence at 8 bis, rue Laurent-Pichat, in an apartment that belonged to the celebrated actress Réjane, one of the idols of his youth. Proust had paid one month's rent on the assumption that he could quickly find more suitable lodgings, a challenge that forced him to prolong his stay until the fall. During this period, Proust became friends with Réjane's son, Jacques Porel, who still suffered from having been gassed during the war at Ypres. Porel and his beautiful wife occasionally dined at the Ritz with Proust and Princesse Soutzo.[44]

Proust's chief complaint about the new apartment was the thinness of the walls, especially without his cork, which had been put in storage while he looked for permanent quarters.[45] It was in this apartment that he overheard the noisy lovers in the room above his, which he described in a letter to Porel and later used for the homosexual encounter of Charlus and Jupien. The enervated Proust writes that he envied "those people who can cry out in such a way that the first time I thought a murder was taking place, although very soon the woman's cry, which was repeated an octave lower by the man, made me realize what was going on."[46] Proust concluded from the sounds heard, he tells Porel, that as soon as the couple's lovemaking ended, they leaped from their bed to take a sitz bath before performing the necessary household chores, which included taking care of children. Then Proust made an unusually frank confession. Although his remarks are vague and give no indication of the identity or sex of his hypothetical partner, he writes that "the absolute absence of any transition exhausts me on their behalf, for if there is anything I loathe *afterward*, or at least *immediately afterward*, it is having to move. Whatever the selfishness required in preserving the warmth of a mouth that has nothing more to receive."[47] Proust's description of his preferences when engaged in sex certainly suggests fellatio. Nothing in the letter indicates a homosexual rather than a heterosexual partner, but such a remark proves at least that Proust discussed such matters openly with a number of people whose discretion he trusted.

In the opening pages of *Sodom and Gomorrah*, published in 1921, Proust uses the same language and concern for cleanliness to describe two men, Jupien and Charlus, who engage in sex, apparently anal intercourse, judging from a kind of mating ritual dance performed by Jupien and the sounds and comments heard by the Narrator. Unseen by the two men, the Narrator witnesses their encounter in the courtyard before sneaking into a hiding place to overhear, as had Proust in the apartment, the sounds of their mating:

> From what I heard at first in Jupien's quarters, which was only a series of inarticulate sounds, I imagine that few words had been exchanged. It is true that these sounds were so violent that, if they had not always been taken up an octave higher by a parallel plaint, I might have thought that one person was slitting another's throat within a few feet of me, and that subsequently the murderer and his resuscitated victim were taking a bath to wash away the traces of the crime. I concluded from this . . . that there is another thing as noisy as pain, namely pleasure, especially when there is added to it . . . an immediate concern about cleanliness.[48]

This scene between Jupien and Charlus, and other homosexual encounters that occur later in the book, demonstrate the unprecedented nature of Proust's narrative. Balzac only hints at Vautrin's desire for Lucien de Rubempré; in *Sodom and Gomorrah*, Proust actually describes, at least through sounds and a minimum of dialogue, homosexuals having sex. *Time Regained* offers a sadistic homosexual tryst in Jupien's brothel similar to the scene witnessed at Le Cuziat's establishment, but leavened, as we have seen, with touches of humor.

The many pages Proust devoted to various types of homosexuals and their determined efforts to find partners made it difficult for those who wished to avoid the taboo subject to deny the existence of a significant colony of homosexuals, who, wrote Proust, were they to relocate in order "to create a Sodomist movement and to rebuild Sodom," would "take wives, keep mistresses in other cities where they would find . . . every diversion that appealed to them. . . . In other words, everything would go on very much as it does today in London, Berlin, Rome, Petrograd or Paris."[49]

Did Rochat's dreariness and taciturn nature drive Proust to consider homicide as the only means to rid himself of the tenacious young man? The novelist had already attempted on two occasions to dispatch Rochat to a foreign country and a new career. Each time Rochat's dreams of finding a lucrative business position had fallen through and he had come running back to his protector in Paris. The Narrator, who considers the once desirable Albertine a "burdensome slave" now that she inhabits his apartment, dreads the prospect of committing a violent act to rid himself of her:

> Every person we love, indeed to a certain extent every person, is to us like Janus, presenting to us a face that pleases us if the person leaves us, a dreary face if we know him or her to be at our perpetual disposal. In the case of Albertine, the prospect of her continued society was painful to me in another way in which I cannot explain in this narrative. It is terrible to have the life of another person attached to one's own like a bomb which one holds in one's hands, unable to get rid of it without committing a crime.[50]

As a third attempt to dislodge Rochat, Proust asked his wealthy childhood friend Horace Finaly, now director of the Banque de Paris et des Pays-Bas, to find Henri a job in the Buenos Aires branch of the bank.[51] On June 4, 1921, Rochat finally left France on a ship bound for Argentina. In a letter to a friend, Proust expressed his amazement at having at last succeeded in finding a satisfactory position for Rochat in a faraway place: "I have found him a very good post in America, a considerable feat on my part, I may say, considering what he is like. I always bungle the things I want for myself, but sometimes, very rarely, I succeed in doing something for others."[52]

A short time later Proust told the princesse Soutzo that, upon his departure for South America, Rochat had expressed a single regret: that he had to leave Paris without ever having seen her. "He said this with no hint of familiarity, as he would have spoken of not having seen the Mona Lisa."[53]

Ever the curious writer, Proust had followed Rochat's courtship of the young woman who lived in the rue des Acacias and who was "more or less" his fiancée. When Rochat had the opportunity to leave for Buenos Aires, he coldheartedly jilted the girl.[54] Proust called on her in an attempt to console her, playing the same role he had assumed years earlier when the marquis Louis d'Albufera, about to be married, had dumped his mistress Louisa de Mornand.[55]

Certain aspects of Rochat can be found in the character Morel, the son of the Narrator's uncle's valet, who becomes Charlus's great love. Morel is engaged to Jupien's niece, who, like Rochat's fiancée, belongs to the servant class. As we have seen, Morel is bisexual, as was Rochat: Morel "was sufficiently fond of both women and men to satisfy either sex with the fruits of his experience of the other."[56] Rochat's sexual escapades proved costly for Proust, whose letters reveal that Rochat contracted a venereal disease from prostitutes he had paid with the money that Proust had given him to finance one of his aborted repatriations. Proust then had to pay for the medical treatment that cured the secretary of the disease.[57]

Although Morel could be "expansive and friendly" and had a "charming side to him," the Narrator concludes that "his must be a vile nature, that he would not shrink from any act of servility if the need arose, and was incapable of gratitude. In which he resembled the majority of mankind."[58] Morel's intentions for his fiancée are indeed sinister: He intends to use her as a procuress and prostitute her to wealthy lesbians.

> Since, in everything but his art, [Morel] was astonishingly lazy, he was faced with the necessity of finding someone to keep him; and he preferred that it should be Jupien's niece rather than M. de Charlus, this arrangement offering him greater freedom and also a wide choice of different kinds of women, ranging from the apprentices, perpetually changing, whom he would persuade Jupien's niece to procure for him, to the rich and beautiful ladies to whom he would prostitute her. That his future wife might refuse to lend herself to these ploys, that she could be to such a degree perverse, never entered Morel's calculations for a moment.[59]

When Morel fails in his attempts to rape the girl and she refuses to follow his suggestion that "she might make friends with other girls whom she would then procure for him," he becomes enraged at her resistance and decides to break with her.[60]

Proust must have sent Hahn an unvarnished account of Rochat's caddish behavior toward his fiancée, although Rochat can hardly have been as vile as Morel is depicted to be. From Deauville, where Hahn was conducting Saint-Saëns's *Phryné* and Gounod's *Médecin malgré lui* for the summer season, he sent a note to express his disgust with Rochat for having become "mendacious and mean."[61]

We do not know what became of Rochat after he sailed for South America. Apparently, Proust never heard from again. Céleste and Proust were clearly happy to have him finally off their hands. The novelist expressed his relief by saying: "Here we are, Céleste. Peace and quiet at last."[62]

While Proust had continued to tolerate the presence of the "useless" Rochat, he occasionally thought of another handsome valet, the blond Swede, Ernest Forssgren, who had served him briefly before emigrating to America. The lasting impression that Forssgren had made on the writer was that of a Ruy Blond, as opposed to the brown-haired Rochat, whom Proust characterized as his Ruy Brun.[63]

Forssgren's "summary" of George D. Painter's biography of Proust informs us that Le Cuziat served as head footman at Prince Orloff's in 1914–15 and that, after Forssgren was hired as valet, Le Cuziat himself nicknamed Forssgren "Le Parisien."[64] Le Cuziat had not been engaged for sexual favors by Prince Orloff, whose heterosexual credentials appear to be beyond reproach, but he had earlier been employed for such purposes by the Polish prince Constantin Radziwill, whose homosexuality was widely known. It was in the context of Radziwill's handsome, androgynous valets that Proust remembered Ernest Forssgren most vividly, because he brought to mind the prince's footmen, selected for their stature, good looks, and anticipated moral complacency.

According to Painter, Le Cuziat inspired a comic homosexual encounter found in *Sodom and Gomorrah*.[65] It involves the princesse de Guermantes's usher, called the "barker," because he announces the guests as they arrive at her grand soirées. The barker had been walking one day along the "Champs-Elysées when he met a young man whom he had found charming but whose identity he had been unable to establish. Not that the young man had not shown himself as obliging as he had been generous. All the favours the usher had supposed that he would have to bestow upon so young a gentleman, he had on the contrary received." The mysterious young gentleman was none other than the duke of Châtellerault, who posed "as an Englishman, and to all the passionate questions with which he was plied by the usher, desirous to meet again a person to whom he was indebted for so much pleasure and largesse, the Duke had merely replied, from one end of the Avenue Gabriel to the other: 'I do not speak French.'" A short time later the duke receives his first invitation to a party at the princesse de Guermantes's. The duke "having to respond to all the smiles, all the greetings waved to him from inside the drawing-room," fails to notice the usher, who

> from the first moment . . . had recognised him. In another instant he
> would know the identity of this stranger, which he had so ardently
> desired to learn. . . . Upon hearing the guest's reply: "Le Duc de
> Châtellerault," he was overcome with such pride that he remained for
> a moment speechless. The Duke looked at him, recognised him, saw
> himself ruined, while the servant, who had recovered his composure
> and was sufficiently versed in heraldry to complete for himself an
> appellation that was too modest, roared with a professional vehe-
> mence softened with intimate tenderness: "Son Altesse Monseigneur
> le Duc de Châtellerault!"[66]

The employment of handsome young footmen for sex—Forssgren would no doubt have been shocked to learn—reminded Proust of young Ernest, whose tall stature, masculine beauty, and distinguished bearing made him an ideal candidate. Proust was quick to deny that he hired Forssgren for any such purposes, but a letter written a few years after Forssgren's employment with Proust offers a glimpse of the wealthy homosexual milieu in which Le Cuziat operated, at first selling his own favors as part of his wages and then setting up a brothel for his former employers and their acquaintances with similar sexual preferences. In his memoirs, Forssgren vehemently denies any knowledge of Proust's homosexuality and, by extension, his own.[67] The letter in question was a reply to one from the duchess of Clermont-Tonnerre, who, as we have seen, was herself to become "notorious as one of the so-called 'amazons,' women artists and writers of postwar Paris who defied sexual convention."[68]

Praising Mme Clermont-Tonnerre's letter for its vivid style, Proust compared her writing to a painting by Jean-Antoine Watteau and a poem by Paul Verlaine, because each depicted a *Fête galante,* which in turn reminded him of handsome blond footmen wearing liveries of blue velvet. "Blue" is perhaps an allusion to the "slang phrase *ballets bleus* for orgies with young men."[69] The vision of such footmen sets off a series of comments about those recruited by Prince Constantin Radziwill, who, although married, kept a bevy of youths on staff to satisfy his sexual desires. Robert de Montesquiou had remarked of him: "To speak of women would be uncivil / In the house of Constantin Radziwill." Of Polish origin and immensely wealthy, the prince kept a staff of twelve handsome valets, to each of whom he gave a pearl necklace.[70] Proust promised to tell the duchess on their next meeting about his own "Ruy blond," adding quickly that his valet was not destined to the same purposes as those who worked for Prince Constantin.

Proust's Ruy blond was Ernest Forssgren, as he makes clear in the next sentence of the letter, which evokes his last trip to Cabourg, accompanied by Céleste Albaret and Forssgren. "He made an indelible impression on the Comte Greffulhe, who saw him at Cabourg in 1914 and never forgot him, which I believe is very unusual for Comte Greffulhe where footmen are concerned (needless to say, his admiration was merely that of a master for the professional qualities of a servant)." Proust goes on to say that the only scandal Constantin's former footmen spoke of was "not as you might think, that between Prince Constantin and one of the blue statues, but between him and Lady Pirbright. The footmen in blue velvet worshipped their Master." The scandal had erupted when the lady was caught fellating the prince. Proust had relayed this bit of gossip to Hahn years earlier in a letter sent from Cabourg during the summer of 1911.[71]

In the letter about the blond footmen, Proust recalled yet another prickly occasion when a new, uninitiated valet, outraged by the lusty prince's advances, attempted to throw his lordship out the window. The prince's wife intervened, scolding the "recalcitrant valet, 'If you didn't want to do that, you had only to refuse. But you shouldn't try to kill people over such matters.' A maxim that would prevent many wars." In a subsequent letter, Proust asked the duchess to destroy his: "Not so much because of Ruy Blas . . . or the number of dukes compromised, as for a quite different reason, namely my absolute insistence . . . that none of my letters should be kept, let alone published."[72]

Proust, who by now had become truly famous, was naïve in thinking that he could prevent publication of his letters. He continued to ask the recipients to return or destroy those that might damage his reputation, and yet—as we have seen—he himself failed to destroy one of the most compromising letters that he ever wrote, the one to Agostinelli, returned to the sender because the young man died the day Proust wrote it.

CHAPTER ELEVEN

Love Is Divine

As Proust began transposing the experiences of his love affairs and infatuations into the novel, he found inspiration in the recently published letters of Alfred de Musset, who had been his favorite poet during adolescence.[1] Of Musset's tempestuous love affairs, the most famous with George Sand, Proust observed that his "loves survive only because he had made them the matter of his poems." At first, Proust found the writing difficult, apparently because he had not yet conceived the plot and structure of his work, but he had long known the essence of what he wanted to convey: "Everything [I am writing] is fiction, laboriously though, for I have no imagination, but everything is filled with a meaning that I have carried for a long time within me, for too long because I have forgotten some of it, my heart has grown cold, and I have fashioned for it, with difficulty, these awkward conduits that enclose it, but from which warmth emanates."[2]

By the end of his long quest, the emanating warmth had become the light that illumines because Proust made his Narrator a representative of the utopian figure of the artist, of men and women of great achievement, who not only saves himself from aridity and aimlessness but also benefits his readers by transcribing for them, just as Musset had done, the experience of his loves: "What we have to bring to light and make known to ourselves is our feelings, our passions, that is to say the passions and feelings of all mankind." Thus does the egotist become an altruist by converting the years wasted in vain pursuits into a transcendent work of art:

> Our love is not only the love of an Albertine, it is a portion of our own mind more durable than the various selves which successively die within us and which would, in their egotism, like to keep it to themselves, it is a portion of our mind which must, however much it hurts us, detach itself from individuals so that we can comprehend and restore to it its generality and give this love, the understanding of this love, to all, to the universal spirit.[3]

He now sees that he was right, contrary to his grandmother's wishes, to neglect Elstir at Balbec in order to pursue Albertine. "A woman whom we need and who makes us suffer elicits from us a whole gamut of feelings far more profound and more vital than a man of genius who interests us." Although he did learn many lessons about architecture, painting, and fashion from Elstir, the tortures he suffered because of his jealous obsession with the elusive Albertine are more important to his future work because the girl is the instrument by which grief becomes knowledge and sorrow is converted to joy. Proust offers this lesson as the secret to the art of living:

> Every individual who makes us suffer can be attached by us to a divinity of which he or she is a mere fragmentary reflection, the lowest step in the ascent that leads to it, a divinity or an Idea which, if we turn to contemplate it, immediately gives us joy instead of the pain which we were feeling before—indeed the whole art of living is to make use

of the individuals through whom we suffer as a step enabling us to draw nearer to the divine form which they reflect and thus joyously to people our life with divinities.[4]

The writer must sound the deepest regions of his being in order to fathom his entire experience, the depth of which is determined by the degree to which he has suffered: "A writer's works, like the water in an artesian well, mount to a height which is in proportion to the depth to which suffering has penetrated his heart." Such inner delving requires courage, since the writer must acknowledge the truth and abandon "cherished illusions" about love, "so that now, instead of soothing oneself for the hundredth time with the words: 'She was very sweet,' one would have to transpose the phrase so that it read: 'I experienced pleasure when I kissed her.' "[5] In a 1919 letter to Violet Schiff, Proust used the abandonment of cherished illusions to define his craft: "Art is a perpetual sacrifice of sentiment to truth."[6] The Narrator shares this goal, as he sets out to emulate and surpass Bergotte, whose books were earlier described as "mirrors of absolute truth."[7]

What truth or truths do we see in the mirror held up to us by Proust's own book? The opening pages of *In Search of Lost Time*, referred to in a letter by Proust as his "overture," depict his Eden and serve as the genesis of the fictional universe that he unfolds before our eyes. This new world features, among other things, the androgynous birth of Eve from Adam, one of a number of ancient myths of a primordial hermaphrodite who existed before the division of the sexes into male and female: "Sometimes, too, as Eve was created from a rib of Adam, a woman would be born during my sleep from some misplacing of my thigh."[8] Proust returns to this theme in *The Captive*, shortly after the passage on watching Albertine as she sleeps. The carnal act of love is depicted, in solemn tones and biblical references, as reconstituting the ancient unity of the perfect creature: "O mighty attitudes of Man and Woman, in which there seeks to be united, in the innocence of the world's first days and with the humility of clay, what the Creation made separate, in which Eve is astonished and submissive before Man by whose side she awakens, as he himself, alone still, before God who has fashioned him!"[9]

In *Time Regained,* as the Narrator prepares to write his book, many of the images suggest that he must become, like Elstir before him, a new Adam, like the first who embodied the female as well as the male. In a letter to Dr. Samuel Pozzi, the gynecologist whom his brother Robert had assisted for a decade, Proust stated his belief in the androgynous nature of the writer's voice: "A writer must forget that he has a sex and speak for all" his characters.[10] To the Narrator, Elstir's "studio appeared like the laboratory of a sort of new creation of the world." Like Adam, who had the responsibility of bestowing names on things when the world was first made, "it was by taking away their names or giving them other names that Elstir created [things] anew."[11] Elstir's seascapes are characterized by the mingling of the male and female elements of the land and sea so that they are indistinguishable one from the other, thus creating a "multiform and powerful unity, the cause (not always clearly perceived by themselves) of the enthusiasm which Elstir's work aroused in certain collectors."

In the Narrator's love for Albertine, sexuality, in its jealous, obsessive form, presented an obstacle to the attainment of his highest goals, rendering him, like Swann before him, sterile as a writer. The Narrator, while still in his selfish, egotistical mode, has a bleak view of the human condition:

> The bonds between ourselves and another person exist only in our minds. Memory as it grows fainter loosens them, and notwithstanding the illusion by which we want to be duped and with which, out of love, friendship, politeness, deference, duty, we dupe other people, we exist alone. Man is the creature who cannot escape from himself, who knows other people only in himself, and when he asserts the contrary, he is lying.[12]

After years of solitude in a sanatorium, the Narrator returns to Paris, where a series of involuntary memories, like that of the madeleine, lead to the recovery of his will; this in turn makes him determined to learn his craft and comprehend his life's experience in order to transform it into a book.

In *Time Regained,* the Narrator sees his errors, corrects them, and finds the right path to reach his goal. Art alone allows us to know the essence of another person's experience. Music, painting, and literature go far beyond the boundaries set by physical love and jealous possession of the beloved: "As the spectrum makes visible to us the composition of light, so the harmony of a Wagner, the colour of an Elstir, enable us to know that essential quality of another person's sensations into which love for another person does not allow us to penetrate."[13] The Narrator, like Swann, before him, had always come closest to finding the "open sesame" when meditating on Vinteuil's music: "Was this perhaps the happiness which the little phrase of the sonata promised to Swann and which he, because he was unable to find it in artistic creation, mistakenly assimilated to the pleasures of love?"[14] Unlike Swann, the Narrator has been able to correct course and discover himself as a writer, which brings him great joy.

The terrible suffering caused by the unfathomable distance that separated him from Albertine results in her having fertilized and impregnated him with the material for his future book: "Certainly, it was to her face, as I had seen it for the first time beside the sea, that I traced back certain things that I should no doubt include in my book. And in a sense I was right to trace them back to her, for if I had not walked on the front that day, if I had not got to know her, all these ideas would never have been developed." He recognizes the irony of the situation: Albertine inspired these pages whose meaning she "would quite certainly never have understood. It was, however, for this very reason . . . that she was so different from me, that she had fertilised me through unhappiness and even, at the beginning, through the simple effort which I had had to make to imagine something different from myself. Had she been capable of understanding my pages, she would, for that very reason, not have inspired them."[15] Endowed with creative ability, he now bears within himself the substance of future work.

The concluding section of *In Search of Lost Time* contains other androgynous analogies describing the writer's task. The Narrator, set to begin his novel, compares himself to Scheherazade, who must continue her narrations under the constant threat of death. He will construct his book with the same care that the old family servant Françoise took in preparing and cooking her succulent "bœuf mode" and yet also in the simple, diligent way that she constructed a dress.[16] Much earlier in the story Proust used such an analogy to describe the hero's first attempt to write, which consisted only of a few pages describing the steeples of Martinville. The fledgling author was so pleased with himself that he felt like a hen that has just laid an egg and begun to crow at the top of her voice.[17]

By presenting the androgynous characteristics of the creative process, Proust follows an ancient tradition of celebrating the fecundity of bisexuality. In mythology bisexuality was a theme associated with gods and fertility cults; it spawned a number of creation myths wherein an androgynous birth begat the divine and human races. A medieval concept depicts the inner being as androgynous by dividing the soul and mind into "a feminine sensory part on one hand and masculine reason and will on the other."[18] This notion still has some currency today; we often hear about female intuition or a man who is attempting to get in touch with his feminine side.

This belief in the bisexual nature of people—that each of us possesses male and female characteristics—was commonplace in late-nineteenth-century France, especially in artistic and scientific circles, which Proust knew so intimately. However, by the turn of the century, according to Françoise Cachin, "the fin-de-siècle androgynous dream appears to have resulted more from the negation of sex than from the potential resources of its double nature."[19] With Proust the opposite clearly prevails; the coexistence of masculine and feminine traits within an individual constitutes a positive, enhancing condition, as seen in the explanation of Charlus's profound understanding and appreciation of art. The idea of the rich resources provided by the androgyne's double nature appeals to Proust as a symbol of the integral nature of the artist whose duty it is to create new worlds. We have seen Proust, in step with the modern era's growing interest in psychology, finding androgynous vestiges in the world of dreams, domain of the subconscious.[20]

Proust recognized the androgynous aspects of his own endeavor at its inception, as can be seen in *The Notebook of 1908:* "Work makes us something of a mother. Sometimes, feeling myself near death, I said to myself, feeling the child that was forming within me and not knowing if I had the strength required to give birth, I would say, with a sad and sweet smile, to the child within me: 'Will I ever see you?' "[21]

Years later, in the darker, requiem-like passages of the concluding pages of *Time Regained,* as the weary Narrator comes closer to the acceptance of death and the idea that he may indeed not have enough time to construct his vast cathedral of a novel, he compares himself to a weary mother whose child has needs that surpass her capacities:

> The idea of my work was inside my head, always the same, perpetually in the process of becoming. But even my work had become for me a tiresome obligation, like a son for a dying mother who still, between her injections and her blood-lettings, has to make the exhausting effort of constantly looking after him. Perhaps she still loves him, but it is only in the form of a duty too great for her strength that she is aware of her affection.[22]

Proust did find the strength to be a good "mother" to his demanding child, even at the expense of his life, which he sacrificed, like Bergotte in the novel, to the production of his great work. Here is what he wrote about the process in the closing section of his long quest: "The writer feeds his book, he strengthens the parts of it which are weak, he protects it, but afterwards it is the book that grows, that designates its author's tomb and defends it against the world's clamour and for a while against oblivion."[23]

The Narrator's obsessive and vain pursuits of Albertine, undertaken because of his jealousy, described as pathological and demonic, had brought only suffering, which he now will transpose into art, a process that releases happiness. Pain becomes joy as he converts the particular to the general by writing a book that will take its place in the common stockpile of truth and beauty:

> The work is a promise of happiness, because it shows us that in every love the particular and the general lie side by side and it teaches us to pass from one to the other by a species of gymnastic which fortifies us against unhappiness by making us neglect its particular cause in order to gain a more profound understanding of its essence. . . . Even at a time when we are in love and suffer, we feel so strongly during the hours in which we are at work that the individual whom we love is being dissolved into a vaster reality.[24]

A similar connection between truth, work, and joy can be found in a letter dating from the period when Proust was finally coming out of the long period of illness, depression, and deep mourning resulting from the loss of his mother in 1905. In February 1907 Marcel wrote to Lucien Daudet, who was in a discouraged and dark mood, and attempted to lift his friend's spirits by suggesting that he think of himself "simply as an instrument capable of whatever experiments in beauty or truth you wish to perform, and your gloom will evaporate." By doing this, Daudet was sure to find "joy and a great eagerness for life and work."[25]

Thanks to the discovery of the Narrator's vocation, made possible by a series of involuntary memory experiences, like that of the madeleine and tea, and by his newfound determination, the Narrator evolves, as did Proust, from an obsessively jealous, miserable creature incapable of working to an energetic, focused, and altruistic writer:

> How different was my attitude now! The happiness which I was feeling was the product not of a purely subjective tension of the nerves which isolated me from the past, but on the contrary of an enlargement of my mind, within which the past was re-forming and actualising itself, giving me . . . something whose value was eternal. What

I was seeking to protect was pleasure still, but no longer pleasure of an egotistical kind. It was an egotism that could be made useful to other people.[26]

Selfish, possessive love at last yields to the generous, compassionate work of the writer, who knows that his necessary withdrawal from society in order to create will appear egocentric, "for all the fruitful altruisms of nature develop in an egotistical manner."[27] John Updike has called this statement "a kind of Godless Golden Rule and the germinating principle of art."[28] The true germination of Proust's vast novel could begin only when he finally discovered the story and structure suitable to sustain and illustrate his aesthetics and ethics.

In the essay "John Ruskin," published in 1900 in the *Gazette des Beaux-Arts,* Proust had insisted on the universality of Ruskin's writings and his search for truth: "For the man of genius cannot give birth to immortal works except by creating them in the image, not of his mortal being, but of the humanity he bears within himself. . . . The work of Ruskin is universal. He sought the truth, and found beauty even in chronological tables and social laws."[29] Proust saw in Ruskin the confirmation of his own idealistic goals held since youth and first ratified by Alphonse Darlu in his philosophy class at Condorcet.

Early in the novel Proust had defined genius, represented by Bergotte, as the power to transform oneself into a mirror.[30] As we have seen, the youthful Narrator identified Bergotte's works as "mirrors of absolute truth," an example the mature hero recalls at the end of his quest: "For I had already realised long ago that it is not the man with the liveliest mind, the most well-informed, the best supplied with friends and acquaintances, but the one who knows how to become a mirror and in this way can reflect his life, commonplace though it may be, who becomes a Bergotte."[31] His books originate in "that part of the Eternal Mind which is the author of the works of Bergotte."[32] A statement regarding the positive moral influence of a writer who may at times behave badly is also found in the passage on Bergotte's genius: "Great artists often, while being wicked, make use of their vices in order to arrive at a conception of the moral law that is binding upon us all."[33] Proust's concern for morality, even though he and his characters may perform wicked acts, often involving sexual sadism and profanation, is evident in the Narrator's conversion to altruism at the end. In the early stages of the novel's development, Proust had entertained the idea of using as the general title *The Vices and Virtues of Combray.*

Time Regained contains a high moral message that points the way to "happiness" and the creation of something "whose value" is "eternal." The right path or way (*côté*) lies in the opposite direction from that of egotistical pleasures. The Narrator sees that the lessons learned, at the expense of pain and waste of time, can be converted into altruistic, transcendent art worthy of being called great and universal because it endows us with a treasury that enriches each succeeding generation as it draws from and contributes to the accumulated wealth of human achievements.

In Search of Lost Time is an open-ended novel built on the model of the universe. Proust's vision is indeed cosmic in that he seeks to create a fictional universe that, like the real one, is constantly expanding, "perpetually in the process of becoming."[34] This novel's ballooning, evolving nature constitutes one of its most modern aspects. Edmund Wilson praised Proust's book for being nothing less than the literary equivalent of Albert Einstein's theory of relativity: "He has recreated the world of the novel from the point of view of relativity: he has supplied for the first time in literature an equivalent on the full scale for the new theory of physics." Wilson saw the grandmother as the golden mean of the novel, "playing for Proust the same rôle that the speed of light does for Einstein: the single constant value which makes the rest of the system possible."[35] The Narrator credits his mother and grandmother with having instilled in him the moral value of not judging others: "I had inherited from my mother and grandmother their incapacity for rancour even against far worse offenders, and their habit of never condemning anyone."[36]

Unconditional love exists in the novel only between parents and their children: the grandmother and the mother for each other and for the Narrator, and Vinteuil for his daughter: "However much M. Vinteuil may have known of his daughter's conduct it did not follow that his adoration of her grew any less."[37] There is a substantial amount of evidence that Proust saw his novel as a monumental love letter to the person he cherished most: his mother. *In Search of Lost Time* has its origins in an imaginary conversation that Proust had with his deceased mother about the failings of the critic Charles Augustin Sainte-Beuve. In the novel he does not let the mother die. The Narrator expresses his great love for his grandmother in the only passage in which God is invoked: "And I asked nothing more of God, if a paradise exists, than to be able, there, to knock on that wall with the three little raps which my grandmother would recognise among a thousand . . . and that he would let me stay with her throughout eternity, which would not be too long for the two of us."[38] Proust often discussed with Céleste his enduring love for his mother: "If I were sure to meet my mother again, in the Valley of Jehosaphat or anywhere else, I would want to die at once."[39]

Time Regained reunites what had been separated and rendered sterile in the wasteland created by sexual jealousy. Proust often uses images of sterility and desiccation to represent the Narrator's mistaken paths and his inability to write. Having earlier stated that we exist alone, Proust creates in the novel's finale a kind of literary Grand Unified Theory by putting everything that had been shattered and sundered back together again. We see this in the analogies used to recombine the two sexes into one powerful androgynous creator and in his belief in the fundamental unity of everything that exists—a unity that the artist and the scientist seek to render visible. Fashion, culture, biology, and so on—even our personalities—all come from the same cosmic stock reserves:

> I had always considered each one of us to be a sort of multiple
> organism or polyp, not only at a given moment of time—so that when

a speck of dust passes it, the eye, an associated but independent organ, blinks without having received an order from the mind, and the intestine, like an embedded parasite, can fall victim to an infection without the mind knowing anything about it—but also similarly, where the personality is concerned and its duration through life, I had thought of this as a sequence of juxtaposed but distinct "I's" which would die one after the other or even come to life alternately, like those which at Combray took one another's place within me when evening approached. But I had seen also that these moral cells of which an individual is composed are more durable than the individual himself.

He realizes that he has "seen the vices and the courage of the Guermantes recur in Saint-Loup," in addition to Saint-Loup's "own strange and ephemeral defects of character." Now, observing Bloch, he realizes that he too is "animated by the same wrath against his father-in-law as had animated his own father against M. Nissim Bernard and even interrupted his meals to deliver the same tirades against him." Recalling "the conversation of Cottard and Brichot and so many others," the Narrator "felt that, through the influence of culture and fashion, a single undulation propagates identical mannerisms of speech and thought through a whole vast extent of space," leading him to conclude that "throughout the whole duration of time great cataclysmic waves lift up from the depths of the ages the same rages, the same sadnesses, the same heroisms, the same obsessions, through one superimposed generation after another."[40]

After having particularized his characters, Proust places them all in the vast, evolutionary sweep of the universe. As is true for Einstein, his great contemporary, matter for Proust is neither created nor destroyed, but it is the artist's duty to fashion new visions, new worlds out of the same matter. Long before he began writing what became *In Search of Lost Time*, he expressed this concept of the cosmic stock reserves of materials—spiritual, biological, psychological—in the preface to his translation of Ruskin:

No one is unique, and fortunately for the sympathy and understanding which are such great pleasures in our life, our individualities
are shaped within a universal framework. If we could analyze the soul
as we analyze matter, we would see that under the apparent diversity
of minds as well as of things there are but a few simple substances and
irreducible elements, and that into the composition of what we believe
to be our personality enter elements that are quite common and that
are met again to some degree everywhere in the universe.[41]

A major contributor to the impression of connectedness, of unity
created in his novel, is Proust's brilliant use of analogies and meta-
phors, which he sees as the key stylistic element. Metaphor makes of
each thing and each person a mirror:

Had not nature herself—if one considered the matter from this point
of view—placed me on the path of art, was she not herself a beginning
of art, she who, often, had allowed me to become aware of the beauty
of one thing only in another thing, of the beauty, for instance, of noon
at Combray in the sound of its bells, of that of the mornings at
Doncières in the hiccups of our central heating? The links may be
uninteresting, the objects trivial, the style bad, but unless this process
has taken place the description is worthless.[42]

In the course of the Narrator's quest to discover his vocation as a
writer, he fails on several occasions to heed signs—such as the involuntary memory phenomenon of the madeleine scene or the mysterious apparition of the three trees near Hudimesnil—that seem to
beckon to him, urging him to begin work on his book.[43] Each of these
experiences hints at the existence of the sublime harmony of all things
of which he is given only a glimpse. When he finally makes the often
postponed trip to Venice, he finds reminiscences of Combray in the
Italian city: "I received there impressions analogous to those which I
had felt so often in the past at Combray, but transposed into a wholly
different and far richer key."[44]

The Proustian cosmos is holographic because its totality can be recreated from any single part: it all hangs together like a beautiful tapestry. Wallace Fowlie saw this clearly: "The miracle of Proust's novel is the relationship established between every character, every scene, every theme, within the entire work."[45] A passage in *The Guermantes Way* speaks of this kind of tightly woven tapestry that we may discover in the recollections of our past. Here it is memory that does the weaving in a manner that anticipates the Narrator's ultimate conception of the novel he intends to write:

> Thus the empty spaces of my memory were covered by degrees with names which in arranging, composing themselves in relation to one another, in linking themselves to one another by increasingly numerous connexions, resembled those finished works of art in which there is not one touch that is isolated, in which every part in turn receives from the rest a justification which it confers on them in turn.[46]

The holographic nature of *In Search of Lost Time* results, in large measure, from the brilliant orchestration of the themes and the magisterial deployment of metaphor and analogies, based on Proust's conception of his novel as a giant mirror of the universe. Here the Narrator relates another experience he shared with the author, the failure of the first readers to understand the innovative nature and purpose of the drafts that they had been given to read:

> Before very long I was able to show a few sketches. No one understood anything of them. Even those who commended my perception of the truths which I wanted eventually to engrave within the temple, congratulated me on having discovered them "with a microscope," when on the contrary it was a telescope that I had used to observe things which were indeed very small to the naked eye, but only because they were situated at a great distance, and which were each one of them in itself a world.[47]

Like the universe that it is meant to reflect, the form of Proust's novel is the circle, a timeless symbol of unending unity. Nearing the end of the quest, the hero discovers that other important entities of his life's experience, in this case the geographic ones, are also circular. In *Time Regained,* Gilberte reveals to him that the two ways, that, in his youth, he had loved to walk on different days—Swann's way and the Guermantes way—are not, as he had always thought, separate, leading off into different directions, but parts of the same circular path.[48] The linking of the two ways represents the symbolic unification of his entire experience—as does Mlle de Saint-Loup, the daughter of Gilberte Swann and her husband, Robert de Saint-Loup.

After describing Mlle de Saint-Loup's features, the Narrator states: "I thought her very beautiful: still rich in hopes, full of laughter, formed from those very years which I myself had lost, she was like my own youth."[49] Time manifests itself in the girl as the intersecting lines of his past join to form in her the "star-shaped crossroad" of his life. All the threads of his past, both geographical and biological, are bound together in Mlle de Saint-Loup. The family lines and bloodlines of his characters—even those he thought forever separated by an unbreachable wall of social distinctions—are joined in this ultimate girl in flower: "And to complete the process by which all my various pasts were fused into a single mass Mme Verdurin, like Gilberte, had married a Guermantes." The insistence on "all my pasts" reminds us of the multiple nature of Proust's conception of memory. This is the ultimate resolution and the incarnation of the themes sounded in the opening pages of the book, pages situated entirely outside the plotline of the story (the Narrator does not know who he is, where he is, when he is) and that serve to suggest the rich, deep layers of experiences whose memories lie buried within our bodies and our psyches: "When a man is asleep, he has in a circle round him the chain of the hours, the sequence of the years, the order of the heavenly bodies."[50] The final images of the novel thus unite his entire past, out of which he will construct a new world: "The truth is that life is perpetually weaving fresh threads which link one individual and one event to another, and that these threads are crossed and recrossed, doubled and redoubled to thicken the web, so that between any slightest point of our past and all the others a rich network of memories gives us an almost infinite variety of communicating paths to choose from."[51]

Proust maintained that each work of art or scientific discovery represents a new world, a small mirror reflecting the infinite, and thus is profoundly emblematic and unifying. In a 1909 letter to his fellow writer and childhood friend Maurice Duplay, Proust said that Duplay, like each of us, mirrors the entire universe: "As in everything that you write, each word reflects the monad that says it, but this monad is itself a reflection of the universe."[52] Proust's vision is cosmic: he believes that all works of art and science are manifestations of universal harmony. The duty of the artist is to capture the vision of this unity and create its aesthetic or scientific equivalent. Proust's statements to this effect imply a belief in the idea of progress and perfectibility, of the gradual creation by past, present, and future artists and scientists of a fundamental unity consisting of all the fragments of true discoveries and corresponding to the ideal universe, a harmonious unity of all that exists. At the end of his quest the Narrator accepts the moral duty of the artist as one does a religious obligation—"to accept it like a discipline, build it up like a church"—and realizes that he has assumed nothing less than the challenge to create a new cosmos, "my attempt to transcribe a universe which had to be totally redrawn."[53]

Perhaps we should let Charlus and the Narrator have nearly the last words on the subject of love. Charlus had defended Mme de Sévigné's apparently excessive love for her daughter by maintaining that "what matters in life is not whom or what one loves . . . it is the fact of loving."[54] The Narrator, having lost Albertine, reaches the same conclusion as Charlus and states it more eloquently:

> Never should I find again that divine thing, a person with whom I could talk freely of everything, in whom I could confide. Confide? But did not others offer me greater confidence than Albertine? With others, did I not have more extensive conversations? The fact is that

confidence and conversation are ordinary things in themselves, and what does it matter if they are less than perfect if only there enters into them love, which alone is divine.[55]

I do not agree with Edmund White's rather simplistic conclusion that Proust despised love.[56] The type of love that Proust condemned was, as we have seen, that exemplified by Jean Racine's masterpiece *Phèdre,* in which sexual jealousy is the overwhelming emotion that precipitates the tragedy. It is clear from all that we have seen that Proust's possessiveness and his jealousy from his high school days and onward into adulthood deprived him of friends and frightened away companions like Hahn and Daudet, who clearly loved him.

In spite of his denials of any responsibility for Agostinelli's death, Proust may have felt that his jealousy and his possessiveness were important factors in making his secretary decide that he must flee 102 boulevard Haussmann without giving his employer notice. Had Proust been more the true benefactor and less the jealous suitor, perhaps Agostinelli would have met a different fate. Proust, who has few equals in his knowledge of the human psyche, certainly understood that jealous love is closer to hatred than to true love and is therefore malign. Proust's comparison of sexual jealousy to reciprocal torture suggests that he would endorse La Rochefoucauld's maxim that "if one judges love by most of its manifestations, it resembles hatred more than friendship."[57] During Proust's worst moments of jealous rage and despair he may have wished for Agostinelli's death, just as the insanely jealous Phèdre wishes for Hippolyte's. We have seen the Narrator express this sentiment:

> It is because human bodies contain within themselves the hours of the past that they have the power to hurt so terribly those who love them, because they contain the memories of so many joys and desires already effaced for them, but still cruel for the lover who contemplates and prolongs in the dimension of Time the beloved body of which he is jealous, so jealous that he may even wish for its destruction.[58]

In the novel Proust warns us against the dangers of such maniacal passion, which results in the tragic death of the fugitive Albertine and had prevented the Narrator, like Swann before him, from realizing himself fully. The Narrator finally understands that he did love Albertine, "my great love," but had been unable to appreciate his own happiness when he had it in his possession: "I had not the perspicacity to recognise happiness. And the cause of this happiness at the knowledge of her returning home, of her obeying me and belonging to me, lay in love and not in pride."[59]

It seems to me that such failure is unfortunately common. In the Narrator's case, he recognizes his errors only when it is too late: "It seemed to me that, by my entirely selfish love, I had allowed Albertine to die just as I had murdered my grandmother." He is horrified that because of the erosive work of time and habit, he will ultimately, as we have seen, be forced to relinquish the memory of them both to the general law of oblivion. "It is not because other people are dead that our affection for them fades; it is because we ourselves are dying. . . . My new self, while it grew up in the shadow of the old, had often heard the other speak of Albertine; through that other self, through the stories it gathered from it, it thought that it knew her, it found her lovable, it loved her; but it was only a love at second hand."[60]

Nothing and no one is ever completely lost, however. Even though a lover may vanish from our conscious, willful memory due to the effacing, numbing forces of time and habit, our bodies remain faithful to some degree by retaining pale vestiges of the forgotten one. These body memories are described in a passage where, many years after Albertine's death, the Narrator is Gilberte's guest at Tansonville:

> The love of Albertine had disappeared from my memory. But it seems that there exists too an involuntary memory of the limbs, a pale and sterile imitation of the other but longer-lived, just as there are animals or vegetables without intelligence which are longer-lived than man. Our legs and our arms are full of torpid memories. And once,

when I had said goodnight to Gilberte rather early, I woke up in the middle of the night in my room at Tansonville and, still half asleep, called out: "Albertine!" It was not that I had thought of her or dreamt of her, nor that I was confusing her with Gilberte, but a memory in my arm, opening like a flower, had made me fumble behind my back for the bell, as though I had been in my bedroom in Paris. And not finding it, I had called out: "Albertine!," thinking that my dead mistress was lying by my side, as she had often done in the evening, and that we were both dropping off to sleep.[61]

As Proust began to relinquish his mortal ties to this world, he found consolation for his regrets and pains in the knowledge that those who came after him would enjoy the fruits of his labor. In spite of the solemn, somber words of Proust the man struggling to complete his ambitious work, the ultimate product of his awesome labors in the conversion of pain to literature is made quite clear by the frequent use of the word *joy* in the passages describing the discovery of his vocation and his determination to settle down and work. This feeling of exhilaration and triumph resulting from all the effort and suffering so impressed Iris Murdoch that she made it an important plot element in *The Good Apprentice*. Near the end of Murdoch's novel, Edward, one of the main characters, resumes his reading of *In Search of Lost Time:*

"Oh—Proust—" Edward had been looking for the passage which had so amazed him . . . about Albertine going out in the rain on her bicycle, but he couldn't find it. He had turned to the beginning. [*Longtemps, je me suis couché de bonne heure.*] What a lot of pain there was in those first pages. What a lot of pain there was all the way through. So how was it that the whole thing could vibrate with such a pure joy? This was something which Edward was determined to find out."[62]

The Good Apprentice ends with Edward setting out on his own Proustian quest. This joy, whose source Edward seeks to discover, stems in part, I believe, from the affection that Proust shows for all his characters, even those whom he finds most at fault. He loves and wants to redeem them all, a sentiment that constitutes a powerful moral force, endowing his characters with life and making them real. Pamela Hansford Johnson sees this as the great lesson of *In Search of Lost Time:* "There is no novel in the world that changes its readers more profoundly.... Above all it teaches compassion, that relaxing of the mind into gentleness which makes life at once infinitely more complex and infinitely more tolerable." And, she continues, "Proust makes the reader love [the Narrator] so that Proust himself, perhaps more than any writer except Shakespeare, becomes an intimate."[63]

In the closing pages, Proust urges us to comprehend, develop, and deploy our own remarkable faculties. He intends his entire enterprise to persuade us that we are incredibly rich instruments, but that most often we let our gifts lie dormant or we squander them, as did Swann and Charlus, and as the Narrator came perilously close to doing. The joy that so many readers feel at the conclusion of the book derives also from the long-delayed triumph of the hero and the realization that we too can, by following his example, attempt to lead the true life. Here is one of several blueprints Proust provides for discovering the true life by assuming the task of the artist and bathing in the fountain of youth:

> This work of the artist, this struggle to discern beneath matter, beneath experience, beneath words, something that is different from them, is a process exactly the reverse of that which, in those everyday lives which we live with our gaze averted from ourselves, is at every moment being accomplished by vanity and passion and the intellect, and habit too, when they smother our true impressions, so as entirely to conceal them from us, beneath a whole heap of verbal concepts and practical goals which we falsely call life. In short, this art which is so complicated is in fact the only living art. It alone expresses for others and renders visible to ourselves that life of ours which cannot effectually observe itself and of which the observable manifestations

need to be translated and, often, to be read backwards and laboriously deciphered. Our vanity, our passions, our spirit of imitation, our abstract of intelligence, our habits have long been at work, and it is the task of art to undo this work of theirs, making us travel back in the direction from which we have come to the depths where what has really existed lies unknown within us. And surely this was a most tempting prospect, this task of re-creating one's true life, of rejuvenating one's impressions.[64]

In Search of Lost Time is, to my mind, comedy of the highest order that amuses, delights, and frequently dazzles as we follow the Narrator on his quest. After many ups and downs and wrong turns, the story has a happy ending in which the myriad themes—major and minor—beautifully orchestrated throughout, are gloriously resolved in the grand finale. And as one expects of any good comedy, a wedding, while it doesn't take place, is at least announced. Mlle de Saint-Loup, as befits her symbolic status as the incarnation of the Narrator's entire life, instead of "marrying a royal prince," as her social-climbing mother Odette Swann had plotted and schemed for all these years, "chose for her husband an obscure man of letters."[65] A letter to Jacques Boulenger written in the final months of Proust's life makes it clear that he intended his hero to be Mlle de Saint-Loup's husband, thereby marrying not only his past but his lost youth as well: "At least your morality will be satisfied, for you'll see that, at the end of the book, my hero, the denigrator of Sodom, is about to marry. Future *Sodoms* will be almost entirely about my hero's passions for women, moreover, I mean to give them titles less inspired by Vigny."[66]

Perhaps Proust had a sequel in mind.

Notes

ONE *Promiscuous Proust*

Epigraph: "Marcel Proust par lui-même," *CSB*, 336.

1. Jacques-Émile Blanche, *Mes Modèles: Souvenirs littéraires* (Paris: Stock, 1984), 100.
2. See *Letters of Marcel Proust*, trans. and ed. Mina Curtiss (New York: Random House, 1949), 3–4.
3. Marcel Proust, *Écrits de Jeunesse, 1887–1895*, sel. and ed. Anne Borrel (Illiers-Combray: Institut Marcel Proust International, 1991), 41.
4. *SL* 1: 10–11. Proust's ellipses, which he often uses to create suspense before the conclusion of a sentence. All ellipses are mine unless otherwise indicated.
5. Quoted in *Écrits de Jeunesse*, 38.
6. Parents, priests, teachers, and doctors, including Proust's doctor father, Adrien, condemned this common sexual activity. See Adrien Proust and Gilbert Ballet, *L'Hygiène du neurasthénique* (Paris: Bibliothèque d'hygiène thérapeutique, 1897), 154.
7. *Corr.* 21: 554. The emphasis is Proust's.
8. For the letter and Halévy's comments, see *Marcel Proust: Correspondance avec Daniel Halévy*, ed. Anne Borrel and Jean-Pierre Halévy (Paris: Éditions de Fallois, 1992), 42–44.
9. *The Fugitive* 5: 883.
10. See *Jean Santeuil*, ed. Pierre Clarac and Yves Sandre (Paris: Gallimard, 1971), 4: 709, 857. Proust began this work when he was twenty-four and never completed it. The manuscript, consisting of drafts and sketches, was discovered and published posthumously as *Jean Santeuil*, after the name of its hero, who resembles its author in many ways.
11. *Swann's Way* 1: 14, 222–23.
12. See ibid., 1: 198–99.

13. *Time Regained* 6: 4–5.

14. *SL* 4: 37. In the inscription Proust wrote in the copy of *Swann's Way* he gave to Robert Dreyfus, he evoked the days when the two had played with the "girls of the Champs-Élysées and the dances, when we each loved a different girl but whose names each ended in 'i'." *Corr.* 18: 288–89.

15. *Swann's Way* 1: 569.

16. In a letter identifying Mlle Benardaky as the model for Gilberte, Proust was eager to point out that "naturally, the freer passages involving Gilberte at the beginning of *Within a Budding Grove* have nothing whatever to do with the person in question, for I never had any but the most proper relations with her." *SL* 4: 41. The wrestling scene with its premature ejaculation is clearly what worried Proust. The kind of erotic arousal he describes could easily have occurred while wrestling with another boy.

17. *Within a Budding Grove* 2: 90.

18. *Proust-Halévy Corr.*, 43–44.

19. Curtiss, *Letters of Marcel Proust*, 4.

20. See Theodore Zeldin, *France, 1848–1945* (Oxford: Oxford University Press, 1973), 1: 306. Zeldin also observes that the attempts to "extirpate [masturbation] were so enormous they can only be likened to a new version of the medieval witchhunts."

21. Graham Robb, *Strangers: Homosexual Love in the Nineteenth Century* (New York: Norton, 2003), 75.

22. Peter Gay, *Freud: A Life for Our Time* (New York: Norton, 1988), 48.

23. Edmond de Goncourt and Jules de Goncourt, *Journal: Mémoires de la vie littéraire* (Paris: Robert Laffont, 1989), entry for April 16, 1883, 2: 1003.

24. *Corr.* 21: 550–51.

25. The word Proust uses for unclean is *malpropre* and for normal *habituel*. For this letter, see *Corr.* 21: 552–53.

26. Proust did not include "Avant la nuit" in *Les Plaisirs et les Jours*, no doubt because of its scandalous nature. This story has recently been translated into English by Joachim Neugroschel in *The Complete Short Stories of Marcel Proust* (New York: Cooper Square, 2001), 181–85.

27. *Complete Short Stories*, 183.

28. *Écrits de Jeunesse*, 149–51. Graham Robb notes in *Strangers* that the terms " 'warm brothers' or 'warm friends' had been in use for homosexual love since at least the early 1770s. 'Warm' implies affection, though Magnus

Hirschfeld traced the expression to the supposedly higher skin temperature of homosexuals" (94).

29. Robert Dreyfus dated the piece as having been written before October 15, 1888.

30. *Écrits de Jeunesse*, 121–22.

31. *SL* 1: 19–20.

32. Ibid., 1: 21.

33. The incident is described in *Proust-Halévy Corr.*, 169–72.

34. Paul Morand, *Le Journal inutile*, ed. Laurent Boyer and Véronique Boyer (Paris: Gallimard, 2001), 1: 198.

35. Jean-Yves Tadié, *Marcel Proust* (Paris: Pierre Belfond, 1983), 107.

36. Henri Bonnet, *Alphonse Darlu: Maître de philosophie de Marcel Proust* (Paris: Nizet, 1961), 7–8.

37. *SL* 1: 24.

38. *The Captive* 5: 270.

39. *SL* 1: 25.

40. Ibid. Proust's ellipsis.

41. *Corr.* 2: 464.

42. Fernand Gregh, *L'Âge d'or: Souvenirs d'enfance et de jeunesse* (Paris: Grasset, 1947), 326–27 n. 2.

TWO *Mighty Hermaphrodite*

Epigraph: "Marcel Proust par lui-même," *CSB*, 336.

1. Proust wrote a similar letter when Marie Benardaky's brother was killed in the war: "These transpositions into another sex of a face one has loved fascinate me. That's why I would so much like to have known young Benardaky, who was killed at the beginning of the war and whose sister, perhaps without knowing it, was the intoxication and despair of my youth." *SL* 4: 37.

2. Robert de Billy, *Marcel Proust: Lettres et conversations* (Paris: Éditions des Portiques, 1930), 173–74.

3. Quoted by Claude Francis and Fernande Gontier, *Marcel Proust et les siens: Suivi des souvenirs de Suzy Mante-Proust* (Paris: Plon, 1981), 122.

4. *SL* 1: 205.

5. *Sodom and Gomorrah* 4: 417. See also *Time Regained* 6: 445: "Almost every aged Charlus is a ruin in which one may recognise with astonishment, beneath all the layers of paint and powder, some fragments of a beautiful woman preserved in eternal youth."

6. *SL* 3: 268.

7. *Sodom and Gomorrah* 4: 480.

8. *The Complete Short Stories of Marcel Proust*, trans. Joachim Neugroschel (New York: Cooper Square, 2001), 183–84. We saw in the previous chapter that this story also uses an aesthetic argument to justify lesbian love. Elisabeth Ladenson suggests that Proust's first publications treating homosexuality deal with lesbianism because there was greater tolerance in society for this kind of sexual expression. See her provocative study, *Proust's Lesbianism* (Ithaca, N.Y.: Cornell University Press, 1999), 68. We have seen, however, that Proust was eager to write about male homosexuality; it was his literary classmates at Condorcet who censored the publication of "Glaukos."

9. Quotations in this paragraph and the next two of the Narrator's remarks on the evolution of society's attitude on homosexuality from the days of Socrates to the modern era are from *The Captive* 5: 270–71. Proust expounded upon this idea in a letter to his financial adviser Lionel Hauser, with whom he often discussed philosophy and morality: "There have been times when physical and moral well-being was the very fount of preeminence in all things, and of genius. Plato's young disciples (who differed from yours in loving young men rather than women, but that was the fashion of the day) were certainly beings in whom body, mind and a sense of justice were developed in harmony through physical, intellectual and moral exercises. And there is nothing to say that this sovereign health, this moral perfection, cannot one day be reborn. Meanwhile, what strikes me most about the modern world is the opposite, alas." For this and more, see *SL* 4: 43–44.

10. Here is another passage on the same theme: "Everything we think of as great has come to us from neurotics. It is they and they alone who found religions and create great works of art." *The Guermantes Way* 3: 414. Proust says elsewhere that if Charlus had nurtured his talent and written, not only would he have found many admiring friends, but he would also have found the work therapeutic because it would have "drained" him of the "evil" caused by his irascible nature and jealous obsessions. *The Captive* 5: 292. It is, of course, the Narrator who will succeed—whereas

his surrogate fathers, Swann and Charlus, fail—by overcoming his destructive jealous obsession with Albertine and discovering his true vocation as a writer.

11. Research done at the Kinsey Institute for Sex Research and elsewhere has shown this commonly held belief to be false. For my article "Proust's Views on Sexuality," based on my having asked Dr. Paul Gebhard, Kinsey's successor, to score the accuracy of Proust's statements about homosexuality, see *Adam International Review,* nos. 413–15 (1979): 56–62.

12. *The Captive* 5: 388.

13. *Sodom and Gomorrah* 4: 29–30.

14. *The Captive* 5: 274.

15. Francis and Gontier, *Marcel Proust et les siens,* 117–18.

16. See *Sodom and Gomorrah* 4: 492.

17. Chantal Bischoff, *Geneviève Straus: Trilogie d'une égérie* (Paris: Éditions Balland, 1992), 139.

18. Léon Daudet, *Salons et journaux,* in *Souvenirs et Polémiques* (Paris: Robert Laffont, 1992), 474.

19. Paul Morand, *Le Journal inutile,* ed. Laurent Boyer and Véronique Boyer (Paris: Gallimard, 2001), 2: 629.

20. For an interesting case of a hermaphrodite documented and photographed in Paris by Paul Nadar in the 1860s, see *Nadar,* ed. Françoise Heilbrun and Philippe Néagu (New York: The Metropolitan Museum of Art, 1995), 96–98, including fig. 93, pls. 94, 95, which offer explicit visual details of the woman's dual genitalia. There is no indication that Proust or his father or brother saw these photographs.

21. *Sodom and Gomorrah* 4: 434.

22. Marie Delcourt, *Hermaphrodite: Mythes et rites de la bisexualité dans l'Antiquité classique* (Paris: Presses Universitaires de France, 1958), 45–46.

23. *Sodom and Gomorrah* 4: 516.

24. Ibid., 4: 552–53, 419.

25. See "Marcel Proust par lui-même," *CSB,* 336. Proust was around twenty years old when he filled out the second of two such questionnaires. The Proust Questionnaire, as the set of questions and answers is now known, has recently been published in a facsimile edition: *The Proust Questionnaire* (New York: Assouline, 2005).

26. For Proust's objection to the word *homosexual*—"what is sometimes, most ineptly, termed homosexuality"—see *Sodom and Gomorrah* 4: 9.

27. See Elisabeth Ladenson's *Proust's Lesbianism.* Harold Bloom made this

observation regarding Proust's androgyny and his definition of homosexuality: "My own experience of *Search,* particularly of its major or Albertine sequence (*The Captive* and *The Fugitive*), is that the narrator's stance could only be called that of a male lesbian, which is itself a variant of the androgynous imagination Proust both manifests and celebrates." See Bloom, *The Western Canon: The Books and School of the Ages* (New York: Harcourt Brace, 1994), 399.

28. *Time Regained* 6: 20.

29. Ibid., 6: 20–21.

30. *The Fugitive* 5: 903. Not long after this passage, we find the Narrator summarizing the same idea in a maximlike statement: "Homosexuals would be the best husbands in the world if they did not put on an act of loving other women." *The Fugitive* 5: 930.

31. *Time Regained* 6: 21.

32. For the complete passage and Proust's elaboration on the influence of nature and nurture on Mme de Vaugoubert's sexual alteration, see *Sodom and Gomorrah* 4: 61–63.

33. Ibid., 4: 1–44.

34. Ibid., 4: 9, 37. The internal quotation is from Victor Hugo's poem "Les Voix intérieures."

35. *Sodom and Gomorrah* 4: 38.

36. Dreyfus's remarks are quoted in *Les Écrits de jeunesse,* 37– 39.

37. *SL* 2: 23–24; see 24 n. 3.

38. Ibid., 2: 37–38.

39. Louisa de Mornand, "Mon Amitié avec Marcel Proust," *Candide,* November 1, 1928, quoted in Philippe Michel-Thiriet, *The Book of Proust,* trans. Jan Dalley (London: Chatto and Windus, 1989), 207. George Painter states that Proust and Louisa did have intercourse: "Proust made love to her, first platonically, then physically." See *Marcel Proust: Letters to His Mother,* trans. and ed. George D. Painter (London: Rider, 1956), 42.

40. André Gide, *Journal, 1889–1939* (Paris: Gallimard, 1951), 1: 691–92. Proust's word, which I have translated as "platonically" was "spirituellement."

41. Henri Bonnet, *Les Amours et la sexualité de Marcel Proust* (Paris: Nizet, 1985), 31.

42. *Corr.* 8: 104.

43. Alfred C. Kinsey, Wardell B. Pomeroy, and Clyde E. Martin, *Sexual Behavior in the Human Male* (Philadelphia: Saunders, 1948), 639.

Epigraph: "Marcel Proust par lui-même," *CSB*, 337.

1. *Corr.* 1: 440 n. 1.
2. Ibid., 1: 442. The ellipsis is Proust's.
3. This relationship is the basis in part of that between the homosexual baron de Charlus, modeled largely on Montesquiou, and the bisexual violinist Charles Morel. For Proust on having missed his true vocation as a match-maker, see *SL* 4: 11.
4. Two recent compact discs provide the opportunity to enjoy Hahn's talent as a composer and performer. Susan Graham's acclaimed recording *La Belle Époque: The Songs of Reynaldo Hahn* is devoted exclusively to his songs, including "Si mes vers avaient des ailes." Hahn himself can be heard singing and playing on *Reynaldo Hahn: Composer, Conductor, Singer, and Accompanist: Recordings, 1908–35*.
5. *Sodom and Gomorrah* 4: 32.
6. Bernard Gavoty, *Reynaldo Hahn: Le Musicien de la Belle Époque* (Paris: Éditions Buchet / Chastel, 1976), 90.
7. Hahn's emphasis on the word *homosexual*. Both letters, written in 1893, are quoted in Gavoty, *Hahn*, 91.
8. *Sodom and Gomorrah* 4: 432.
9. *Corr.* 2: 488.
10. See ibid., 1: 310, 311 n. 2.
11. See "Portraits of Painters and Composers," *The Complete Short Stories of Marcel Proust*, trans. Joachim Neugroschel (New York: Cooper Square, 2001), 83–87.
12. *SL* 1: 88.
13. Ibid., 1: 75. Proust's biographers, myself among them, have assumed that Marcel and Reynaldo were indeed lovers. We have no proof of any of Proust's actual sexual activities, except his admissions in the letters, quoted in an earlier chapter, about his practice of masturbation and, in those same letters, his invitations to Bizet and Halévy to join him for sexual acts.
14. *Corr.* 11: 40. It is well known that the great love of Proust's life was his mother, a subject that his biographers have treated extensively. For recent psychological interpretations of this relationship and its influence on Proust's personality and his writings, see Malcolm Bowie, *Proust,*

Freud, and Lacan: Theory as Fiction (Cambridge: Cambridge University Press, 1987); Elisabeth Ladenson, *Proust's Lesbianism* (Ithaca, N.Y.: Cornell University Press, 1999); and a study that I find particularly illuminating, Inge Wimmer, *Proust and Emotion: The Importance of Affect in "À la recherche du temps perdu"* (Toronto: University of Toronto Press, 2003).

15. *Marcel Proust: Lettres à Reynaldo Hahn,* ed. Philip Kolb (Paris: Gallimard, 1956), 20.

16. Many of these drawings, some quite elaborate and often humorous, are reproduced in Philip Kolb's edition of *Lettres à Reynaldo Hahn*. I am grateful to Caroline Szylowicz for pointing out that the drawings are not always part of the letters next to which they are reproduced. None of these contain the figure with the elongated nose, but Kolb describes these drawings in his twenty-one-volume edition of Proust's correspondence. See, for example, *Corr.* 7: 71 n. 11, 269 n. 12; 10: 30 n. 4.

17. See Claude Gandelman, "The Drawings of Marcel Proust," in *Adam International Review,* nos. 394–96 (1976): 39–45.

18. The poem's original title is in English.

19. *SL* 1: 90.

20. *Corr.* 1: 379.

21. *Swann's Way* 1: 320.

22. Ibid., 1: 327.

23. Robert Soupault, *Marcel Proust du côté de la médecine* (Paris: Plon, 1967), 194–95. This view matches my own. For the scant information known about hints of matrimonial plans for Proust, see William C. Carter, *Marcel Proust: A Life* (New Haven: Yale University Press, 2000).

24. Quoted in Gavoty, *Hahn,* 103.

25. *Marcel Proust, 1871–1922: An Exhibition of Manuscripts, Books, Pictures, and Photographs,* Manchester, Whitworth Art Gallery, 1956, exhibition, no. 8.

26. In a July 1896 letter to Reynaldo, Proust wrote, "I am not, like the Lemaires, hostile to all places where we cannot be together." See *SL* 1: 127 and n. 1; *Swann's Way* 1: 205–8.

27. *Swann's Way* 1: 207.

28. See *Jean Santeuil,* trans. Gerard Hopkins (New York: Simon and Schuster, 1956), 363–64; *Corr.* 1: 429–30 n. 2.

29. Hahn's *Trio for Violin, Cello, and Piano in F Major,* eventually became a symphonic suite entitled *Illustration pour le Jardin de Bérénice: June 1895–January 1896.* See *Corr.* 7: 331–32 and n. 4.

30. *Lettres à Reynaldo Hahn,* 15.

31. *Corr.* 2: 493.

32. *SL* 2: 101–2.

33. *SL* 1: 101 and n. 2. The line of verse is from Alfred de Vigny's *La Maison du Berger.*

34. Harrison lived from 1853 to 1930. In my description of Proust's stay at Beg-Meil and the origins of *Jean Santeuil,* I am particularly indebted to Philip Kolb's article "Historique du premier roman de Proust," in *Saggi e ricerche di letteratura francese* 4 (1963): 217–77.

35. Ibid., 226.

36. Although Elstir bears vestiges of Harrison, he evolved to embody aspects of other painters whose works Proust admired, such as Monet, Manet, and Renoir.

37. A *Jean Santeuil* text inspired by Beg-Meil and Lake Geneva contains a sketch of a key theme of the future work: the phenomenon of memory ignited by a physical sensation; the examination of this sensation leads Jean to conclude that our true nature is outside time. See *Jean Santeuil,* 406–10. The title, "Impressions Regained," is not Proust's; he rarely provided titles for the drafts of *Jean Santeuil.* For more details about the development of this passage on involuntary memory, see Carter, *Marcel Proust.*

38. *Corr.* 1: 430 n. 3.

39. *SL* 1: 349–50, 351 n. 1. See *Within a Budding Grove* 2: 592, where Elstir says of Carquethuit in Brittany: "I know nothing in France like it, it reminds me rather of certain aspects of Florida." Harrison knew Florida, having spent some years there making topographic drawings. Harrison's description of Penmarch may have inspired Proust's description of Elstir's masterpiece *Le Port de Carquethuit.*

40. See, for example, this letter where Proust speaks of Saint-Saëns, "a composer, I dislike." *SL* 4: 39.

41. In addition to the letter quoted above, in which Proust acknowledges the origin of the "little phrase," there is a draft of the scene in which the Saint-Saëns sonata is identified as the music that Swann and Odette come to consider the "national anthem of their love." See *À la recherche du temps perdu,* 4 vols. (Paris: Gallimard, 1987), 1: 910, 935, 941. The use of the music as national anthem remained in the novel and is one of Proust's cleverest ways of showing how Swann always reduces art to eroticism. Another is his identification of Odette as a Botticelli woman.

42. *SL* 3: 322. On inscribing Jacques de Lacretelle's copy of *Swann's Way*, Proust identified Saint-Saëns's composition as the source of Swann and Odette's song. *SL* 4: 39. I believe that Proust's later remark—"a composer I dislike"—had as much to do with Saint-Saëns's jingoistic behavior during the war, behavior condemned by Proust, as it did with his appreciation of the composer's talent.

43. *Jean Santeuil*, 660.

44. *Swann's Way* 1: 308, 335.

45. *SL* 1: 118–19. This letter dates from March 1896. Proust begins to address Hahn with the more intimate *tu* for *you*. He signed the letter "Ton Marcel" (Your Marcel). See *Corr.* 2: 52. He soon reverted to the *vous* form of address, which the two men continued to use.

46. *The Guermantes Way* 3: 512.

47. "Thus, like an evil deity, his jealousy inspired Swann, driving him on towards his ruin." *Swann's Way* 1: 518.

FOUR *Jalousie*

1. *Corr.* 1: 451 and n. 1.

2. Lucien Daudet, *Autour de Soixante Lettres de Marcel Proust*, *Les Cahiers Marcel Proust* 5 (Paris: Gallimard, 1929), 31.

3. Ibid., 30.

4. *Corr.* 2: 68.

5. *Time Regained* 6: 20.

6. *Corr.* 2: 71 and n. 3.

7. Hahn had already begun taking notes in his journal for *La Grande Sarah*, his biography, written many years later, of the much-adored actress.

8. *Within a Budding Grove* 2: 213.

9. *SL* 1: 127; see 129, n. 2.

10. Ibid., 1: 132.

11. *Corr.* 2: 100–101.

12. *SL* 1: 133–35.

13. *The Captive* 5: 194.

14. ["Éros et Vénus,"] *CSB*, 388. For "The End of Jealousy" see *The Complete Short Stories of Marcel Proust*, trans. Joachim Neugroschel (New York: Cooper Square, 2001), 150–70.

15. *Swann's Way* 1: 438–39. There are many similar analogies referring to

Swann's love for Odette as a disease. He dies eventually of stomach cancer.

16. *Corr.* 18: 217.

17. *Swann's Way* 1: 516, 518.

18. Ibid., 1: 522.

19. *Corr.* 17: 433.

20. Harold Bloom, *The Western Canon: The Books and School of the Ages* (New York: Harcourt Brace, 1994), 396, 400. See the chapter "Proust: The True Persuasion of Sexual Jealousy."

21. *The Captive* 5: 115, 129; *Time Regained* 6: 530.

22. *Marcel Proust: Mon Cher Petit, Lettres à Lucien Daudet*, ed. Michel Bonduelle (Paris: Gallimard, 1991), 119–20.

23. *SL* 1: 175.

24. See Graham Robb, *Strangers: Homosexual Love in the Nineteenth Century* (New York: Norton, 2003), 27, 24. Robb tells us that in nineteenth-century France, the charge of public indecency and corruption of the young, often applied to sodomites, carried a maximum penalty of six months.

25. See Theodore Zeldin, *France, 1848–1945* (Oxford: Oxford University Press, 1973), 1: 313.

26. Robb, *Strangers*, 28.

27. Cornelia Otis Skinner, *Elegant Wits and Grand Horizontals* (Boston: Houghton Mifflin, 1962), 233.

28. Maurice Duplay, *Mon Ami Marcel Proust: Souvenirs intimes, Cahiers Marcel Proust* n.s. 5 (Paris: Gallimard, 1972), 50; André Gide, *Journal, 1889–1939* (Paris: Gallimard, 1951), 1: 692.

29. Edmond de Goncourt and Jules de Goncourt, *Journal: Mémoires de la vie littéraire* (Paris: Robert Laffont, 1989), 3: 571, 963, 1141. "Platré" is a derisive reference to Lorrain's powdered cheeks. A somewhat blunter English analogue would be "Look at the flaming queen!"

30. Ibid., 3: 590–91.

31. *SL* 1: 262.

32. See Duplay's memoir, *Mon Ami Marcel Proust*, 110–13.

33. *Corr.* 20: 430 n. 2.

34. The Narrator refers to a number of duels he fought over the Dreyfus Affair. See *Sodom and Gomorrah* 4: 11, *The Captive* 5: 387. Duels also feature in *Jean Santeuil;* see *Jean Santeuil*, ed. Pierre Clarac and Yves Sandre (Paris: Gallimard, 1971), 4: 684–93, 726–31.

35. Jean Bothorel, *Bernard Grasset: Vie et passion d'un éditeur* (Paris: Grasset, 1989), 76–77; *Corr.* 13: 389–90. See also *SL* 3: 203–4 and n. 22. Similar remarks are found throughout Proust's correspondence. See, for example, *SL* 4: 401–2, where Proust writes: "I thought my delightful dueling days were back again, but it seems that our assailants were not the sort of people with whom one fights."

36. *Corr.* 20: 614. Six years later, in 1903, Proust acted, with Régnier, as a second when the actor Auguste Le Bargy challenged the playwright André Picard to a duel. The novelist and the poet were able to reconcile the two men, thus avoiding a duel. See *SL* 3: 133 n. 2.

37. *Corr.* 21: 161.

38. Bonduelle, *Mon Cher Petit*, 130.

39. Reynaldo Hahn, *Notes: Journal d'un musicien* (Paris: Plon, 1933), 54.

40. Robert Dreyfus, *Souvenirs sur Marcel Proust, accompagnés de lettres inédites* (Paris: Grasset, 1926), 152–53.

41. From film interview by Roger Stéphane and Roland Darbois, *Portrait-Souvenir: Marcel Proust*, directed by Gérard Herzog, 1962.

42. *SL* 1: 189. For the Narrator's rapturous description of life in the barracks, see *Within a Budding Grove* 2: 75–76.

43. Duplay, *Mon Ami Marcel Proust*, 50.

44. *SL* 1: 158.

45. *Corr.* 2: 448.

46. Ibid., 2: 417–18.

47. *À la recherche du temps perdu*, 4 vols. (Paris: Gallimard, 1987), 3: 807, variant b. Kitchener (1850–1916) served with great military distinction in the Middle East and Africa and was promoted to field marshal in 1914. For Julius Caesar's alleged homosexual behavior, see Louis Crompton, *Homosexuality and Civilization* (Cambridge: Harvard University Press, 2003), 80, 101–2.

48. *Corr.* 19: 574–75. Souday is quoted ibid., 19: 576 n. 12. Proust also addressed the issue of snobbery in this letter, saying that "society people were so stupid" that when it was time to illustrate the duchesse de Guermantes's wit, the only model he could find was that of a commoner Mme Straus. The scene in which the Narrator thinks he has mistakenly received an invitation to a grand social event came from the memoirs of M. d'Haussonville père. "These are perhaps the only two times in my entire work when I did not completely make things up."

49. "Le Destin," signed and dated "Reynaldo Hahn, October 1898, Dieppe, Chez Mme Lemaire." See *Corr.* 3: 474 n. 2.

50. *Corr.* 2: 472–73. The phrase beginning "undying embers" alludes to Vigny's poem "La Maison du Berger." Ibid., 2: 474 n. 4.

51. *SL* 2: 21. Proust had originally planned to dedicate the translation to Hahn, but in 1903, when Dr. Proust died, Marcel decided to complete the work and dedicate it to his father's memory. The dedication ends on a humorous note that, in spite of its levity, cannot disguise Proust's disappointment in himself for not being engaged in original work: "Come, my little Master, don't make funs of the pony in his new Anglomaniac 'exercises' which are pretty perilous for him. And above all very boring."

52. Ibid., 2: 22–23.

53. Ibid., 2: 447.

54. *Carnet 1908,* 49; *The Captive* 5: 125. Not only are knowledge and possession of the other impossible, it is the very impossibility of ever being satisfied that fuels the desire: "One only loves that in which one pursues the inaccessible, one only loves what one does not possess." Ibid., 5: 517.

55. Céline Cottin, "A l'ombre de Marcel Proust," interview by Paul Guth, *Le Figaro littéraire,* September 25, 1954, 4.

56. See *Corr.* 20: 236, 334.

57. *The Captive* 5: 81.

58. *SL* 3: 128. In another letter dating from 1912, Proust told Hahn, "You know that you are always with me, that I converse with you all night; thus it would be entirely inadequate for me to say to you that I am thinking about you." *Corr.* 11: 70.

59. *Corr.* 21: 658.

60. Fénelon's secret concerning his sexuality is discussed in a later chapter. It is possible that revelations remain in store. Reynaldo Hahn's private diary will not be published until 2025. Proust's letters to Bertrand de Fénelon have been for many years in the hands of a private collector who refuses to divulge their contents.

61. Clovis Duveau, "Proust à Orléans," *Bulletin Marcel Proust* 33 (1983): 12.

62. *Pleasures and Regrets,* trans. Louise Varese (New York: Crown, 1948), 250–51. Translation modified. For the original text, see *Jean Santeuil,* 4: 130–31.

63. *Time Regained* 6: 310.

FIVE *A Nun of Speed*

1. *Corr.* 7: 285–86.
2. *SL* 2: 325.
3. *The Captive* 5: 132.
4. *SL* 2: 332 n. 1.
5. Élisabeth de Clermont-Tonnerre, *Robert de Montesquiou et Marcel Proust* (Paris: Flammarion, 1925), 101.
6. Céleste Albaret, *Monsieur Proust*, as told to Georges Belmont, trans. Barbara Bray (New York: New York Review of Books, 2003), 122. See *SL* 4: 181 n. 1.
7. Paul Morand, *Le Journal inutile*, ed. Laurent Boyer and Véronique Boyer (Paris: Gallimard, 2001), 1: 431 and n. 1. For a discussion of Natalie Clifford Barney's reaction to Proust's depiction of lesbians, see Elisabeth Ladenson, *Proust's Lesbianism* (Ithaca, N.Y.: Cornell University Press, 1999). Barney was an American expatriate whose salon gathered many of the era's most prominent Amazons.
8. *Corr.* 7: 295, 19: 712.
9. These details from Proust's visit are from Mme de Clermont-Tonnerre's memoirs, *Robert de Montesquiou et Marcel Proust*, 101–2. Clermont-Tonnerre also wrote a second memoir about Proust and his circle: *Marcel Proust* (Paris: Flammarion, 1948).
10. When the article was published in 1919 in a volume of Proust's articles and essays, the title was changed to "Journées en automobile" (Motoring days) and placed in the section on French churches. See *CSB*, 63–69.
11. For the Narrator's description of the steeples of Martinville, based largely on "Impressions de route en automobile," see *Swann's Way* 1: 255–56. Agostinelli is present as himself in the article for *Le Figaro* but absent from the version created for the novel.
12. *The Fugitive* 5: 658–59.
13. "Journées en automobile," *CSB*, 67.
14. *SL* 2: 338 and n. 2. See *The Fugitive* 5: 799, and *Time Regained* 6: 15, where the Narrator receives, in similar circumstances, a letter of congratulation "in a plebeian hand and a charming style" from an unknown person who signs his name Sanilon. There the similarity ends. The Narrator later discovers that Sanilon is a pseudonym used by Theodore, who had been a choirboy and grocer's boy at Combray. The industrious Theodore also prostituted himself to Legrandin. See *Time Regained* 6: 15.

15. Morand, *Journal inutile*, 2: 136, 487.

16. See ibid., 1: 78–79, 261–62.

17. Proust and Blanche were to remain friends, although they often quarreled, which is not surprising, given each man's eccentricities and difficult temperament. On one occasion Blanche took back the famous
portrait of Proust, which was originally full-length, and, without the
subject's permission, cut off the bottom half, thereby removing Proust's
legs and a dog sitting next to him. Then Blanche forgot to return it,
obliging Proust to go to Blanche's studio and take back the portrait by
force. Ibid., 1: 475.

18. Fernand Gregh recollected having often seen Proust, his eyes half-closed,
humming Fauré's "enchanting music" to "Chant d'automne" (Autum-
nal). See Gregh, *L'Âge d'or: Souvenirs d'enfance et de jeunesse* (Paris:
Grasset, 1947), 167.

19. *Carnet 1908*, 56.

20. *Corr.* 6: 216.

21. See Louis de Robert, *Comment débuta Marcel Proust* (Paris: Gallimard,
1969, 105–6); Clermont-Tonnerre, *Montesquiou et Proust*, 146. For
Proust's notation "le petit monstre Gabardine de Robin," see *Le Carnet de
1908*, 54.

22. *SL* 2: 405–6.

23. Ibid., 2: 399.

24. Morand, *Journal inutile*, 1: 282.

25. *The Fugitive* 5: 903. See also *Time Regained* 6: 20.

SIX *Where Fair Strangers Abound*

Epigraph: *Sodom and Gomorrah* 4: 209.

1. See *Carnet 1908*, 99, 101, and 59, where he is mentioned in a passage with
Fénelon, another model for Saint-Loup.

2. *SL* 2: 434 n. 1. During the tennis matches, Marcel had stayed on the
sidelines, flirting with his friend Gaston de Caillavet's fiancée, Jeanne
Pouquet, one of the primary models for Gilberte Swann.

3. *Carnet 1908*, 58. Proust also addressed skeptics who might find Gérard
de Nerval's similar depiction of "double love" difficult to believe. He
noted that "I" or the Narrator felt stirrings that were "quintuple." *Carnet*

1908, 66. The reference was to Nerval's *Sylvie.* See *Carnet 1908,* 66 and n. 118.

4. *Corr.* 9: 197. See *SL* 2: 452.

5. *Sodom and Gomorrah* 4: 569.

6. The new Penguin translation has changed Scott Moncrieff's original English title *Within a Budding Grove* to *In the Shadow of Young Girls in Flower,* which is an accurate translation of the original *A l'ombre des jeunes filles en fleurs.*

7. *Within a Budding Grove* 2: 506, 663.

8. Ibid., 2: 511.

9. Ibid., 2: 563, 561.

10. *Corr.* 15: 257. The two parts of the novel involving Balbec are *Within a Budding Grove* and *Sodom and Gomorrah.*

11. *The Fugitive* 5: 851; see also 5: 873: "My love for Albertine had been but a transitory form of my devotion to youth." The passage continues to stress the subjective, illusory nature of our infatuations: "We think that we are in love with a girl, whereas we love in her, alas! only that dawn the glow of which is momentarily reflected on her face."

12. Wherever the letter strayed, it has never been found. See *SL* 4: 434; the translation has watered down the original by omitting the word *horrors.* See *Corr.* 9: 88.

13. See Paul Verlaine, *Œuvres poétiques complètes* (Paris: Gallimard, 1999), 1387–1416.

14. *SL* 2: 418–19.

15. *The Fugitive* 5: 583, 597. The 1989 Pléiade edition, with its copious notes and many previously unpublished drafts, offers no new information on this episode.

16. For the passages involving this incident, see *The Fugitive* 5: 583, 598–99. The original has "avait l'air si bon" which might be better rendered as "kind," but also "good," in the sense of honorable.

17. Barbara W. Tuchman, *The Proud Tower: A Portrait of the World before the War, 1890–1914* (London: Folio, 1995), 309.

18. *SL* 2: 336. For Charlus's remark about the dignity and courage of those accused in the scandal, see *Sodom and Gomorrah* 4: 471.

19. *SL* 2: 386.

20. Françoise Leriche provided this information in the introduction to her edition of *Sodome et Gomorrhe* (Paris: Livre de poche, 1993), xxv.

21. In 1906 and 1907 Proust had asked Auguste Marguillier whether there were any essays by the American art critic Bernard Berenson available in French translation. Kolb writes that Proust may have known through Robert de Rothschild or a member of his circle that his cousin Baroness Léon Lambert had entreated Berenson to explain homosexuality to her. Berenson had responded by writing an essay in which he was completely frank about his homosexuality. See *Corr.* 7: vii and n. 14; see also *Corr.* 7: 26, 27, and n. 6.

22. Richard Ellmann, *Oscar Wilde* (New York: Knopf, 1988), 341.

23. Philippe Jullian, *Oscar Wilde*, trans. Violet Wyndham (New York: Viking, 1969), 66.

24. Ellmann, *Wilde*, 344.

25. Ibid., 346.

26. Quoted in André Gide, *Oscar Wilde: In Memoriam, De Profundis*, trans. Bernard Frechtman (New York, Philosophical Library, 1949), v. See also, André Gide, *Journal, 1889–1939* (Paris: Gallimard, 1951), 1: 28; Ellmann, *Wilde*, 355.

27. Ellmann, *Wilde*, 357.

28. Jullian, *Oscar Wilde*, 241–42.

29. *SL* 3: 4. See also *Corr.* 19: 124, where Proust says that George Eliot was the "cult of my adolescence."

30. The grandsons first told their story to Wilde's French biographer Philippe Jullian. Their account has been repeated since by other biographers, including Richard Ellmann. See Jullian, *Oscar Wilde*, 241– 42; Ellmann, *Wilde*, 347. George D. Painter corrects the address to 9 boulevard Malesherbes. George D. Painter, *Marcel Proust*, vol. 1, *The Early Years* (Boston: Little, Brown, 1959), 209.

31. Robert de Billy, *Marcel Proust: Lettres et conversations* (Paris: Éditions des Portiques, 1930), 89.

32. In French, the sentence contains 894 words. In Scott Moncrieff's English translation, the sentence runs to 958 words; *Sodom and Gomorrah* 4: 21– 24.

33. Edmond de Goncourt and Jules de Goncourt, *Journal: Mémoires de la vie littéraire* (Paris: Robert Laffont, 1989), 3: 821.

34. H. Montgomery Hyde, *The Trials of Oscar Wilde* (London: W. Hodge, 1948), 99.

35. Wolf Von Eckardt, Sander L. Gilman, and J. Edward Chamberlin, *Oscar*

Wilde's London: A Scrapbook of Vices and Virtues, 1880–1900 (New York: Anchor, 1987), 259.

36. H. Montgomery Hyde, *Oscar Wilde: A Biography* (New York: Farrar, Straus and Giroux, 1975), 118.

37. Ellmann, *Wilde*, 282.

38. *SL* 2: 360.

39. Ibid., 2: 365. Translation slightly modified.

40. Ibid., 2: 365–66, 371.

41. Roger Duchêne remarks that Proust, as in his university days, remained a literary man and a philosopher. *L'Impossible Marcel Proust* (Paris: Robert Laffont, 1994), 583.

42. *SL* 2: 372 and n. 1. Proust often noticed unexpected refinement and distinction among members of the working class. Agostinelli would provide another example, as would Céleste Albaret, whom Proust would come to regard, despite her remarkable ignorance on a number of subjects, as a kind of genius.

43. *SL* 2: 373–74.

44. *Sodom and Gomorrah* 4: 611. *Tristesse d'Olympio,* by Victor Hugo, evokes memories of the poet's passionate love for the actress Juliette Drouet. "In Wilde's dialogue *The Decay of Lying* (translated into French in 1906), Vivian says: 'One of the greatest tragedies of my life is the death of Lucien de Rubempré.'" *SL* 2: 374 n. 2.

45. *Jean Santeuil,* ed. Pierre Clarac and Yves Sandre (Paris: Gallimard, 1971), 4: 872. Jean's attitude influences his mother to be more tolerant without compromising her own moral standards. M. Sandré, on the other hand, would have chased such creatures from his house by beating them with a stick. In the later novel, the Eulenburg case is followed closely by Charlus because of his "own tendencies." See *Sodom and Gomorrah* 4: 471. From the early sketches, Charlus, like almost all Proust's "homosexual" characters, is capable of heterosexual experience, like Wilde, who was married with children. Guercy, an earlier version of Charlus, remains married for fifteen years until his wife dies. See *CSB*, 265. Charlus is also a widower.

46. Harold Bloom, *The Western Canon: The Books and School of the Ages* (New York: Harcourt Brace, 1994), 404–5.

47. *SL* 2: 442–43.

48. *Corr.* 21: 409. See Charlus's scatological outburst against Mme de Saint-Euverte, said to have been directly inspired by Montesquiou, in *Sodom*

and Gomorrah 4: 135–38. Montesquiou sent Proust a letter in which he called his passage on the hawthorns in bloom at Combray a "mixture of litanies and sperm." See *Corr.* 11: 66; *SL* 3: 65.

49. This is Tadié's thesis; Jean-Yves Tadié, *Marcel Proust* (Paris: Pierre Belfond, 1983), 900. Painter, citing no source, has Proust scream this very sentence at Céleste Albaret and her family when he gives them history lessons in the evening: "At his bedside he gave lessons in French history to Céleste, Marie Gineste, Yvonne Albaret, and Odilon, scolding them when he was displeased with the awful menace: 'I'll drown you in an ocean of *merde!*'" George D. Painter, *Marcel Proust*, vol. 2, *The Later Years* (Boston: Little, Brown, 1965), 344.

50. *SL* 3: 268. See *Sodom and Gomorrah* 4: 479.

51. *SL* 3: 270.

52. Gide, *Journal*, 1: 694.

53. *SL* 4: 405–6. For the Schlumberger quotation see 406 n. 4.

54. The concluding volume of *À la recherche du temps perdu* was published posthumously in 1927.

55. *Corr.* 20: 272, 275, 565.

56. *Timed Regained* 6: 11–12.

57. Ibid., 6: 80–81.

58. *SL* 3: 346. See also the letter to his brother in which he says that he had not meant to be "pro nor anti" but merely "objective." Ibid., 4: 156. This and two other letters written the same year maintain that Proust's characters had run away with him. For example, he wrote Natalie Clifford Barney that "the nature of his characters has made my book something less 'objective' than I would have liked." *Corr.* 19: 543. For the other letter, see ibid., 19: 514.

59. For example, here are three such passages on homosexuality: "Each man's vice (we use the term for the sake of linguistic convenience) accompanies him after the manner of the tutelary spirit who was invisible to men so long as they were unaware of his presence"; *Sodom and Gomorrah* 4: 18. " . . . their [homosexuals'] vice, or what is improperly so called"; *Sodom and Gomorrah* 4: 24. "No doubt the life of certain inverts appears at times to change, their vice (as it is called) is no longer apparent in their habits"; *Sodom and Gomorrah* 4: 34.

60. See, for example, *Time Regained* 6: 20 and 76, where Saint-Loup's homosexuality is said to be "hereditary."

61. "Publication" is to be taken literally here: "made public." Gide had

published parts of *Corydon* in a private edition in 1911 and the full work in another private edition in 1920. See Michael Lucey, *Gide's Bent: Sexuality, Politics, Writing* (New York: Oxford University Press, 1995), 69.

62. Paul Morand, *Le Journal inutile,* ed. Laurent Boyer and Véronique Boyer (Paris: Gallimard, 2001), 1: 291.

63. *Sodom and Gomorrah* 4: 255–56.

64. Morand, *Journal inutile* 2: 52.

65. Ibid., 1: 536.

66. *Jean Santeuil,* trans. Gerard Hopkins (New York: Simon and Schuster, 1956), 52. Proust changed the family name of the sisters to Kossichef, to indicate their Russian origin, but depicts the Benardaky family's circumstances and even gives their Paris address. In his inscription of Jacques de Lacretelle's copy of *Swann's Way,* Proust mentions Marie as the model for Gilberte in the gardens of the Champs-Élysées. *SL* 4: 39.

67. *The Fugitive* 5: 808–9.

68. *Sodom and Gomorrah* 4: 32.

69. Tadié, *Marcel Proust,* 561. According to Antoine Bibesco, Nahmias and his sisters, Anita and Estie, were all models for Albertine. See Philippe Michel-Thiriet, *The Book of Proust,* trans. Jan Dalley (London: Chatto and Windus, 1989), 209.

70. *Within a Budding Grove* 2: 441.

71. *Sodom and Gomorrah* 4: 52. "But the gods are immediately perceptible to one another, like as quickly to like, and so too had M. de Charlus been to Jupien." *Sodom and Gomorrah* 4: 18.

72. Ibid., 4: 32. *Invert* is Proust's preferred term for homosexual. See also *Within a Budding Grove* 2: 4–5.

73. Paul Morand, *Le Visiteur du soir, suivi de quarante-cinq lettres inédites de Marcel Proust* (Geneva: La Palatine, 1949), 26.

74. *Carnet 1908,* 49 and n. 15.

75. *The Guermantes Way* 3: 243.

76. *The Captive* 5: 397.

77. *SL* 4: 374.

78. *Corr.* 20: 286.

79. *SL* 4: 164.

80. Morand, *Le Visiteur,* 26. *Bimetallism* as a slang term for bisexuality had its origin in the practice of using two metals, such as gold and silver, jointly as a money standard.

81. *SL* 1: 129.

82. Morand, *Journal inutile,* 1: 247, 284.

83. *Sodom and Gomorrah* 4: 29.

84. See ibid., 4: 6, 9, and for the variety of complementary sexual types, 30–31.

85. *Corr.* 13: 367. Kolb is uncertain of the date of this letter but suggests that it was written in November 1911.

86. Ibid., 12: 248–49.

87. See ibid., 8: 208.

88. *SL* 3: 67–68. The only known photograph of Nahmias shows him in his ninetieth year. Still looking remarkably handsome and fit, Nahmias seems to have escaped the vicissitudes of old age described so memorably by Proust in the "masked ball" section of *Time Regained.* Nahmias lived until he was ninety-four. The photograph was published by Henri Bonnet in his article "Nahmias fils (1886–1979)," *Bulletin de la Société des Amis de Marcel Proust et de Combray* 35 (1985): 383.

89. *The Captive* 5: 79–80.

90. *SL* 3: 85–87.

91. Alphonse Daudet's memoir about his struggle with the excruciatingly painful tertiary stage of syphilis has recently been translated by Julian Barnes: *In the Land of Pain* (New York: Knopf, 2003).

92. *Swann's Way* 1: 412. See *The Guermantes Way* 3: 816–19 for the scene in which Swann is forced by the duchesse to reveal that he is terminally ill and she, to her horror, realizes that if she listens to him, she'll be late for a dinner party. In 1913, in a similar but much less traumatic context, Proust wrote Nahmias that his failure to show up for a rendezvous left "me in a state of agitation worthy of Swann's" when he rushed to Prévost's looking for Odette, who had not met him as expected. *Corr.* 12: 103.

93. For a letter in which Proust used identical language, à la Charlus, to scold young Marcel Plantevignes, see *Corr.* 8: 208.

94. See William C. Carter, *Marcel Proust: A Life* (New Haven: Yale University Press, 2000), 321. For the corresponding scene in the novel, see *The Guermantes Way* 3: 758–69.

SEVEN *Lovesick*

1. *SL* 3: 261.

2. Céleste Albaret knew about Agostinelli's passion for sports and his

daredevil nature through her husband, Odilon, who had worked with Agostinelli periodically since 1907. Albaret, *Monsieur Proust,* as told to Georges Belmont (Paris: Éditions Robert Laffont, 1973), 232–33. Agostinelli, she reports, "était audacieux et casse-cou"—was reckless and a daredevil. Barbara Bray, in her translation (New York: New York Review of Books, 2003), 190, omits "daredevil." This fascination with sports and machines of speed is a trait given to Albertine in the novel.

3. Albaret, *Monsieur Proust* (2003), 189. The only known photograph of Anna can be seen in Céleste Albaret's memoirs.

4. *SL* 3: 265.

5. *À la recherche du temps perdu,* 4 vols. (Paris: Gallimard, 1987), 1: 122. The English translation avoids the vulgarity, substituting for it a well-known and innocuous English verse, "Frogs and snails and puppy-dogs' tails . . ." *Swann's Way* 1: 172. In another example of the subjectivity of attraction, the Narrator has difficulty comprehending Saint-Loup's infatuation with Rachel. The actress-*cum*-prostitute is not attractive when seen up close and has a face that is pockmarked. See *The Guermantes Way* 3: 231.

6. *SL* 3: 265.

7. Ibid., 3: 165, 221 and n. 1.

8. See *The Captive* 5: 514–16; "Portrait of a Friend," *Jean Santeuil,* trans. Gerard Hopkins (New York: Simon and Schuster, 1956), 198–205; *The Guermantes Way* 3: 563–69.

9. Céleste Gineste was born in Auxillac on May 17, 1891. *Corr.* 12: 118 n. 2. Albaret, *Monsieur Proust* (2003), 4.

10. *Corr.* 21; 660 n. 2. See Albaret, *Monsieur Proust* (2003), 4.

11. *Corr.* 12: xxi, 211–12.

12. *SL* 3: 197. Proust wrote a similar letter to André Foucart, saying that his return to Paris was "absurd" but that he had left someone there whom he saw "seldom" but being away from whom caused him a "terrible anxiety." Because of this intense feeling, he had found the view of the people at the casino and the hotel "unbearable." *Corr.* 21: 655–66.

13. *SL* 3: 195.

14. *Corr.* 12: 248–49.

15. Ibid., 12: 322.

16. Paul Morand, *Le Journal inutile,* ed. Laurent Boyer and Véronique Boyer (Paris: Gallimard, 2001), 1: 253.

17. *SL* 3: 198–99, 200.
18. *Sodom and Gomorrah* 4: 21.
19. *The Fugitive* 5: 672.
20. *Corr.* 9: 100, 3: 160.
21. *SL* 2: 268.
22. *The Captive* 5: 137.
23. *Jean Santeuil*, 1.
24. *Corr.* 12: 252.
25. *The Guermantes Way* 3: 447.
26. *Time Regained* 6: 315. There is a variation on this theme toward the end of the novel: "The writer feeds his book, he strengthens the parts of it which are weak, he protects it, but afterwards it is the book that grows, that designates its author's tomb and defends it against the world's clamour and for a while against oblivion." *Time Regained* 6: 508.
27. *Corr.* 13: 228–29.
28. In a letter to Émile Straus on June 3, 1914, Proust quotes himself as having said this. *SL* 3: 261.
29. Albaret, *Monsieur Proust* (2003), 190, 192.
30. *Corr.* 13: 340.
31. *SL* 3: 209.
32. *Corr.* 12: 336, 13: 367, 19: 725. De Noailles's letter has not come down to us. For a similar letter to Jean-Louis Vaudoyer, see ibid., 12: 291.

EIGHT *Grieving and Forgetting*

1. See Céleste Albaret, *Monsieur Proust,* as told to Georges Belmont, trans. Barbara Bray (New York: New York Review of Books, 2003), 190. The date of the Agostinellis' departure was determined by Kolb in *Corr.* 12: 15.
2. *SL* 3: 214.
3. See *The Fugitive* 5: 587, 615–16. For the correspondence between Proust and Nahmias regarding the pursuit of Agostinelli, see *Corr.* 12: 355–66.
4. *The Fugitive* 5: 615–16.
5. *SL* 3: 190 and n. 2.
6. *Corr.* 18: 404–5.
7. Ibid., 13: 186–87.
8. See the letter to Lionel Hauser, ibid., 13: 213 and 214 n. 2.

9. *SL* 3: 256–58. The emphasis is Proust's.

10. *Corr.* 13: 221 n. 8.

11. For Proust's transposition of his letter to Agostinelli into one from the Narrator to Albertine under similar circumstances, see *The Fugitive* 5: 612–15.

12. *Corr.* 13: 190 n. 6.

13. *SL* 3: 258–59. Agostinelli ignored Proust's request to return all his letters, later destroyed by the young man's family, who said they were love letters. See Jean-Yves Tadié, *Marcel Proust* (Paris: Pierre Belfond, 1983), 280 n. 3. The one surviving letter, returned since Agostinelli died before he could receive it, does not read like a love letter. Had Proust wanted the letters back in order to use them in his novel? This is Philip Kolb's thesis. If he is right, then the novelist had already decided to use Agostinelli as one of the models for Albertine before the pilot's death. The fact that Proust preserved this letter may be an indication of his intention to use it in the novel. See *Corr.* 13: 220– 21, 223 n. 25.

14. *Time Regained* 6: 328.

15. See *The Captive* 5: 91.

16. See *Time Regained* 6: 166–68.

17. The idea that Agostinelli drowned because "he had never learned to swim" apparently originated with Painter, who does not cite a source for this information. See George D. Painter, *Marcel Proust*, vol. 2, *The Later Years* (Boston: Little, Brown, 1965), 213. None of the earlier accounts say that Agostinelli could not swim. Robert Vigneron maintains that Agostinelli was known to be a good swimmer. For press accounts of Agostinelli's death, see Vigneron, "Genèse de Swann," *Études sur Stendhal et sur Proust* (Paris: Nizet, 1978), 101; *Corr.* 13: 242 n. 3.

18. The Narrator learns of Albertine's death in a telegram sent by Mme Bontemps. *The Fugitive* 5: 642.

19. Albertine has mysterious rings bearing eagles with outspread wings, which, when inverted, closely resembles the *V* symbol for velocity. See *The Captive* 5: 75; *The Fugitive* 5: 624.

20. *Corr.* 13: 238. See *SL* 3: 260, n. 3.

21. Ibid., 13: 225 and n. 2.

22. *SL* 3: 260.

23. *Corr.* 13: 241, 243; *SL* 3: 267.

24. *SL* 3: 265.

25. *Corr.* 13: 228 and n. 3.

26. *SL* 3: 267–68. In a letter to Émile Straus, written three days after Agostinelli's death, Proust said Agostinelli was an "extraordinary person who possessed perhaps the greatest intellectual gifts I have ever known." Ibid., 3: 261. For the Narrator's appreciation of Albertine's intelligence, see *The Fugitive* 5: 668.

27. *Corr.* 13: 254.

28. Ibid., 13: 239.

29. *SL* 3: 293.

30. *The Fugitive* 5: 673.

31. *Corr.* 13: 228; *SL* 3: 261. Proust made the same remark to Gautier-Vignal. See Louis Gautier-Vignal's memoir, *Proust connu et inconnu* (Paris: Laffont, 1976), 243.

32. See *La Prisonnière*, ed. Jean Milly (Paris: Flammarion, 1984), 11. There are other traces of "Albertine" episodes in *Le Carnet de 1908;* see Kolb's generous notes. Albertine assumes and enlarges the role of a much earlier character that Proust had sketched under the name Marie.

33. *Corr.* 20: 500.

34. *The Fugitive* 5: 674. Earlier, Albertine had predicted that she would die by drowning: "The sea shall be my tomb." *Sodom and Gomorrah* 4: 272. For a more comprehensive portrait of Alfred Agostinelli and what he contributed to the character of Albertine, see the chapters "The Death of an Aviator" and "The Artist and the Aviator" in my book *The Proustian Quest* (New York: New York University Press, 1992), 133–85. There I correct what I believe to be J. E. Rivers's exaggerated assessment of Agostinelli's contributions, especially to the figure of the aviator in the novel, which is purely symbolic and has nothing to do with Agostinelli. See Rivers, *Proust and the Art of Love: The Aesthetics of Sexuality in the Life, Times, and Art of Marcel Proust* (New York: Columbia University Press, 1980). I find Rivers much stronger on the history of sexuality and its sociological implications for the world described in Proust's novel. Harold Bloom rightly objects to readings like Rivers's as well: "Biographical scholars have cleared away the nonsense that allegorizes [the Narrator's] affair with Albertine into Proust's relationship with Alfred Agostinelli." Bloom, *The Western Canon: The Books and School of the Ages* (New York: Harcourt Brace, 1994), 404.

35. See *Carnet 1908*, 48 and n. 5, and 135–36 n. 23. All Proust's fictional

lovers suffer from this "incapacity for happiness," with variations on the theme of obsessive jealousy over heterosexual or homosexual infidelities: Swann and Odette, Saint-Loup and Rachel, the Narrator and Albertine, and Charlus and Morel.

36. *The Fugitive* 5: 874. One finds variations on this theme throughout *The Fugitive,* where the Narrator grieves and then recovers from the loss of Albertine. Here is one aphoristic example: "It is the tragedy of other people that they are merely showcases for the very perishable collections of one's own mind." *The Fugitive* 5: 751.

37. *SL* 3: 409.

38. Paul Morand, *Le Journal inutile,* ed. Laurent Boyer and Véronique Boyer (Paris: Gallimard, 2001), 2: 513.

39. *The Fugitive* 5: 805.

40. *SL* 3: 280–81.

41. Ibid.

42. For a discussion of this and other Forssgren documents that have recently come to light, see *The Memoirs of Ernest Forssgren, Proust's Swedish Valet,* ed. William C. Carter (New Haven: Yale University Press, 2006).

43. *The Fugitive* 5: 809.

44. *SL* 3: 280–81. This reads, as passages in the letters often do, like a draft for the texts from the novel already quoted about mourning and forgetting, a new self that replaces the grieving one, and so on. See *The Fugitive* 5: 805.

45. *Time Regained* 6: 287, 516.

46. Ibid., 6: 524.

47. Clive Bell, *Proust* (London: Hogarth, 1928), 89.

48. *Corr.* 14: 137, 140, 135. Proust leaves the friend unnamed in the letter. In 1916 Proust asked Adèle Larivière, traveling in the south, to sign Proust's name in the book in the church of Saint-Pierre in Monte Carlo at the mass for the anniversary of Agostinelli's death. See ibid., 15: 175.

49. Ibid., 14: 201. We recall that when Proust was exploring Normandy in 1907, he sought a "provincial Balzacian town" for a story that he wanted to write. See *SL* 2: 332 n. 1.

50. Tadié, *Marcel Proust,* 732; *Corr.* 15: 31 and 32 n. 8.

51. *The Fugitive* 5: 689.

52. *Time Regained* 6: 310.

53. *Sodom and Gomorrah* 4: 231–32. The most-developed appearance by a real person in the novel is that of Céleste Albaret, who, in addition to

having contributed traits to the servant Françoise, appears as herself. See *Sodom and Gomorrah* 4: 331–37; *The Captive* 5: 12–13, 167. In the second of these passages, the Narrator's lack of interest in Albertine's intellectual qualities matches Proust's own indifference to the intellectual acumen of the young men that he paid to serve him and keep him company: "Albertine had developed to an astonishing degree. This was a matter of complete indifference to me, a woman's intellectual qualities having always interested me so little that if I pointed them out to some woman or other it was solely out of politeness. Céleste's curious genius alone might perhaps appeal to me."

54. *Time Regained* 6: 530.

NINE *The Night Prowler*

Epigraph: Questionnaire, *CSB,* 336.

1. *Corr.* 17: 343.
2. Céleste Albaret, *Monsieur Proust,* as told to Georges Belmont, trans. Barbara Bray (New York: New York Review of Books, 2003), 194.
3. Painter demoted Orloff from prince to count, a mistake repeated by many others, including Céleste Albaret. George D. Painter, *Marcel Proust,* vol. 2, *The Later Years* (Boston: Little, Brown, 1965), 263. See *The Memoirs of Ernest Forssgren, Proust's Swedish Valet,* ed. William C. Carter (New Haven: Yale University Press, 2006).
4. For Céleste Albaret on Le Cuziat, see *Monsieur Proust,* 192–98. All subsequent quotations of Céleste in this chapter are from this passage.
5. See Theodore Zeldin, *France, 1848–1945* (Oxford: Oxford University Press, 1973), 1: 307–8.
6. In the Paris of Proust's era, "Female brothels would obtain male prostitutes for clients who wanted them." Arno Karlen, *Sexuality and Homosexuality: A New View* (New York, Norton, 1971), 248.
7. *Sodom and Gomorrah* 4: 650–51, 655.
8. Albaret, *Monsieur Proust,* 193. In a 1917 letter to Mme Catusse, Proust mentions that he has "made a lot of poor souls happy" by his gifts of furniture. *Corr.* 16: 312. Mme Catusse no doubt would have been shocked had she known the fate of the "profaned" furnishings.
9. *Within a Budding Grove* 2: 208–9.

10. This explains why no known correspondence between Proust and Le Cuziat exists. There is only one letter that mentions, in passing, "Albert," identified as Le Cuziat by Philip Kolb. See *Corr.* 21: 366.

11. *The Fugitive* 5: 904.

12. All the information about Proust's being caught in the police raid are from Laure Murat, "Proust, Marcel, 46 ans, rentier: Un individu 'aux allures de pédéraste' fiché à la police," *La Revue littéraire* 14 (May 2005): 82–93. I am grateful to my friend J. P. Smith for bringing this article to my attention shortly before this book went to press.

13. *Corr.* 17: 143.

14. See Paul Morand, *Poèmes* (Paris: Gallimard, 1973), 17–18. I have incorporated into my translation of the "Ode" the shorter version given in *SL* 4: 95–96 n. 7. All quotations regarding Proust's reaction to the "Ode" are from this letter.

15. Paul Morand, *Le Journal inutile*, ed. Laurent Boyer and Véronique Boyer (Paris: Gallimard, 2001), 2: 79.

16. *SL* 4: 95.

17. Albaret, *Monsieur Proust*, 196.

18. *Carnet 1908*, 69.

19. *The Fugitive* 5: 664.

20. Albaret, *Monsieur Proust*, 197.

21. Even the detestable Verdurins are the donors of anonymous charitable gifts. See *The Captive* 5: 436, 440. Proust always shows compassion for his characters by trying to understand the reasons for their actions and by finding redeeming qualities. The Narrator attributes his inability to condemn others to the influences of his mother and grandmother. *Within a Budding Grove* 2: 445.

22. *The Captive* 5: 439.

23. *Time Regained* 6: 184–200.

24. *SL* 3: 120.

25. *Time Regained* 6: 245, 339.

26. Ibid., 6: 182–85, 195–201.

27. Henri Bonnet, *Les Amours et la sexualité de Marcel Proust* (Paris: Nizet, 1985), 79–85.

28. Bonnet said that the key word in the notebook, which he transcribed as *pleasure*, meaning orgasm, is illegible and therefore dubious. Ibid., 80 n. 1.

29. Albaret, *Monsieur Proust*, 86–86, 203. Tennessee Williams, a writer with a similar phobia, also took stringent precautions when engaging male prostitutes, which he routinely did wherever he traveled. Williams describes, as an example, the time he hired a young man named Lyle in a New Orleans establishment where the "go-go boys double as waiters as well as hustlers." The boys paraded around wearing "G-strings only—so you can be pretty sure what you're getting. I would recommend, however, that penetration be avoided, as they are most probably all infected with clap in the ass. And I'd also recommend that you get them to bathe as their hours are long and sweaty. And that you have a pubic pesticide such as A–200." When "the young Lyle" showed up in Williams's room for the rendezvous, the playwright feasted his eyes upon the boy but strictly limited his contact: "[Lyle] has a softly nubile look and a soft Southern voice—and I contemplate no intimacy beyond the tactile—I mean the relatively chaste knowledge of his skin surface with my fingers. This restriction is particularly prudent since I am allergic to penicillin and the last thing I need is a clap." Tennessee Williams, *Memoirs* (New York: Doubleday, 1972), 75. Proust's fear of physical contact apparently surpassed that of Williams.

30. Jean Cocteau, *Le Passé défini*, ed. Pierre Chanel (Paris: Gallimard, 1983), 1: 288–89 and n. 1. In the same passage, Cocteau maintains that the reason Proust became so upset over Morand's "Ode" was that the French word for "routs," "*raouts*," suggested by its look and sound *rats* (which is the same in French as in English). We have seen, however, that Proust's fear of being caught in a police raid at Le Cuziat's was well founded.

31. *Sodom and Gomorrah* 4: 416, 300.

32. Cocteau, *Passé défini*, 1: 289; *The Guermantes Way* 3: 109–10.

33. Cocteau, *Passé défini*, 1: 305.

34. Ibid., 1: 290.

35. André Gide, *Ainsi soit-il*, in *Journal, 1939–49: Souvenirs* (Paris: Gallimard, Pléiade, 1966), 1223. According to the Proust biographer André Maurois, Bernard Faÿ, the "author of *In Search of a Lost Soldier*," who "knew Proust during the war," also confirmed the sadistic use of rats. See Maurois, *The World of Marcel Proust*, trans. Moura Budberg with the assistance of Barbara Creed (New York: Harper and Row, 1974), 255.

36. For Morand on Proust's photographs, see *Journal inutile*, 1: 398, 475; 2: 142.

37. Albaret, *Monsieur Proust*, 305.

38. *Corr.* 18: 509.

39. Morand, *Journal inutile*, 1: 398.

40. See Maurice Sachs, *Le Sabbat: roman* (Paris: Gallimard, 1960), 285, 287. See also Pierre Assouline, *Gaston Gallimard: Un Demi-siècle d'édition française* (Paris: Éditions Balland, 1984), 175–77. For more on Sachs's escapades and misadventures, see Henri Raczymow's biography, *Maurice Sachs; ou, Les travaux forcés de la frivolité* (Paris: Gallimard, 1988).

41. See Assouline, *Gaston Gallimard*, 175–77.

42. Morand, *Journal inutile*, 1: 715.

43. See Painter, *Proust*, 2: 268–69. Painter gives the wrong month for Sachs's reminiscence, *Historiette*, which appeared under the rubric, "L'Air du mois." It was in the May 1938 issue, not July, pages 863–64, of *La Nouvelle Revue Française*.

44. See *Le Sabbat*, 285, 287.

45. Albaret, *Monsieur Proust*, 196.

46. Morand, *Journal inutile*, 1: 231.

47. Louis Gautier-Vignal, *Proust connu et inconnu* (Paris: Laffont, 1976), 246–47. A friend and neighbor of the elderly Marcel Plantevignes's, who was one of Proust's young men from the 1908–10 Cabourg period, told me that, according to Plantevignes, Proust was indeed impotent.

48. *Corr.* 18: 330–31. In a letter written a decade earlier (October 30, 1908), Proust hinted that he was still sexually active: "I eat, I sleep, I drink . . . I screw, but I am ill." Ibid., 8: 265. Since he is paraphrasing a remark by another writer, and given ambiguous reference to his health at the end of the letter, it is impossible to know whether he was being serious about his sexual activity.

49. Cocteau says that the cigarette is another telltale sign that the girls are really men. According to him, no young woman would have smoked in public during the period in question. See *Le Passé défini*, 1: 298.

50. *Sodom and Gomorrah* 4: 381–82.

51. *Time Regained* 6: 528.

52. Morand, *Journal inutile*, 1: 281.

53. *Swann's Way* 1: 331.

54. *The Fugitive* 5: 904; *The Guermantes Way* 3: 497–98.

Epigraph: *The Fugitive* 5: 715.

1. This account is taken from Wixler's interview "Proust au Ritz: Souvenirs d'un maître d'hôtel," *Adam International Review* 40, nos. 394–96 (1976): 14–21.
2. *Corr.* 17: 514.
3. There are two errors in Wixler's account at this point, but they do not undermine the rest of his story. He says that he went to boulevard Hauss-mann and Céline Cottin showed him in to the writer's room, where he saw Proust lying in his bed, which was strewn with pieces of paper. According to Wixler's own chronology, Proust was then living at rue Hamelin, and Céleste Albaret had replaced Cottin as the housekeeper at the outbreak of the war.
4. For all quotations regarding the Ritz dinner see *Corr.* 17: 343, 344 n. 10, and 387.
5. Paul Morand, *Le Journal inutile*, ed. Laurent Boyer and Véronique Boyer (Paris: Gallimard, 2001), 1: 253; 2: 595. See Ernest Forssgren's "Summary of Painter" in *The Memoirs of Ernest Forssgren, Proust's Swedish Valet*, ed. William C. Carter (New Haven: Yale University Press, 2006), for another of Proust's moves.
6. Maurice Duplay, *Mon Ami Marcel Proust: Souvenirs intimes, Cahiers Marcel Proust* n.s. 5 (Paris: Gallimard, 1972), 95.
7. *Corr.* 17: 360–61, 384, 483.
8. Céleste Albaret, *Monsieur Proust*, as told to Georges Belmont, trans. Barbara Bray (New York: New York Review of Books, 2003), 188.
9. Morand, *Journal inutile*, 1: 599. The emphasis is Morand's. Morand, in a sense, anticipated Elisabeth Ladenson's study *Proust's Lesbianism* (Ithaca, N.Y.: Cornell University Press, 1999).
10. *Corr.* 21: 651. This sentiment was to be reinforced by the heroic French soldiers, les "poilus," in the war about to begin. As the nobleman and officer Saint-Loup remarks, "As I say, the people, the working men, are the best of all, but everybody is splendid." *Time Regained* 6: 91.
11. *Sodom and Gomorrah* 4: 578.
12. *SL* 3: 124. See also the letter to Mme Vallette in *Corr.* 19: 55–56.
13. *Time Regained* 6: 61.

14. *Sodom and Gomorrah* 4: 156.

15. *The Fugitive* 5: 669.

16. *SL* 4: 151.

17. Ibid., 3: 332. Proust wrote in a 1909 letter: "My solitary life has enabled me to recreate in my thoughts those I have loved." Ibid., 2: 454.

18. Albaret, *Monsieur Proust*, 188.

19. *The Fugitive* 5: 923.

20. *Swann's Way* 1: 487–88.

21. *The Fugitive* 5: 592.

22. *Within a Budding Grove* 2: 252. For more on Proustian comedy, see Harold Bloom's excellent essay "Proust: The True Persuasion of Sexual Jealousy," in *The Western Canon: The Books and School of the Ages* (New York: Harcourt Brace, 1994), 396–412. Bloom rightly underscores Proust's great skill at comedy: "I wonder sometimes why Proust is unique in seeing and representing the high comedy, rather than the low farce of sexual jealousy. The meditative process of *In Search of Lost Time* carried him to a perspective in which [the Narrator's] jealous sufferings can be seen as exquisitely, if still painfully, comic," 397.

23. *The Guermantes Way* 3: 657.

24. *Corr.* 18: 355, 17: 405.

25. *The Captive* 5: 81–82. See also ibid., 5: 235: "I admired Albertine's paintings. The touching pastimes of a captive, they moved me so that I congratulated her upon them."

26. Albaret, *Monsieur Proust*, 188.

27. *Corr.* 18: 122 and n. 2.

28. Harold Nicolson, *Peacemaking 1919* (New York: Grosset and Dunlap, 1965), 275–76.

29. Ibid., 318–19.

30. Morand, *Journal inutile*, 1: 259.

31. *The Captive* 5: 412, 408–9.

32. Ibid., 5: 399–402.

33. "Un amour malheureux qui finit" (an unhappy love that is coming to an end), *Corr.* 18: 199–200.

34. Ibid., 18: 205. See also ibid., 19: 36–37.

35. Albaret, *Monsieur Proust*, 79.

36. Morand, *Journal inutile*, 1: 608.

37. Mauriac met Proust for the first time on February 4, 1918, at a party given

in honor of Francis Jammes. He visited Proust at rue Hamelin on February 28, 1921. I have combined the several entries from Mauriac's memoirs describing these two encounters. See François Mauriac, *Œuvres autobiographiques* (Paris: Gallimard, 1990), 263, 276, 283–84.

38. See, for example, *Corr.* 18: 230.
39. Ibid., 19: 104.
40. Jean Cocteau, *Le Passé défini*, ed. Pierre Chanel (Paris: Gallimard, 1983), 1: 305–8.
41. Cocteau, *Le Passé défini*, 1: 269, 305. For Ladenson's interpretation of this remark in relation to Albertine's sexuality, see *Proust's Lesbianism*, 104–8.
42. *SL* 3: 34.
43. Cocteau, *Le Passé défini*, 1: 305–8.
44. *Corr.* 17: 153.
45. *Corr.* 18: 279.
46. Ibid., 18: 330–31.
47. The letter, edited by Kolb, is quoted in full by Jean-Yves Tadié, *Marcel Proust* (Paris: Pierre Belfond, 1983), 695–96. Emphasis is Proust's.
48. *Sodom and Gomorrah* 4: 12.
49. Ibid., 4: 44.
50. *The Captive* 5: 235–36. See also ibid., 5: 500–501: "I had clipped her wings, and she had ceased to be a winged Victory and become a burdensome slave of whom I would have liked to rid myself."
51. *Marcel Proust–Gaston Gallimard: Correspondance*, ed. Pascal Fouché (Paris: Gallimard, 1989), 365 n. 2.
52. *SL* 4: 238.
53. *Corr.* 20: 357.
54. In a letter of July 16, 1921, Proust told Sydney Schiff that his secretary, "who was to marry a concierge's daughter," had "broken off his engagement" before departing for South America. *SL* 4: 238.
55. Céleste Albaret, who is the source for Proust's visit to Rochat's fiancée, provides no details. Albaret, *Monsieur Proust*, 189.
56. *Sodom and Gomorrah* 4: 419.
57. *Corr:* 18: 243, 284–85.
58. *Sodom and Gomorrah* 4: 420.
59. *The Captive* 5: 59–60.
60. Ibid., 5: 255.
61. *Corr.* 20: 405.

62. Albaret, *Monsieur Proust*, 189.

63. The term is an "allusion to Victor Hugo's eponymous valet, Ruy Blas." *SL* 4: 181 n. 1. Proust had apparently first heard Montesquiou use the title to designate handsome blond footmen.

64. See *The Memoirs of Ernest Forssgren*.

65. Painter, *Marcel Proust*, vol. 2, *The Later Years* (Boston: Little, Brown, 1965), 262–63.

66. *Sodom and Gomorrah* 4: 46, 49–50. Homosexuals in the Paris of Proust's day cruised the same popular areas frequented by prostitutes. These included the banks of the Seine, the Tuileries gardens, the Palais-Royal, and the Champs-Élysées. See Bryant T. Ragan, Jr., "The Enlightenment Confronts Homosexuality," in *Homosexuality in Modern France*, ed. Jeffrey Merrick and Bryant T. Ragan, Jr. (New York: Oxford University Press, 1996), 12; Graham Robb, *Strangers: Homosexual Love in the Nineteenth Century* (New York: Norton, 2003), 157.

67. See *The Memoirs of Ernest Forssgren*.

68. *SL* 4, 180–81 n. 1.

69. Ibid., 4: 181 n. 4.

70. See Philippe Michel-Thiriet, *The Book of Proust*, trans. Jan Dalley (London: Chatto and Windus, 1989), 216.

71. See *Corr.* 10: 333.

72. *SL* 4: 182.

ELEVEN *Love Is Divine*

1. *CSB:* 336.

2. *Carnet 1908*, 45 and n. 461, 69.

3. *Time Regained* 6: 316, 301; see also 315 and *The Captive* 5: 504: "It is inconceivable that a piece of sculpture or a piece of music which gives us an emotion that we feel to be more exalted, more pure, more true, does not correspond to some definite spiritual reality, or life would be meaningless."

4. *Time Regained* 6: 316, 303–4. See also *Within a Budding Grove* 2: 563–64, where the Narrator observes that "the emotions which a perfectly ordinary girl arouses in us can enable us to bring to the surface of our consciousness some of the innermost parts of our being, more personal,

more remote, more quintessential than any that might be evoked by the pleasure we derive from the conversation of a great man or even from the admiring contemplation of his work."

5. *Time Regained* 6: 318, 300.

6. *Corr.* 18: 296.

7. *Swann's Way* 1: 133.

8. Ibid., 1: 3.

9. *The Captive* 5: 97.

10. Lawrence Joseph, "Marcel Proust et 'Docteur Dieu': Lettres inédites à Samuel Pozzi," *Bulletin Marcel Proust* 51 (2001): 27.

11. For this passage, see *Within a Budding Grove* 2: 564–67.

12. *The Fugitive* 5: 607.

13. *The Captive* 5: 206.

14. *Time Regained* 6: 272.

15. Ibid., 6: 328. Cf. *The Fugitive* 5: 669: "A woman is of greater utility to our life if, instead of being an element of happiness in it, she is an instrument of suffering, and there is not a woman in the world the possession of whom is as precious as that of the truths which she reveals to us by causing us to suffer." See *Time Regained* 6: 303–4 for more on the conversion of pain caused by obsession to the joy of creating a work of art.

16. *Time Regained* 6: 509, 510–11. For the reference to Scheherazade, see ibid., 6: 524. In the early notes for *Le Temps retrouvé*, images of feminine creativity predominate. See Marcel Proust, *Matinée chez la Princesse de Guermantes: Cahiers du Temps retrouvé*, ed. Henri Bonnet in collaboration with Bernard Brun (Paris: Gallimard, 1982), 300.

17. *Swann's Way* 1: 257.

18. According to metaphysical tradition, the figure of the androgyne presides over births. See Elémire Zolla, *The Androgyne: Reconciliation of Male and Female* (New York: Crossroad, 1981), 66, 70; for the metaphysical conception of cosmic man as an androgyne, see 48. The theme of androgyny is found even in the church of Saint-Hilaire, whose steeple is one of the principal unification symbols of the novel. Hilaire was originally a female saint whose name, through morphological changes, became that of a man. See *Swann's Way* 1: 145.

19. Françoise Cachin, "Monsieur Vénus et l'Ange de Sodome: L'Androgyne au temps de Gustave Moreau," *Nouvelle Revue de Psychanalyse* 7 (1973): 63–69.

20. For a succinct analysis of some of the major similarities and differences between the ideas of Sigmund Freud and Proust, see Malcolm Bowie, *Freud, Proust and Lacan: Theory as Fiction* (Cambridge: Cambridge University Press, 1987). Bowie makes this observation about the primordial Adam and family and social pressures on the young: "Bisexuality remembers the protozoic Eden more completely, and rediscovers its many pleasures more readily, but is preyed upon, as all sexual dispositions are, by that other prehistory—of training and coercion, seduction and counterseduction—which is the life of the human infant within the family" (95).

21. *Carnet 1908*, 69.

22. *Time Regained* 6: 522. See also ibid., 6: 508, where the future work must be nourished like a child. The translation is not accurate here. Proust's *suralimenter*, which means "to feed up" or to nourish as fully as possible, is rendered as *cosset*. The new Penguin translation gets it right: "feeding it [the book] up like a child." Marcel Proust, *Finding Time Again*, trans. Ian Paterson (London: Allen Lane, 2002), 342. Rivers quotes Leo Bersani, who sees the entire concluding sequence of *Time Regained* as suggesting the stages of pregnancy by "the joyful conception of the idea [for the book] at the Guermantes *matinée*, the weakness and dizziness on the staircase some time later, and a painful delivery." Rivers, *Proust and the Art of Love*, 253.

23. *Time Regained* 6: 508.

24. Ibid., 6: 312.

25. *SL* 2: 252–53.

26. *Time Regained* 6: 513.

27. Ibid.

28. John Updike, "Remembrance of Things Past," *Horizon* 14, no. 4 (1972): 105.

29. Marcel Proust, *On Reading Ruskin*, trans. and ed. Jean Autret, William Burford, and Phillip J. Wolfe (New Haven: Yale University Press, 1987), 29–38.

30. *Within a Budding Grove* 2: 175.

31. *Time Regained* 6: 45. See also *Swann's Way* 1: 133.

32. *Within a Budding Grove* 2: 179. In drafts for the novel, we find notes developing the idea that the individual is an ephemeral manifestation of eternal laws. In a variation on the theme, Proust wrote: "A single poet who has endured since the beginning of the world . . . and so unique that even his physical portraits seem under the name of Baudelaire, Hugo,

Vigny to be only the different profiles of the same admirable face. The works themselves could be framed together like the scattered pieces of the same universe." *Matinée*, 366; see also 184–85, 352. Proust had expressed the idea of a universal soul many years earlier in his essay "Contre l'obscurité," published in *La Revue blanche* on July 15, 1896: It is "another law of life" that the "universal or eternal" can be realized "only in individuals. In works of literature as in life, human beings, however general they may be, must be strongly individualized (cf. *War and Peace, The Mill on the Floss*) and it can be said of them, as of each one of us, that it is when they are most themselves that they realize most fully the universal soul." "Against Obscurity," *Marcel Proust: Against Sainte-Beuve and Other Essays*, trans. John Sturrock (New York: Viking, 1988), 139. Stéphane Zagdanski has come to the realization indirectly through Jorge Luis Borges's remark that "Dante and Ulysses are one and the same man." This applies just as well, he adds, to "Homer and Proust." Zagdanski, *Le Sexe de Proust* (Paris: Gallimard, 1994), 92.

33. *Within a Budding Grove* 2: 181.

34. *Time Regained* 6: 522.

35. Edmund Wilson, *Axel's Castle* (New York: Scribner, 1931), 189, 163. *Swann's Way* was published in 1913, during the time when Einstein's theories were coming to be widely known, providing the first new model for the physical world since the time of Newton. The articles in which Einstein expounded his theory of relativity, of which Proust had no knowledge at the time, were published between 1905 and 1916. See John D. Erickson, "The Proust-Einstein Relation: A Study in Relative Point of View," in *Marcel Proust: A Critical Panorama*, ed. Larkin B. Price (Urbana: University of Illinois Press, 1973), 247–76. Proust and Einstein were conceiving their great works at approximately the same time. I have found a remarkable similarity between Proust's and Einstein's definitions of the artist and between their religious beliefs. See my "Proust, Einstein, et le sentiment cosmique religieux," *Bulletin de la Société des Amis de Marcel Proust et de Combray* 37 (1987): 52–62. One explanation for the universal appeal of Proust is found in another unifying element of his vision: he sees the roles of the artist and the scientist as being the same, that of seeking the truth. The only distinction is in their methods of finding it. See the chapter "The Cosmos Builder" in William C. Carter, *The Proustian Quest* (New York: New York University Press, 1992), 207–39.

36. *Within a Budding Grove* 2: 444–45.

37. *Swann's Way* 1: 208–9.

38. *Sodom and Gomorrah* 4: 220. In the novel the mother and the grandmother are both modeled on Proust's mother.

39. Albaret, *Monsieur Proust*, 143.

40. *Time Regained* 6: 353. For an earlier version of this "idea of Existences that are more vast than those of individuals, of a sole Spirit, scattered throughout space, and of immortal Characters perpetuating themselves throughout Time," see *Matinée*, 400–401. This passage gives us a glimpse of Proust using his own nature and experience for various characters, in this case Bloch. He writes that for Bloch's outbursts he can use "if need be myself imitating Papa and Mama's despotism."

41. Preface to *La Bible d'Amiens* in *On Reading Ruskin*, 10. See also "Contre l'obscurité," *CSB*, 394. Cf. earlier passages on unity, and this: "All poets seemed to me to constitute only one Poet whose different names apply to Gérard de Nerval in his time as a vagabond, to Baudelaire reminiscing." *Matinée*, 184–85. In a note to himself about death, Proust reiterates his belief that the individual is an ephemeral manifestation of eternal laws. *CSB*, 352; see also 366, 401. Proust intended his highly particularized and vivid characters Elstir and Vinteuil to serve an emblematic function as well: "[Elstir] a great artist with a fictitious name who symbolizes the Great Painter in my book as Vinteuil symbolizes the Great Composer (such as Franck)." *SL* 3: 337.

42. *Time Regained* 6: 290.

43. For example, the steeples of Martinville in *Swann's Way* 1: 253–57, the three trees at Hudimesnil in *Within a Budding Grove* 2: 404–7.

44. *The Fugitive* 5: 844.

45. Wallace Fowlie, *A Reading of Proust* (Chicago: University of Chicago Press, 1985), 68.

46. *The Guermantes Way* 3: 737.

47. *Time Regained* 6: 520.

48. Joan Rosasco has described the utopian nature of the circular topography of Combray; see "Le Texte et sa doublure," in *Proust et le texte producteur*, ed. John Erickson and Irène Pagès (Paris: Guelph, 1980), 93–113.

49. *Time Regained* 6: 507.

50. *Swann's Way* 1: 4.

51. All quotations regarding Mlle de Saint-Loup are from *Time Regained* 6: 502–7.

52. *Corr.* 9: 72.

53. *Time Regained* 6: 507–8, 528. For an analysis of Proust's abundant use of planetary imagery, see the chapter "The Cosmos Builder" in my *Proustian Quest*.

54. *Within a Budding Grove*, 2: 468.

55. *The Fugitive* 5: 671.

56. Edmund White, *Marcel Proust* (New York: Viking, 1999), 154.

57. La Rochefoucauld, *Œuvres complètes* (Paris: Gallimard, 1964), 412.

58. *Time Regained* 6: 530. For the desirability of destroying such love, see *The Captive* 5: 122: "We live only with what we do not love, with what we have brought to live with us only in order to kill the intolerable love, whether it be for a woman, for a place, or again for a woman embodying a place." Compare Oscar Wilde's observation: "Each man kills the thing he loves."

59. *The Fugitive* 5: 655; see also ibid., 5: 573.

60. Ibid., 5: 676, 805.

61. *Time Regained* 6: 11.

62. Iris Murdoch, *The Good Apprentice* (New York: Viking, 1986), 521. French sentence bracketed in original.

63. Pamela Hansford Johnson, "The Novel of Marcel Proust," in *Marcel Proust: Letters to His Mother*, trans. and ed. George D. Painter (London: Rider, 1956), 32.

64. *Time Regained* 6: 299–300.

65. Ibid., 6: 501.

66. *SL* 4: 345.

Index

Proust's preoccupation with homosexuality, 170
Moreau, Gustave, 86
Mornand, Louisa de, 17, 27–28, 102, 104, 179
Mouton, Jean, 154
Murdoch, Iris, 202–3
Musset, Alfred de, 102, 184

Nahmias, Albert, fils: meets Proust at Cabourg, 79–80; becomes Proust's secretary and intimate friend, 103; bisexuality of; as model for Albertine, 103–4; Proust's infatuation and possessiveness over, 108–11; rumors of affair between Proust and, 116–17; sent by Proust in pursuit of Agostinelli, 123–25
Nicolson, Harold, 169–70
Nietzsche, Friedrich, 1
Noailles, Countess Anna de, 80, 122

Offenbach, Jacques, 7, 32
Orloff, Prince Alexis, 140, 180

Painter, George D., 154, 180, 181
Parent, Pierre, 79
Peter, René, 75
Peyrefitte, Roger, 170
Pirbright, Lady Sarah, 183
Plantevignes, Marcel, 108
Plato, 14, 15, 20
Poincaré, Raymond, 49
Porel, Jacques, 107, 153, 155, 175–76
Pougy, Liane de, 76
Pouquet, Jeanne, 102
Pozzi, Dr. Samuel, 22–23, 187
Proust, Dr. Adrien: concerns of regarding Proust's sexuality, 8; sends Proust to brothel, 9, 14; influence on Proust of, 18; with

Jeanne, receives Oscar Wilde, 88; liaison with Marie van Zandt of, 153

Proust, Jeanne, 14, 52, 69, 76, 88, 152
Proust, Marcel: adolescent possessiveness of, 1–2; on need to rebel against family, 4; need to be loved of, 16; fights duel with Jean Lorrain, 60–63; gossips with duchesse de Clermont-Tonnerre, 76; pastimes with male servants of, 76–77; on Georges de Lauris's masculine beauty, 77–78; meets Oscar Wilde, 87–89; love of English and American letters of, 87–88; defends self against insinuation of homosexuality, 92, 108; rebukes Morand for publication of "Ode to Marcel Proust," 145–46; fetish of for photographs, 153–55; prefers company of young men from the working class, 163–65; engages Rochat as secretary, 166; leaves 102 boulevard Haussmann, 175; unconditional love by, 194
—and Alfred Agostinelli: meeting, 69; excursions together, 70–72; Proust falls in love, 114, 115, 117, 118, 119–20; Proust denies homosexual relationship, 117; Proust dispatches Nahmias to pursue Agostinelli and persuade him to return, 123–24; Proust offers airplane and Rolls-Royce for Agostinelli's returns, 126–27; Proust mourns, 129–30, 135–36; Proust investigates activities, 136–37;
—and Lucien Daudet: Proust's infatuation, 47; mad laughter and childish word games together, 47–49;